Richard Be
Plays 6

One Man, Two Guvnors;
Young Marx; The Hypocrite

One Man, Two Guvnors (winner of the 2011 Evening Standard Theatre Best New Play and Critic's Circle Best New Play awards): 'For almost three blissful hours cares are forgotten and gnawing anxieties put aside as you surrender to great waves of healing laughter. It is absolute bliss. [Bean's] script is a bang-on-the-money mixture of wisecracks, sight gags, and fiendish moments of audience participation.' *Telegraph*

Young Marx: 'A wily, fast-paced comedy . . . what makes the piece especially timely is its adroit portrait of an open London where refugees were welcomed and where a wanted man like Marx, in flight from the wave of 1848 revolutions in Europe and mistakenly branded a terrorist, could escape arrest or extradition.' *Independent*

The Hypocrite: 'Serves as a scabrous, bawdy, witty, often flagrantly silly love-letter to Hull and its purported place in a crucial moment of national history . . . it hits the bull's-eye . . . Richard Bean returns to *One Man, Two Guvnors* form with a brilliantly entertaining new farce.' *Telegraph*

Richard Bean became the first playwright in 2011 to win the Evening Standard Award for Best Play for two plays, *The Heretic* and *One Man, Two Guvnors*. The New York production of *One Man, Two Guvnors* was awarded the 2012 Outer Critics' Circle Award for Outstanding New Broadway Play. His recent credits include *Kiss Me* (Hampstead), *The Nap* (Sheffield Crucible), *Great Britain* (National Theatre), *Made in Dagenham*: The Musical (Adelphi Theatre) and *Pitcairn* (Chichester Minerva Theatre/Shakespeare's Globe). Richard's other work includes *Under the Whaleback* (Royal Court. George Devine Award 2002), *The Heretic* (The Royal Court; Evening Standard Best New Play

2011), *Honeymoon Suite* (Pearson Play of the Year), *Harvest* (Critic's Circle Best New Play), *The House of Games* (from David Mamet's film), a new version of Moliere's *The Hypochondriac, The Big Fellah* (Out of Joint), *England People Very Nice* (National Theatre), *The Mentalists* (National Theatre), *The English Game* (Headlong), *Up on Roof and Pub Quiz is Life* (Hull Truck), *In the Club* (Hampstead), *The God Botherers* (Bush Theatre) and *Mr England* (Sheffield Crucible).

Richard Bean
Plays 6

One Man, Two Guvnors
Young Marx
The Hypocrite

With an introduction by Michael Coveney

methuen | drama

LONDON • NEW YORK • OXFORD • NEW DELHI • SYDNEY

METHUEN DRAMA
Bloomsbury Publishing Plc
50 Bedford Square, London, WC1B 3DP, UK
1385 Broadway, New York, NY 10018, USA

BLOOMSBURY, METHUEN DRAMA and the Methuen Drama logo are
trademarks of Bloomsbury Publishing Plc

This collection first published in Great Britain 2020

One Man, Two Guvnors first published 2011 by Oberon Books
Young Marx written by Clive Coleman and Richard Bean
first published 2017 by Oberon Books
The Hypocrite first published 2018 by Oberon Books

Cover design: Ben Anslow
Cover image © Ansel Krut

A catalogue record for this book is available from the British Library.

A catalog record for this book is available from the Library of Congress.

ISBN: PB: 978-1-3501-8365-0
ePDF: 978-1-3501-8366-7
eBook: 978-1-3501-8367-4

Series: Contemporary Dramatists

Typeset by Mark Heslington Ltd, Scarborough, North Yorkshire

To find out more about our authors and books visit
www.bloomsbury.com and sign up for our newsletters.

Contents

Introduction *Michael Coveney*   vii

One Man, Two Guvnors   1
Young Marx   93
The Hypocrite   191

Introduction

One of the many great things about the Richard Bean play that opened at the National Theatre in May 2011 was that you could see where it was coming from but not where it would end.

Using a literal translation of Goldoni's 1746 Venetian classic *Arlechinno, Servitore di Due Padrone* but sticking to many of the *commedia dell'arte* stereotypes, Bean provided a feast of farce that had critics reaching for the stars in bunches of high fives.

But in the second act he suddenly gave his Arlecchino – brilliantly played by James Corden as a starving out-of-work skiffle band player, Francis Henshall – another identity. Would his Columbina, the lubricious Dolly, grab that away date to Majorca with the gross-out guzzler or plump instead for his identical Irish twin?

In what everyone agreed was the funniest play and production at the National Theatre in living memory, and the funniest in the West End (when it transferred, inevitably) since Michael Frayn's *Noises Off*, Bean had found a way of sustaining the onstage farcical energy beyond the hilarious, climactic dinner scene at the end of Act One.

This version is set not in Venice, but in Brighton – a town Keith Waterhouse once said was always in a position to help the police with their enquiries – and a Brighton, what's more, in 1963, the year of the Beatles debut album and of Philip Larkin's 'Annus Mirabilis' (translated in this cheeky show as 'wonderful bottom'): 'Sexual intercourse began in nineteen sixty-three (which was rather late for me) – Between the end of the *Chatterley* ban and the Beatles' first LP.'

The dinner is served in the Cricketers' Arms, a snug Brighton hostelry that features in Graham Greene's *Brighton Rock* and is here conveniently commandeered as an epicentre of door-banging confusion among the temporary residents. And not just them. Bean's waiters are a snooty, insouciant maître d' and his decrepit sidekick, Alfie, who is indeed side-kicked, shoved aside and pushed downstairs ('It's his first day') while trying vainly to serve the soup.

The cruel hilarity of this scene was at one with the vaudevillian style of Nicholas Hytner's production which traded on audience involvement from the off, as Francis sought help with an over-large trunk. The fourth wall stayed down as an appeal went out for food from the hummus brigade in the front stalls and a 'plant' was enlisted to join in and suffer acute humiliation by rampant chicken balls, full body drenching and fire hydrant foam.

An arranged East End marriage has gone wrong and the interested parties have decamped to the seaside to sort things out. That's the idea, at least. In a perfectly oiled farcical machine, famished Francis, so hungry he's eating a honeymoon salad – letters alone? – is hired as a gofer by both the disguised sister of a dead criminal (her twin) and the public school posho who's rubbed him out. And, of course, the posho loves the twin sister who, lurking beneath a Mary Quant hairstyle, resembles Ringo Starr, one of the new pop stars who have made skiffle, and Francis with it, culturally redundant . . . not with it, in fact.

Goldoni had not really got going when he sketched out the first draft of *Arlecchino*, leaving plenty of leeway for improvisation. His 1753 written version was the 'sacred text' which became a classic, and in Girogio Strehler's legendary production for the newly founded Piccolo Theatre of Milan in 1947, a benchmark in modern theatre. That version visited the Edinburgh Festival in 1956, an acclaimed marvel of acrobatics, mime and ensemble playing.

I saw that everlasting production myself in 1987 in Milan with the second of its only two Arlechinnos, Ferruccio Soleri. It was one of the most beautiful shows I've ever seen. But it was also curiously embalmed. Candelabras and footlights, ravishing silken costumes and stunning silhouettes, hyper-elegant choreography. And far too polite for its origins in rough house theatrics.

Goldoni has fared unevenly in the post-war British theatre, but the Scots came up with an ebullient *The Servant o' Twa Maisters* to launch Tom Fleming's Edinburgh Lyceum reign in 1965, and Jason Watkins was an athletic, updated (to modern

Venice) harlequin in a 1999 Young Vic/RSC co-production. But Bean takes the biscuit for pushing the Goldoni envelope with a Brighton postmark.

As another Goldoni translator, Robert David MacDonald, once said, Goldoni was the master of the superficial. There is no subtext. Every action or word changes the play, bang ... until, as here, you stumble on an alliterative nonsense word game, or an unexpected explanation of the difference between monozygotic and dizygotic twins. Which stops the action, but then makes it even funnier.

One Man was Bean's second play for Hytner at the National, piercing two other panoramic British satires: the rainbow racial survey of *England People Very Nice* (2009) and the equally mercurial 'instant-response' to the phone-hacking scandal in newspapers, *Great Britain* (2014). So when Hytner moved on and launched, with his NT executive director Nick Starr, the commercial venture of The Bridge further east along the South Bank, he cannily opened the place in October 2017 with his fourth Bean collaboration, *Young Marx*.

Having written one farce with a broadly pre-ordained template to go on, Bean, with his friend Clive Coleman, a lawyer and sitcom writer of renown, forged an ingenious farcical scenario with Karl Marx and Friedrich Engels forming a sweet and sour double-act around a rocky marriage ('My wife's packing, she's travelling to Italy' / 'Genoa?' / 'Of course I know her, she's my wife'), a gathering of émigré revolutionaries at crossed purposes and an acute economic crisis.

The year is 1850, as Engels is bailing out Marx and his family in congested Soho on his way back to his even more impoverished working classes in Manchester. It's an ingenious exploitation of the funny side of revolutionary politics, with an undertow of personal upheaval as Marx is sucked into a duel on Hampstead Heath before passing the blame for getting the maid pregnant onto his best friend. And then a tragedy.

Underneath is the rumble of three masterpieces of socio-political European writing: Engels's great tract, not yet translated into English; Marx's *Das Kapital*, which he cannot get on with; and Darwin's *On the Origin of Species*, which Marx accidentally christens in a wonderful fracas in the British Library involving a brush with the prematurely aged and bearded biologist poring over his papers.

There's a similar lilt and irreverence to *The Hypocrite* which Bean wrote for his home town Hull's UK City of Culture celebration in the same year. Like Francis in *One Man*, Sir John Hotham serves two masters: his monarch, Charles I, as governor of Hull in 1642; and Parliament, where he was recently Member for Beverley. He also owes money to both sides for beefing up his daughter's dowry.

The whole farrago is set in motion – there's a frenzy of fornication, a flying foreskin (yes, I did say that) and a permanently engaged commode – by the first overt act of the Civil War: Sir John's barring the city gates against the king's attempt to secure the arsenal. Cue local gossip about Hull's rugby league teams. As in *Young Marx*, Bean riffs on history and stirs the pot, like an alternative comedy love child of Tom Stoppard and Peter Barnes.

Michael Coveney

One Man, Two Guvnors

This version of Goldoni's *The Servant of Two Masters* was developed from a comprehensive and detailed literal translation from the Italian by Francesca Manfrin. I'd like to thank Didi Hopkins for her inspirational explanations of Commedia, and all who contributed to the script in the rehearsal room – you know who you are. The lyrics for 'Tomorrow Looks Good from Here' were co-written with Grant Olding.

Richard Bean

One Man, Two Guvnors was first performed at Lyttelton Theatre, National Theatre on 17 May 2011 with the following cast:

Gareth	**David Benson**
Stanley Stubbers	**Oliver Chris**
Francis Henshall	**James Corden**
Alfie	**Tom Edden**
Harry Dangle	**Martyn Ellis**
Lloyd Boateng	**Trevor Laird**
Pauline Clench	**Claire Lams**
Charlie Clench	**Fred Ridgeway**
Alan Dangle	**Daniel Rigby**
Rachel Crabbe	**Jemima Rooper**
Dolly	**Suzie Toase**

Ensemble   **Polly Conway, Jolyon DIxon, Derek Elroy, Paul Lancaster, Fergus March, Gareth Mason, Clare Thomson**

Director Nicholas Hytner
Associate Director Cal McCrystal
Designer Mark Thompson
Lighting Designer Mark Henderson
Music Grant Olding
Sound Designer Paul Arditti
Fight Director Kate Waters

One Man, Two Guvnors was performed at Music Box Theatre, New York on 6 April 2012 with the following cast:

Stanley Stubbers	**Oliver Chris**
Francis Henshall	**James Corden**
Alfie	**Tom Edden**
Harry Dangle	**Martyn Ellis**
Lloyd Boateng	**Trevor Laird**
Pauline Clench	**Claire Lams**
Gareth	**Ben Livingston**
Charlie Clench	**Fred Ridgeway**
Alan Dangle	**Daniel Rigby**
Rachel Crabbe	**Jemima Rooper**
Dolly	**Suzie Toase**

Ensemble   **Brian Gonzales, Eli James, Sarah Manton, Stephen Pilkington, David Ryan Smith, Natalie Smith**

Director Nicholas Hytner
Physical Comedy Director Cal McCrystal
Composer Grant Olding
Designer Mark Thompson
Lighting Designer Mark Henderson
Sound Designer Paul Arditti
Associate Director Adam Penford
Original UK Casting Alastair Coomer CDG
US Casting Tara Rubin Casting CSA

New York Producers Bob Boyett, National Theatre of Great Britain under the direction of Nicholas Hytner and Nick Starr, National Angels, Chris Harper, Tim Levy, Scott Rudin, Roger Berlind, Harriet Leve, Stephanie P. McClelland, Broadway Across America, Daryl Roth, Jam Theatricals, Sonia Friedman, Harris Karma, Deborah Taylor, Richard Willis

Characters

'Charlie the Duck' Clench, *fifties*
Pauline Clench, *his daughter, eighteen*
Harry Dangle, *sixties*
Alan Dangle, *his son, twenties*
Dolly, *an employee of Clench, thirties*
Lloyd Boateng, *a friend to Clench, Jamaican, fifties*
Francis Henshall, *thirties*
Rachel Crabbe, *mid-twenties*
Stanley Stubbers, *late twenties*
Alfie, *waiter, eighty-seven*
Gareth, *head waiter, forty*

Others as required.

Notes on text

I'm not using continental scene changes: i.e. the scene doesn't change on the entrance of a new character; rather, scene changes are restricted to time and location changes.

Act One

Scene One

As the audience take their seats the skiffle band plays. Lights down. 1963, April, mid-morning. A room in **Charlie Clench**'s *house in Brighton. A framed photo of Queen Elizabeth II at coronation upstage.* **Charlie**, *his daughter* **Pauline**, **Harry Dangle**, *his son* **Alan**, **Lloyd Boateng**, **Dolly** *and other friends and family. Hardly anything remains from a buffet of typically English party food. Maybe one lone cheese and pineapple on a stick, and some peanuts. A party can of beer, etc. All very lively and jolly, with the skiffle band playing, laughter, drinks, dancing. The song finishes.* **Pauline** *and* **Alan** *kiss. They toast 'Pauline and Alan'.* **Charlie** *taps a glass for quiet.*

Dangle Happy engagement! Pauline and Alan!

All Pauline and Alan!

Dolly Come on, Charlie! Give us a speech!

All Speech!

Charlie I've only ever spoken three times, formally, in public, in my life, and each time I've been banged up by the judge straight afterwards! For twenty years, me and Pauline's mother were happy, and then, unfortunately, just by chance, we met each other. I done me best bringing up Pauline, on me own, after her muvver . . . (*Chokes.*) . . . sorry . . .

Lloyd – doin' well, Charlie.

Charlie – I've had to be her dad and her mum after her muvver . . . (*Chokes.*)

Pauline – It's alright, Dad.

Charlie . . . after her muvver left me and went to live in Spain. It's a disappointment that Jean can't be here in Brighton at her daughter's engagement party, and a shame she can't even afford a stamp for a card neither. But I'm not gonna go on about it. I'd like to thank Alan's father, my solicitor.

Dangle (*coming forward*)   *Ecce homo!*

Charlie   No Latin! Please! I have enough difficulty understanding you when you're speaking English. But, seriously, without Harry, I wouldn't be here today, I'd be behind bars, where, let's face it, by rights, I oughta be. Over to you, Alan.

He steps back. Applause for **Charlie**. **Alan** *kneels, with a flourish, before* **Pauline**.

Alan   Pauline, I give you my hand. (*He holds out an upturned, closed, cupped hand towards* **Pauline**.)

Dolly (*aside*)   He wants to be an actor.

Alan   Captive within my hand is a bird. This bird is my heart.

Pauline (*to* **Dolly**)   Is it a real bird?

Dolly   No. It's a metaphor.

Pauline (*excited*)   Oh! Lovely!

Alan   I offer you the whole of my life, as your husband.

Dolly (*aside*)   Ooh! I could do with a bit of this myself.

Pauline *opens his hand and takes out the imaginary bird, and presses it to her heart.*

Pauline   I accept your bird heart thing, and I promise to look after it properly. (*She kneels, and offers her hand to* **Alan**.) I got a bird in my hand an' all.

Charlie   – That's two birds now, I'm gonna have to get in a box of Trill!

Pauline   – this bird is *my* heart, the only one I've ever had.

Alan *mimes taking the bird and presses it through his rib cage into his heart. They kiss passionately. Silence. A bit embarrassing. It is broken by the pop of a champagne cork.*

Dangle   May I propose a toast. To love! In Latin –

Charlie   – oh no!

Dangle   *Ars amandi!*

Pauline   No! Pauline.

Alan (*to* **Pauline**)   '*Ars amandi*', is the art of love.

Pauline   I don't understand.

Alan (*aside*)   This is why I love her. She is pure, innocent, unspoiled by education, like a new bucket.

Lloyd   To love!

All   To love!

They toast. The door bell rings.

Charlie   Dolly, get the door.

Dolly   Bookkeeper? Or butler? Make your mind up.

Charlie   And if it's carol singers tell them to piss off. It's only April.

Dolly *exits.*

Lloyd (*to* **Dangle**)   You're Charlie's solicitor then?

They shake hands.

Dangle   Harry Dangle. Dangle, Berry and Bush. My card.

Lloyd (*reading*)   No win, same fee?

Dangle   That's us.

Lloyd   Charlie tells me you're brilliant!

Dangle   Put it this way, I got the Mau Mau off. Are you family, Lloyd?

Lloyd   No, no! An old friend. Me and Charlie go way back.
(*Aside.*) Parkhurst.

Pauline   Dad! Me and Alan, we're gonna go up to my room, to play some records.

Charlie   Do I look like I just came down in the last shower? No! Mingle!

Lloyd *takes* **Charlie** *to one side. Gets out invitation.*

Lloyd   Man! What's going on! Last week I gets this invitation to an engagement party –

Charlie   – put that away.

Lloyd   – of Pauline Clench and Roscoe Crabbe, which was a shock because I always thought Roscoe was ginger.

Charlie   He was ginger! He was as queer as a whisky and Babycham. That was the whole point, it was a gonna be a marriage of convenience, wannit.

Lloyd   But today and it's a different groom man!

Charlie   Because Roscoe's dead. Pauline and this Alan wanted to get engaged, so I thought –

Lloyd   – I've paid for the sausage rolls so why waste them?!

Charlie   Exactly!

Lloyd   Man! They don't call you 'Charlie the Duck' for nothing! Tight man! Tight as!

Enter **Dolly**, *looking serious.*

Dolly   Some geezer from London. Says he's Roscoe Crabbe's minder.

Lloyd   Can't be much of a minder, Roscoe's dead.

Charlie   Is he a face? Does he look handy?

Dolly   To be honest, he looks a bit overweight.

Charlie   Check him out, Lloydie, see if he's tooled up.

Lloyd   Charlie, I don't work for you no more.

Dolly   Leave it to me, boys. (*She exits.*)

Dangle   More guests?

Charlie   Roscoe Crabbe's minder.

Dangle   But I understand there was a knife fight and Roscoe Crabbe was mortally wounded?

Charlie   No! He was killed.

Lloyd   Good riddens!

Charlie   The Old Bill are looking for his twin sister, Rachel, and her boyfriend.

Dangle   Because?

Lloyd   Revenge! The boyfriend testified against Roscoe in court. Put him away for four years. Man! It's obvious! Who is Roscoe gonna get into a fight with on his first day of freedom?

Charlie (*to* **Dangle**, *unnecessarily*)   Rachel's boyfriend.

Enter **Dolly**.

Dolly   He's clean. Shall I let him in?

Charlie (*nods*)   Yeah. (*Exit* **Dolly**.) What can I do?

Lloyd   She's a smashing girl is Rachel! Notin' like that vicious little toerag of a brother!

Charlie   I think Roscoe was a bit whatsaname – you know, what's that word for someone who likes inflicting pain?

Lloyd   Police officer.

Charlie   No!

Dangle   Sadist.

Charlie   That's Roscoe.

Lloyd   Unusual for twins to have such different personalities.

Charlie (*to* **Dangle**)   They was identical twins, you see, Roscoe and Rachel.

Lloyd   They were not *identical* twins! Roscoe was a boy, and Rachel is a girl!

Charlie   So?

Dangle   Identical means identical.

Charlie   What I want to know is, if Roscoe's dead, what's his minder doing on my doorstep.

Enter **Dolly***. Followed by* **Francis Henshall***. He is suited and booted, but the suit is too tight, too short. The room freezes. He is acting tough. He checks the room as if looking for hidden dangers. He's playing the role of hard man minder. Everyone else is still, frozen in fear, waiting for a cue from* **Charlie***.* **Francis** *stops under the picture of the Queen. Points to it.*

Francis   Who's that?

Pauline   That's the Queen.

Francis   What a beautiful woman. Someone should write a song about her.

Pauline   'God Save the Queen'?

Francis   It's a good title.

He picks a peanut from a bowl on the side, throws it in the air and catches it in his mouth.

Pauline   This is my engagement party.

Francis   *Your* engagement party. Phew!

(*To* **Dolly**.) 'Phew' 'cause I'm glad it ain't yours – 'beautiful eyes'.

Dolly   Thank you.

Francis   Don't ever wear glasses. Even if you need to, you know, for reading.

Dolly (*aside*)   I know exactly what he's after, and if carries on like this he's gonna get it. (**Francis** *throws a second peanut and catches that too. To* **Francis**.) What about glasses for driving?

Francis   Are you one of them women's libbers?

Dolly   Would that be a problem?

Francis   I like a woman who can drive. That way I can go out, have a skinful, and get home without killing anyone. Are you married to er –

Dolly   – I'm single, I'm the bookkeeper here.

Francis   So you're a single, working, driving, bookkeeping woman. That's my type. Do want to go to Majorca for a couple of weeks? Think about it.

He throws a third peanut in the air which forces him to run backwards to catch it. He hits the sofa, goes over with it, and pops up the other side.

Got it.

Dangle (*to* **Charlie**)   This man is a clown.

Francis *turns on* **Dangle**, *grabbing his balls.*

Francis   Everybody at the circus loves the clowns. So, when you say 'this man is a clown', what you're really saying is 'I love you'. Are you Charlie the Duck?

Dangle   No.

Francis   No?

Dangle   No.

Francis *lets all the role-playing drop, and becomes low-status apologetic.*

Francis   Oh shit, have I got the wrong house? The invitation –

Gets his invitation out.

Charlie   – I'm Charlie the Duck.

Francis   Right. Ok. You don't look like a duck.

Charlie   Who are you?

Francis   Good idea! Let's do the big questions. Who am I? Why am I here?

Lloyd   What do you want?

Francis   Is there a God? Is He loving or judgemental? Let's hope He's loving, 'cause if He's judgemental, trust me, we're all in the shit.

Charlie   You're Roscoe Crabbe's minder.

Francis   I am. And I have an invitation to his engagement party. This party.

Charlie   Roscoe's dead.

Francis   If Roscoe's dead, who's that sitting outside in the motor, listening to the shipping forecast?

Pauline *rushes to the window.*

Pauline   Oh my God! No!

Charlie   He's risen from the dead has he?

Francis   Yeah. It only took him two days. That's one day quicker than the previous world record. So?! Can he come in? To his own engagement party?

Charlie   I guess.

Francis   I'll go and get him.

He exits, with a wink to **Dolly**. *Voices are now raised . . .*

Pauline   Dad! No! Don't let him in! I love Alan, I don't love Roscoe, I never did.

Charlie   You was perfectly happy with Roscoe six month back.

Dangle   He's missed the boat.

Charlie   Roscoe Crabbe can be as late as he likes. And we have an arrangement.

Alan   An arranged marriage worthy of a Molière farce, contemptible even in the seventeenth century.

Pauline   Yeah, Dad, this is the nineteenth century now!

Charlie   Yeah, well, what do you offer my daughter, Alan? *I wanna be an actor*. You can't get more flakey!

Alan   All I offer is love! My love for your daughter eclipses poetry. My love is ethereal, pure – like . . . like the kind of water you're supposed to put in a car battery.

Enter **Rachel Crabbe**, *followed by* **Francis**. **Rachel** *is dressed as a fashionable young man, looking not unlike a short Ringo Starr.*

Rachel   Long time no see, Charlie.

They shake hands.

Charlie   Yeah. You look well Roscoe. All things considered. This is Lloyd, good friend of mine, Dolly, my bookkeeper, my solicitor, Harry Dangle, he's good.

Rachel   Are you the guy who got the Mau Mau off?

Dangle   It wasn't easy.

Charlie   – and, 'course, you remember Pauline.

Rachel   You look fantastic, Pauline.

Alan *walks in front of* **Pauline**, *placing himself between her and* **Rachel**.

Rachel   Who are you?

Alan   Whole nations will be slain before you take my love from me.

Rachel (*to* **Charlie**)   Why's he talking like an actor?

Dolly   He wants to be an actor.

Rachel   Oh alright. Who are you then?

Alan   I am your nemesis.

Rachel   Francis! What's a nemesis?

Francis   Dunno. Definitely foreign. I think it might be a Toyota.

Rachel *goes over to* **Charlie**, *takes him downstage.*

Rachel   What's going on Charlie?

Charlie   We thought you was dead.

Rachel   If you thought I was dead, why would you go ahead with my engagement party?

Charlie   You know, I'd already paid for the sausage rolls and –

Rachel   – IF YOU THOUGHT I WAS DEAD!

Charlie   – the word was, you were murdered. Pauline's met someone else.

Rachel (*indicating* **Alan**)   Horror bollocks, over there?

Charlie   Yeah.

Rachel *approaches* **Alan**.

Rachel   So, let's have another go. What's your name?

Alan   Alan.

Rachel   I have a prior arrangement with Charlie and Pauline, Alan. It's not love, no, it can't be love. This is good news for you, Alan, because the deal guarantees Pauline complete freedom in affairs of the heart, as long as she is discreet.

Alan   My love for Pauline is not discreet. It shouts from the roof tops 'Look at me, look at me, I am love!'

Dangle   It shall be my son who marries Pauline. Come on, Alan! We're going.

Pauline   Don't leave me here, Alan!

Dangle (*to* **Charlie**)   Mr Charles Clench, you will be hearing from me.

Charlie   I can explain.

Alan   I shall return. Like a storm. And everybody will get wet.

He exits. Door closed.

Charlie   Pauline. Over here. (**Pauline** *is now crying. She goes downstage with* **Charlie**.) Behave!

Pauline   It's 1963, Dad! You can't force me to marry a dead homosexual.

Charlie   He's not dead is he.

Pauline   He is a homosexual though.

Charlie   We've only got his word for that. (**Pauline** *runs off into another room.*) Come back here!

(*To* **Roscoe**.) Gimme a minute, Roscoe.

He follows **Pauline**. *He closes the door. During the next scene* **Francis** *mimes taking out his pulsing heart and offering it to* **Dolly**.

Rachel   Lloyd Boateng. My sister worked the bar for you at the Palm Tree.

Lloyd   Rachel, yeah. What's she doing?

Rachel   She runs this nightclub now. It's her boyfriend's. The Stilletto, Mile End.

Lloyd   I've heard it's rough. Criminals, gangsters, Princess Margaret. I like your sister.

Rachel   And she likes you. A lot. She said you could be trusted.

Francis *now fiddles with the nipples of an African woman sculpture. He thinks this is a private thing between he and* **Dolly** *but* **Lloyd** *and* **Rachel** *watch.* **Charlie** *re-enters.*

Charlie   The kid's upset. She thought you was dead. D'yer wanna sandwich?

Francis   Yes! Yes please. We had to skip breakfast you see.

Rachel   We're going to eat later. What's your understanding of the deal, Charlie?

Charlie   I settle the debt I owed your father, paid to you on the day of your engagement –

Rachel   – six thousand two hundred today.

Charlie   Pauline, as your public wife, gets two grand a year, for attending functions on your arm –

Rachel   – and she gets the house in Debden.

Charlie   And Debden.

Rachel   Have you got the money, Charlie?

Charlie   I can give you a cheque. Six thousand two hundred.

Rachel   Banker's draft. And I'll take the two hundred in cash.

Charlie   Dolly, phone the bank, get 'em to knock up a banker's draft for six grand.

Dolly (*incredulous*)   For six thousand?

Charlie   That's what I said, yeah.

Incredulous, **Dolly** *leaves. On the way she is aware of* **Francis** *goosing her.*

Charlie   Are you boys staying in Brighton?

Rachel   Can you recommend somewhere?

Lloyd   I certainly can. The Cricketers' Arms.

Francis   Do they do sandwiches?

Charlie   Wash your mouth out! It's a pub that does food. Lloyd is the landlord. He's had a three-year training as a chef.

Lloyd (*aside*)   Parkhurst.

Francis   That has got to be the most beautiful sentence in the English language. *A pub that does food.*

Rachel   Francis, go ahead in the motor.

Francis *makes to leave.*

Rachel   Hang on, mate, you don't know where the pub is?!

Francis   Guv! For a pub that does food there will be a star in the sky!

He leaves. **Dolly** *re-enters.*

Dolly   I've got the bank on the phone.

Charlie (*to* **Rachel**)   I don't know why they want to talk to me. What's the problem. (*He exits.*)

Lloyd   Rachel?

Rachel   You're looking pretty good, Lloydie!

Lloyd   Girl?! What all dis wid de rude boy disguise!

Rachel   The Old Bill are looking for me. Can I trust you?

Lloyd   You're like a daughter to me!

Rachel   My brother Roscoe is dead. My boyfriend killed my twin brother, yeah. I should hate Stanley for that. But I love him. Have you ever been in love, Lloyd?

Lloyd   True love? Yes, once.

(*Aside.*) Parkhurst.

Enter **Charlie**, *in coat and hat.*

Charlie   I'm gonna go raise that two hundred folding.

He's gone.

Rachel   Me and Stanley are going to have to go to Australia.

Lloyd   Australia! No, man! Oh my God, no, not Australia?! That's really terrible. Australia?! You poor thing, girl! Why Australia? Do you like opera?

Rachel   Not especially. But we've no choice. We sail from Southampton on Monday. The morning tide. The police will be watching the ports so –

Lloyd   – Brighton's near enough but safer?

Rachel   And Charlie the Duck lives here, and we need money.

Lloyd   I guess. Where is your Stanley now?

Rachel   Brighton, somewhere. I've left a letter for him at the post office with instructions for a rendezvous. I pray to God he's alright.

Scene Two

Outside The Cricketers' Arms. Pub tables and a dustbin. Enter **Francis** *from the pub entrance.*

On the pub table are some unfinished drinks. Some dregs of Guinness, white wine, red wine in a bottle, orange juice and a discarded glass of Snowball.

Francis My father, Tommy Henshall, God rest his soul, he woulda been proud of me, what I done with my life, until today. I used to play washboard in a skiffle band, but they went to see The Beatles last Tuesday night, and sacked me Wednesday morning. Ironic, because I started The Beatles. I saw them in Hamburg. Rubbish. I said to that John Lennon, I said, 'John, you're going nowhere, mate, it's embarrassing, have you ever considered writing your own songs'. So I'm skint, I'm busking, guitar, mouth organ on a rack, bass drum tied to me foot and, the definition of mental illness, cymbals between my knees. So there I am, middle of Victoria Station, I've only been playing ten minutes, this lairy bloke comes over, he says – 'Do you do requests?' I say 'yes', he says, 'I'd like you to play a song for my mother'. I said 'no problem, where is she?' He said, 'Tasmania'. So I nutted him. This little bloke Roscoe Crabbe seen all this and offers me a week's work in Brighton, says he needs a bit of muscle. I tell him this is all fat. But I need a wage, I haven't eaten since last night. But I don't get paid until the end of the week, and I can't stop thinking about *chips*. I'm staying in a pub, and I don't even have enough shrapnel for a *pint*.

He empties all the dregs into one pint pot and downs it in one. He seems to choke on something and then takes out a discarded cigarette from his mouth, looks at it in disgust, and then realising he could smoke it later he tucks it behind his ear. He stands, looks at the dustbin. Puts a hand on the lid.

There might be a discarded bag of chips in here. No! I can't go through the bins! Must stop thinking about *chips*. Come on, Francis! Think about something boring, like . . . Canada.

He gives up. Lifts the lid and starts searching in the bin. Enter **Stanley Stubbers**. *He is followed by a cab driver carrying one big trunk.*

Driver That's as far as I'm going with this, mate. (*He puts the trunk down unceremoniously.*) The fare is five and six.

Stanley   Oh focaccia bread and olives. Don't be a bad egg about it!

He gives the **Driver** *the money.*

Driver   I drive a taxi, mate, I ain't Heracles.

Stanley   It's a trunk. No one's asking you to hold up the sky for all eternity!

Driver   *Atlas* held up the sky. Heracles took over for five minutes so Atlas could go and get the golden apples from the Hesperides' garden.

He leaves. **Stanley** *spots* **Francis**.

Stanley   What's this pub like?

Francis   Ground-breaking. It does food.

Stanley   A pub? That does food?! Buzz-wham, whoever thought of that? Wrap his nuts in bacon and send him to the nurse! What are the rooms like?

Francis   World class.

Stanley   Not that I care. I'm boarding school trained. I'm happy if I've got a bed, a chair, and no one pissing on my face. Could you do me a favour and keep a fag's eye on the trunk, whilst I see if they have any vacancies?

Francis   How much?

Stanley   Half a crown?

Francis (*aside*)   HADDOCK AND CHIPS AND MUSHY PEAS!

Stanley   Yeah, alright.

He goes into the pub. **Francis** *considers the trunk, and the task in hand. Enter an old lady pulling a shopping trolley. She looks en passant at the trunk.*

Francis   Don't even think about it.

The pensioner heads off towards stage right, and then stops, turns and looks. **Francis** *lets out a war cry, and charges her offstage. A vicar/priest walks on and inspects the trunk.* **Francis**'s *charge takes him off stage left. Further upstage* **Francis** *is seen to chase the lady pensioner from stage right to stage left. Immediately* **Francis** *chases the vicar/priest from stage left to stage right. Immediately* **Francis** *returns further upstage chasing the lady, with a full salto somersault or cartwheel.* **Francis** *returns adjusting his tie. As he does this the athlete double walks across the stage.* **Francis** *reacts angrily at the double's stupidity. Enter* **Stanley**.

Stanley (*loud whisper*)   I need what they call in the Guards a batman. What's a decent drink for a geezer like you for a day's graft?

Francis   My current guvnor, that is my *previous* guvnor, used to pay me twenty pounds a week, at the end of the week, which is no use to me.

Stanley   Why not?

Francis   I have to EAT EVERY DAY!

Stanley   I shall pay you five pounds per day, but for today that remuneration would *incorporate* the trunk guarding retrospectively.

Francis (*aside*)   Bloody toffs, eh? Why do we let them get away with it?

(*To* **Stanley**.) Alright, guv, you're on.

Stanley   Do you know where the main post office is in Brighton?

Francis (*aside*)   I have absolutely no idea.

Oh yeah, it's next door to my nan's. My uncle Terry lost a leg in there once.

Stanley   There should be some post for me. You'll need this letter of authorisation.

He gives **Francis** *a letter.*

Francis (*reading*)   To whom it may concern, the bearer is an authorised agent of Stanley Stubbers.

Stanley   Shhh!

Francis   Who's Stanley Stubbers?

Stanley (*whisper*)   Me! But don't call me Stanley Stubbers. I'm going to have to make up a new name for the pub.

Francis (*whisper*)   What's wrong with the Cricketers' Arms?

Stanley (*whisper*)   You're not exactly a Swiss watch are you? A false name for me, because I'm lying low. What do I call you? I don't do first names. First names are for girls and Norwegians.

Francis (*whisper*)   Henshall.

Stanley   Like it! (*Whispering.*) Get my trunk indoors, Henshall, collect my letters, Henshall. I'll be in my room.

He exits into the pub. **Francis** *attempts to move the trunk, but it is too heavy. He requests help from the audience. Two volunteers are brought up onto the stage and are taught correct trunk-lifting technique. Under instruction from* **Francis** *they carry the trunk off into the pub. These are not plants/actors, but genuine punters.*

Francis   Post office.

Rachel   Francis! Where are you going?

Francis   I'm walking round and round in circles to ward off the hunger pangs.

Lloyd   I will cook you the lunch of a lifetime.

Francis   Lunch?! I haven't had breakfast yet.

Rachel   Have you got my trunk out of the car yet?

Francis   I've just done the trunk.

(*Aside.*) Ah! Concentrate, Francis!

(*To* **Rachel**.) Don't worry, Roscoe, I'll get your trunk from the motor now.

Lloyd   I'll get one of the bar staff to give you a hand. (*He exits into the pub. He sees the two volunteers standing offstage.*) What! You two again! I've told you before, it's not that kind of pub. You're barred. Off you go! (*The volunteers return to their seats.*)

Rachel   I need you to go to the post office, and –

Francis   – alright, guv, stop going on about it. You only have to tell me once.

Rachel   I haven't asked you to go to the post office at all yet.

Francis (*aside*)   Oh shit!

Rachel   Lloyd tells me it is just around the corner.

Francis (*aside*)   That's handy.

Rachel   Collect any letters for me or my sister, Rachel Crabbe. This is a letter of authorisation.

Francis   I've got one of those already. I don't need two do I?

Rachel   How come you already have a letter of authorisation?

Francis (*aside*)   This is trickier than I thought. (*He takes the letter.*) You're right. I'm gonna need that.

Rachel   And any letters you collect are private. Is that clear?

Francis   Don't worry, guv, I won't even read them myself.

Rachel   I'm gonna sink a couple of beers then have a lie-down in my room.

She goes in.

Francis (*aside*)   You got to concentrate, ain't ya, with two jobs. Cor! I can do it, long as I don't get confused. But I get confused easily. I don't get confused that easily. Yes I do. I'm my own worst enemy. Stop being negative. I'm not being negative. I'm being realistic. I'll screw it up. I always do. Who screws it up? You, you're the role model for village idiots everywhere. Me?! You're nothing without me. You're the cock-up! Don't call *me* a cock-up, you cock-up!

(*He slaps himself.*) You slapped me?! Yeah, I did. And I'm glad I did. (*He punches himself back.*) That hurt. Good. You started it.

A fight breaks out, where he ends up on the floor. Enter **Alan**.

Alan   What is my life? Am I to eat, drink, sleep, get a good job, marry, honeymoon, have kids, watch them grow up and have kids of their own, divorce, meet someone else, get old and die happy in my sleep like every other inhabitant of Brighton and Hove? What kind of a life is that? No. I am an artist. Character is action. I cannot allow this twice late suitor, who is both dead and late, to come along and end my beautiful dream, like a dead, discarded Russian astronaut dog landing on my head. (*He notices* **Francis**.) My rival's lackey. This will be the beginning of the end.

(*To* **Francis**.) Where is the dog, your guvnor? He will die today.

He takes his jacket off, rolls his sleeves up and takes his watch off as if preparing for a fist fight.

Francis   Do yourself a favour, mate, walk away.

Alan   You have obviously never been in love.

Francis (*counting on his fingers*)   Janice Carter, one; Pamela Costello, two; her gran, three –

Alan   – bring the cur out here, now!

Francis   You want to talk to my guvnor?

Alan   Talk a little, yes, and then slaughter a lot.

Francis   Alright, stay there, I'll go and get him. (*He heads for the pub door. Just as he gets there* **Stanley** *opens it.*)

Stanley   Have you been to the post office yet?

Francis   I was –

Stanley   – who's he?

Francis   He wants a word with my guvnor.

Stanley   But I'm your guvnor.

Francis   Yes. You are aren't you.

Stanley   He wants a word with me, does he?

Alan (*aside*)   My ire is like a forest fire. Fierce, inexorable, enough to ruin several picnics.

Francis (*introducing* **Stanley** *to* **Alan**)   This gentleman is called Alan.

Stanley   Oh bad luck.

Francis   I'll be at the post office. (*He tiptoes backwards out the way, unseen.*)

Stanley   Are you an actor?

Alan   Does it show?

Stanley   The way you stand, at an angle. As if there's an audience, over there.

Alan   My rival in love, Roscoe Crabbe, arrived from London today and is staying here.

Stanley (*aside*)   Bizarre! Roscoe Crabbe is the name of the chap I killed accidentally last Saturday evening, stabbing him three times in the chest with a knife I'd bought earlier.

Alan   He has today claimed my bride, my love, my life!

Stanley   No! Roscoe Crabbe is dead. I know he's dead because a friend of mine knows someone, whose dad works with a chap who says he murdered him.

Alan   I met him not an hour ago. He lives, his every breath tortures me.

Stanley (*aside*)   I suppose when I fled the club he wasn't actually yet dead. Oh Jeez! If Roscoe did survive and is in Brighton, he's here for one reason only, to kill me. Oh my God.

(*To* **Alan**.) He's not staying here. I know him. I would have seen him.

Alan   Oh. I was led to believe. No matter. My card. If you see him tell him that his life will only be spared if he gives up his wedding plans.

He gives him a card.

Stanley   You said your name was Alan? This card says *Orlando* Dangle.

Alan   Equity already had an Orlando Dangle.

Stanley   You *chose* 'Alan'?

Alan   It's 1963, there's a bloody revolution in the theatre and angry young men are writing plays about Alans. What's your name, sir?

Stanley   My name? (*Aside.*) Buggerello! Gonna have to be creative now. Not my best game! (*He looks at the dustbin.*) Dustbin, Dustin.

Alan   Dustin?

Stanley   Yes, Dustin. (*He looks around again at the pub.*) . . . Pubsign.

Alan   Pubsign?

Stanley   Dustin Pubsign. Yes. It's an old Anglo-Saxon guild name. The Bakers baked bread, the Smiths were the blacksmiths and the Pubsigns . . . we made the pub signs.

Alan   It has been a pleasure meeting you, Mister Pubsign.

He exits.

Stanley   Roscoe is in Brighton! I'd be better off lying low in London than lying low in Brighton. Poor dear Rachel must be terrified. My God! Can this be happening? What to do?! I must go to London, find Rachel. Damn it! I can't! I have to wait here for Rachel's letter.

Enter a **Policeman**.

Stanley   Uurgh! Rozzer! (*To the* **Policeman**.) Lovely day for it!

Policeman   Lovely day for what, sir?

Stanley   Fighting crime.

He backs into the pub. The **Policeman** *walks on, though he is suspicious. Enter* **Francis**. *He starts going through the letters of which there are four in all: two letters and two authorisations. Bit of a routine needed here, with four letters, pockets, etc.*

Francis   Authorisation letter. Let's put that in this pocket. Rachel Crabbe. Let's put that in this pocket for now. I'm good at this. I could work for the post office. That'd be three jobs. Authorisation. That goes in the Authorisations' pocket. Stanley Stubbers. (*Puts it in his mouth. Chews a little. Mumbling.*) Don't really need these authorisation letters anymore do I? (*He puts the authorisations in the same pocket as the* **Rachel** *letter.*)

So this pocket is now for Stanley Stubbers's letters. Good. What are these then? I'm getting confused now. Two authorisation letters. If there's two letters they definitely need their own pocket. What's this? Stanley Stubbers. That's the one that tasted quite good.

Puts it in his mouth. Chews a little more.

Mmm.

He takes a proper bite.

Not bad for paper. Bit dry. Could do with a bit more ink. I didn't know paper could taste this good. I might go back to communion.

Really eats the letter. **Stanley** *enters from the pub.*

Stanley   Henshall! Did you get the letters?

Francis   Yes, guv. Yeah, they're all here.

Stanley   How many? Just the one I guess.

Francis   Er . . . let's have a look. (*He goes through the letters.*) There's nothing here for you, guv.

Stanley   What are those letters then?

Francis   These are . . . decoy letters.

Stanley   Decoy letters?

Francis   The post office release them like homing pigeons. They record how many find their way back, and how many get shot down and run over.

Stanley *grabs him by the ear and by the balls.*

Stanley   The truth, Henshall! Or you'll never bugger the dolphin again!

Francis (*in pain*)   These are Paddy's letters.

Stanley   Paddy?

Francis   An old friend of mine, he was collecting letters for his boss, but he hadn't had any LUNCH yet, so I picked his letters up for him, so he could go and have HADDOCK AND CHIPS AND MUSHY PEAS!

Stanley   This letter is for my intended, Rachel Crabbe!

He releases his grip on **Francis***'s testicles and takes the letters.*

Francis   You can't open other people's letters!

Stanley   Why not?

Francis   It's a very deep human thing that's really basic and doesn't need explaining.

Stanley   At boarding school we opened each other's post all the time.

Francis   You also held masturbation relay races. Which is not normal either.

Stanley   No?

Francis   No.

Stanley   Mmm. It felt pretty good at the time.

He walks away from **Francis** *to share the contents with the audience.*

(*Aside.*) It's from Jackie, Rachel's best friend.

(*Reading.*) 'Dear Rachel, the police know you fled to Brighton dressed as a man so *The Evening News* carried an artist's impression of what you might look like in men's clothes. You ended up looking a bit like Ringo Starr, who's already been arrested twice.' (*Aside.*) Rachel, the woman I love, is in Brighton disguised as the percussionist of a popular beat combo! (*Reading.*) 'They also carried a boxing photo of Stanley' –

(*Aside.*) – that's me!

(*Reading.*) 'It's so awful that you have to go to that terrible godforsaken place . . . (*Turns letter over.*) Australia. Love, Jackie. Three kisses.'

(*Aside.*) Three kisses? That's a bit girls-only-Greek-island.

(*To* **Francis**.) Henshall! Have you met Paddy's boss?

Francis   No.

Stanley   Find Paddy, tell him to tell his employer I'm staying here.

Francis   I'll look for Paddy after LUNCH!

Stanley   NO! Now! This is a matter of life or death.

He sneaks back into the pub. **Francis** *addresses the audience from the stage.*

Francis   Has anyone got a SANDWICH?! (*Beat.*) There's a thousand people here and no one's got a York ham and mustard? Bacon, lettuce, tomato? (*Pleading.*) Cheese? Anyone? What? Has he got one . . .?

Plant   Yeah.

Some improvisation opportunity here.

Francis   What kind of sandwich is it?

Plant (*quiet*)   Hummus!?

Francis   Hummus?

Improvisation opportunities here, along the lines of: 'Do you always do this at the theatre?' 'Have you been reading the Guardian*?' Do you not understand that these questions up here are not real questions?', etc.*

Enter **Barman**.

Barman   I got a minute, if you want a hand with that trunk of yours.

Francis (*aside*)   This is Andrew. (*Or actor's actual name.*) He's been standing behind this door for five minutes now. He's only got three lines in the play and you've (*hummus man*) already ruined two of them.

He is caught between a sandwich and duty.

Alright! Let's do it. Let's get the trunk out of the motor.

(*To* **Plant**.) Hang on to that hummus sandwich.

He and the **Barman** *head off upstage left. The* **Barman** *glowers at the hummus man. Enter* **Rachel**. *The* **Barman** *sits upstage looking at his watch, taking no real interest.*

Rachel   Francis! Have you got the letters?

Francis *hands over the opened letter to* **Rachel** *plus one other.*

Francis   There you go, guv, none of yours have been eaten.
I'm going to get your trunk –

He heads off quickly with the **Barman**.

Rachel   – Francis! This letter has been opened!

Francis (*aside*)   Oh no, I need a convincing excuse here.

(*To* **Rachel**.)   I had to open it because I realised that there
was a small, distressed frog trapped inside.

(*Aside.*) Yes! Come on!

Rachel   How did you know there was a small distressed
frog trapped inside a sealed envelope?

Francis (*aside*)   Shit! There was no frog, actually. I had a
letter for me, which I hadn't yet opened, and I opened yours
by mistake.

Rachel   Get my trunk to my room, then come back here.
We need to talk.

She sits and reads the letter and does not notice the trunk business.

It's from a friend of mine. Jackie. I wish I could talk to Jackie
but she doesn't have a telephone at home. I bet one day, in
the future, everyone will have their own phones that they
carry around with them. Oh God no! That would be hell
wouldn't it. Wherever you are your mum might ring, people
selling you stuff, it might ring in the theatre!

Francis *and the* **Barman** *enter. The* **Barman** *is carrying the trunk
on his own.*

Francis (*to* **Barman**)   . . . Yeah, it's a condition of the spine,
they call it ankilosin spondilitis, basically if I lift anything
heavier than a knife and fork I go blind.

The **Barman** *goes into the pub.*

Rachel   Are you stupid?

Francis   No. I could've gone to university, if I'd got the qualifications.

Rachel   What's your ironing like?

Francis   World class. I've got the equivalent of a 2:1 in ironing from Durham.

Rachel   I need a clean shirt. I smell like a doctor's finger. My shirts are in the trunk. Here's the key. (*She gives* **Francis** *the key.*) Has Charlie the Duck been here with the money?

Francis   No.

Rachel   I better go chase him up. (*She exits stage right.*)

Francis   He didn't say the shirts needed ironing urgently. Maybe I could go to the high street and beg for some food.

Francis *heads for the audience but is stopped by* **Charlie**, *who enters from stage left. He is dressed for the bank and wearing a trilby. He is carrying a large bulky envelope.*

Charlie   Is your guvnor in? I've got his bangers here.

Francis   His sausages?

Charlie   Bangers and mash.

Francis *does a look to the audience as if to say my prayers have been answered.*

Francis (*aside*)   Sausage and mash in an envelope?! I've just seen the future!

Charlie   It's cockney rhyming. Bangers and mash – cash.

Francis   Agh! It's not food then?!

Charlie   It's the two hundred folding for your guvnor. Don't let me down.

Francis   WHEN AM I GOING TO EAT?!

Charlie *exits. Enter* **Stanley**.

Stanley   Henshall! Did you find your friend Paddy?

Francis   Er . . . I've arranged to meet him later, on the pier.

Stanley   What's that?

Francis   It's an envelope full of money, for my guvnor.

Stanley   I'm your guvnor.

Francis   You are, aren't you. Go on, take it. I don't care anymore.

Stanley   Must be that pawnbroker down the road. Did he have a hearing aid, a wig and a glass eye?

Francis   For sale?

Stanley   No, as functioning parts of his anatomy.

Francis   He was wearing a hat.

Stanley   Must be him. I left a pocket watch with him, earlier. I like Brighton! Pubs with food, cash delivered, it's a better kind of England!

Francis   I'm going to go in now and get on with your ironing.

Stanley   Initiative. I like it.

Francis   I thought we'd already agreed I'd iron your shirts.

Stanley   No. But have a go. I never understood how irons work. I used to bunk off physics, spent every lesson in the radiation cupboard trying to make my penis glow.

They go in.

Scene Three

Charlie's *house.* **Pauline** *is crying.*

Pauline   I can't marry that tiny, weird-looking, vicious, homosexual, short-arsed runt of a criminal.

Charlie   What you got against him?

Pauline   I want to marry for love.

Charlie   Trust me. You don't wanna marry for love! When your muvver . . . (*Breaks up slightly.*) when she left me I . . . I . . . (*Breaks up.*) –

Pauline   – don't upset yourself, Dad. What you tryna say?

Charlie   I'm tryna say that love passes through marriage quicker than shit through a small dog.

Pauline   But I love Alan.

Charlie   Marry Roscoe and you get a detached house in Essex and he won't ever touch you. You just gotta go to the boxing on his arm, show the world he ain't a nine bob note, and at two grand a year he's paying you more than Bobby Moore's getting.

Pauline   I didn't know he was living with Bobby Moore?

Charlie (*aside*)   They've tried, but they can't make bricks thicker.

Five years ago, you agreed to this agreement.

Pauline   Five years ago I was young and stupid.

Charlie   So what's changed?

Pauline   I'm a lot older now.

Dolly *enters.*

Dolly   Roscoe's back.

Pauline *starts wailing. Enter* **Rachel**.

Charlie   Hello, Roscoe! Come in, son. Did you get your bangers?

Rachel   I did not get my bangers, no. And I didn't get no banker's draft neither.

Charlie   I give the bangers to that geezer of yours. The two hundred.

Rachel   And the six thousand?

Charlie   Let's have lunch, at the Cricketers', I'll have it all signed off by then.

Rachel   What's she singing about?

Charlie   This is her grieving for your death from three days ago. She's always a bit behind.

Rachel   I'd like a word with her, if that's alright. Alone.

Charlie   Alright, Roscoe. Take your time.

He exits.

Rachel   Pauline –

Pauline   – piss off! I hate you! You've ruined my life.

Rachel   I know what would make you feel better.

Pauline   You bleeding well touch me, and I'll scream!

Rachel   I have a secret.

Pauline   I don't want to know anything about your life, I wish you were dead.

Rachel (*aside*)   I can't bear to see her suffer any longer.

I am dead.

Pauline   Are you? No! Really? What's it like?

Rachel   Roscoe, my brother is dead.

Pauline   You're Roscoe's brother?!

Rachel   Sister.

Pauline   I don't understand!

Rachel   All you need to know is that I am a woman.

Pauline   So, hang on, that means I can't marry you, dunnit.

Rachel   More importantly it means you can marry Alan.

Pauline   Can I?!

Rachel   In the near future.

Pauline   I'd better go tell him.

She makes for the door, but **Rachel** *stops her, grabbing her sleeve.*

Rachel   No! My identity must remain a secret. I need your help.

Pauline   I'll do anything to marry Alan. I love him.

Rachel   I too am in love.

Pauline   With Alan?

Rachel   No. His name's Stanley.

Pauline   It's weird innit. Love. I wanna talk about him all the time.

Rachel   That's very true, I try to turn every conversation around to Stanley.

Pauline   So do I. To Alan. Stanley's a very manly name. Alan's kinda heroic. Alan.

Rachel   Yes. Stanley killed my own brother, and yet I love him.

Pauline   Love. Huh. It's like being mad, innit.

Rachel   Insane. Look at me. Dressed in my dead brother's clothes.

Pauline   Maybe this is your way of grieving for him.

Rachel   Yes. I hadn't thought of that. (*They hold hands, consoling each other.*)

We girls have to help each other.

They hug spontaneously. Enter **Charlie**.

Charlie   Sorry, shoulda knocked.

Rachel   Charlie, you can go ahead with plans for our wedding.

Charlie   Right?!

Pauline   But I need time . . . to choose a dress.

Rachel   And the banker's draft is –

Charlie   – Roscoe, trust me, the money's no problem. I'd better go tell Laurence Olivier it's definitely off.

He heads for the door and is gone.

Pauline   Oh bloody heck! What if Dad tells Alan, Alan might think we've had it off.

Rachel   What would Alan do, if he were to think that?

Pauline   He'd go into one. He's known as a dangerous actor.

Rachel   I can look after myself.

Pauline   I know, but still, I'd better get to him before Dad does.

She heads for the door. But is held by the arm by **Rachel**.

Rachel   You swore to keep my secret.

Pauline   How long do I have to go along wiv this lie?

Rachel   Stanley and I are going to have to live in Australia.

Pauline   Oh no! Australia?! Oh no! Oh my God! Australia? Uurgh! How awful!

Rachel   It'll be a terrible outdoorsie life, sustained by lager, barbecues and opera.

Pauline   I sympathise wiv yer, but my Alan, he's suffering right now.

Rachel   Trust me. My plan will deliver to you the husband of your choice –

Pauline   – Alan?

Rachel   Yes, Alan. And the pain you feel now will be forgotten in a couple of weeks' time. The night always seems darkest just before dawn.

Pauline   What?

Rachel   That bit of the night, you know, just before dawn always seems really dark, although it isn't, it's just the contrast with the light of morning.

Pauline   I don't understand!

Scene Four

A first-floor aperitif bar squeezed between two private dining rooms. The dining rooms are named the Compton Room (stage right) and the Bradman Room (stage left). Upstage centre the stairs go down to the ground floor and the kitchens. There are autographed cricket bats on the wall. Upstage left is a life-sized plywood cut-out representation of W.G. Grace with the face cut away. **Francis** *enters from the stairs, in a panic. Goes to the door of the Compton suite.*

Francis   Roscoe is going to have lunch with Charlie up here; Mr Stubbers is in his room having a lie-down; and I've been nil by mouth for sixteen hours. I'm only alive cos me gall bladder's worked out a way of eating me kidneys. But! The good news is it's lunchtime. There's gonna be food everywhere, and all I've got to do is organise a stash, you know, leftovers, the odd whole course going missing. Hide it under here maybe.

He looks under the table. Comes up with a mousetrap.

A mousetrap with a chunk of CHESHIRE CHEESE! My favourite. All white and crumbly. And this bit's only slightly nibbled.

He licks the cheese with an extended tongue. Enter **Stanley**.

Stanley   Henshall!

Francis *jumps in fright, the mousetrap goes off on his tongue. He takes the trap off his tongue.*

Francis   Aaaargh!

Stanley   How come a mousetrap went off on your tongue?

Francis   It's a personal thing, guv.

Stanley   Understand! I too enjoy pain. Have you found Paddy?

Francis   I've arranged to meet him after LUNCH.

Stanley   I've got no time to waste on lunch. I'm going down to the pier to look for him myself.

Francis (*aside*)   Now this suits me! Get this guvnor out the way while I serve the other one.

Stanley   By the way, what does Paddy look like?

Francis   He's a big lad, smells of horses.

Stanley   Smells *of* horses? Or smells *like a* horse? The former is respectable and an indication of family money, the latter is just poor hygiene.

Francis   At the end of the day, it's the same thing ain't it.

Stanley (*a mini epiphany*)   Good point.

Francis   Now take your time, guv. There's two piers, I can't remember which pier he said now. Do you want me to order food for you, for later?

Stanley   Order what you like. When I dine I need to eat in private, waited on by you and you alone. What's this Don Bradman Room like? (*He looks into the Bradman Room.*) Perfect. I'll eat in there. (*Takes out envelope of money.*) I don't want to take all this cash with me. Can I trust you with it, Henshall?

Francis   Is it edible?

Stanley   I doubt it.

Francis   It's safe with me then, guv.

Stanley   I'll slip out the back.

He slopes off down the service stairs. Enter **Gareth** *and* **Alfie**.
Gareth *is thirty-something and a trained head waiter type.* **Alfie** *is
meant to be old, slow and doddery.*

Gareth   My name's Gareth. I'm the head waiter. This is
Alfie.

Alfie   I'm eighty-six.

Gareth   No you're not. You're eighty-seven.

Alfie   I thought I was eighty-six.

Gareth   No. That was last year. Be patient with Alfie please,
he's a bit deaf, so don't turn your back, he's gonna lip read.

Alfie   I ain't never going back there! (*To* **Francis**.) It was a
bloody massacre.

Gareth   He was at Gallipoli. He has balance problems, he's
waiting on a cataract operation, and he's got one of them
new fangled pacemakers for his heart.

Francis   Is that all I need to know?

Gareth   One other thing.

Francis   What's that?

Gareth   It's his first day. I've been told to set places for Mr
Clench and your guvnor.

Francis   In there, the Compton Room, and my other
guvnor will eat alone in the Bradman Room later, and
they've both insisted that I personally wait on their tables.

Gareth (*impressed*)   You've got two employers?

Francis   Yeah. I'm that good. I was trained by the
legendary French waiter Jean-Jacques Jim.

Gareth   In France?

Francis   Of course.

Gareth   Which town?

Francis   Ashby de la Zouch.

Gareth   That's near Loughborough.

Francis   It is now.

(Alternative here for those who don't know Ashby de la Zouch is for **Francis** *to mumble some cod French such as 'Je croissant de la pont de hohihon'.* **Gareth** *repeats this line whatever it is later in the scene.)*

Alfie   Do these guvnors of yours know you've got two jobs?

Francis   No, that is our secret for today.

Gareth   What's in it for me and Alfie?

Francis   It's less work for you and you still get paid.

Gareth   What about our tips?

Francis   You'll get ten bob from me at the end of the afternoon.

Gareth   Deal! Alfie! Set one place in the Bradman Room. I'll get some wine lists.

Alfie *starts walking towards the Bradman Room, very slowly, rattling the cutlery on the plate in an extreme manner. He can't get the door open as his hands are full so tries to open it with one buttock. Enter* **Lloyd** *with menu.*

Lloyd   How many courses do you think Roscoe and Charlie will want?

Francis   Seven.

Lloyd   Seven. A la carte?

Francis   No! They're gonna eat indoors.

Lloyd   The menu is in French. How many languages do you speak?

Francis   I speak two languages actually. English *and* French. The menu, *por favor*.

Lloyd   *Por favor* is Spanish.

Francis (*aside*)   Bloody hell! I can speak three languages.

He is given the menu. He spends a couple of beats looking at it, frowning, sweating.

Lloyd   Alfie!

Francis   He's in the Bradman.

Lloyd   What's he doing in there?

Francis   Apparently the gentleman from room ten wants to eat in private. In there later.

Lloyd   Oh. He'll need a menu then. (*He goes to the threshold of the Bradman Room.*) Alfie! (**Alfie** *is in the doorway.*) Jesus! Put this menu and wine list on the table. (**Lloyd** *gives* **Alfie** *a menu and wine list.*)

(*To* **Francis**.) Are you ready to order then?

Francis (*closing the menu with a snap*)   Yes! Can I have a lot of hot food, and, you know, just keep it coming.

Lloyd   My pleasure.

He exits down the stairs. Enter **Gareth** *from the Compton.*

Francis   So, Gareth. Alfie! Bring the food to here, this table, and I'll serve it.

Gareth   Alright. Alfie, bring the soup to here.

Alfie *exits.*

Enter **Charlie** *and* **Rachel**. **Francis** *puts a finger to his lips to inform the waiters.*

Exit **Gareth**.

Rachel   You haven't got the money have you, Charlie?

Charlie   Roscoe, this is my problem, I'll have its arse slapped by three o'clock. *And*, I'm paying for lunch, I insist.

Rachel   Francis! Charlie said he gave you some cash earlier. In an envelope.

Francis (*aside*)   Oh no! I can see what's going to happen! Roscoe's gonna take Mister Stubbers's money! That's a disaster! No, wait, it is Roscoe's money. Yes!

(*To* **Rachel**.) There you go. (*Hands it over.*)

I've set two places in here, the Denis Compton Room.

Charlie   I can't have nothing to do with Denis Compton. He was a Gooner.

Francis   Denis Compton played cricket for Arsenal?

Charlie   Football. In the winter. I'm Spurs ain't I. I can't eat in there, someone might see me.

Rachel   Let's eat in there, the Bradman Room.

Francis   NO!

Rachel   Why not?

Francis   The gentleman from room ten has already booked this room.

Rachel   He's not here is he. When room ten arrives, he can have the Compton Room. You got anything against the Aussies, Charlie?

Charlie   No. As it happens, I quite like opera. And obviously they're not Arsenal, so they're not scum.

He strides into the Bradman Room, **Rachel** *follows and closes the door.*

Francis (*aside*)   Oh shit!

Enter **Alfie** *slowly up the stairs with the soup, shaking, and looking like he might lose his balance as he goes.*

Francis   Come on, Alfie, you can do it!

Alfie   This soup must be made of lead, it's bloody heavy.

He gets to the top, still struggling with his balance. Tureen of soup on a tray.

Francis   Let me help, I'll take that.

*He lifts the tureen off the tray. This overbalances **Alfie** and he tumbles backwards down the stairs unnoticed by **Francis**. He heads to the Bradman Room and has his hand on the door handle when **Stanley** opens the upstage right door from the bedrooms, and sneaks in.*

Stanley   Henshall!

Francis   Guv?! You're back, that was quick.

Stanley   I went round to the Palace Pier, couldn't find anyone who smelt like a horse, and the other pier was on fire.

(*Aside*.) Truth is, Brighton is swarming with rozzers.

(*To **Francis**.) I'll eat now.

Francis   Now?!

Stanley   Yes. Now. What have you got there?

Francis   Your soup.

Stanley   But I wasn't even here yet.

Francis   That's how good I am.

Stanley *strides towards the door of the Bradman Room.*

Francis   Change of plan, guv. You're actually in that room there. The Compton Room.

Stanley   Why's that?

Francis   There's an Australian honeymoon couple in here.

Stanley   Ooh. Mills and Boon! Bring that soup in, I'm starving. I could eat my own pants.

Francis (*aside*)   Oh no! What am I gonna do?!

Stanley *walks into the Compton Room.* **Francis** *follows and is about to go in when* **Rachel** *opens the door from the Bradman and collects cutlery from the table.* **Francis** *slams the Compton door.*

Rachel   Francis, there's only one place setting in here. What you got there?

Francis   Your soup.

Rachel   Giss it here, then. What's the matter wiv you?

She exits back into the Bradman Room.

Francis   I haven't eaten for sixteen hours!

Enter **Gareth** *with water jug.*

Francis   Gareth! I've got two guvnors, two rooms, I need more of everything. Now! Quick.

Enter **Alfie** *with the charcuterie plate.*

Alfie (*panting, out of breath*)   Here's yer cold meats.

He hands over the plate to **Francis**. **Francis** *takes a slice of salami and eats it.* **Alfie** *turns up his pacemaker.*

Francis   What do they call that sliced sausage there?

Alfie   Pepperonly.

Francis   Beautiful.

Alfie   Sliced donkey.

Francis   I like a bit of donkey. You sound out of breath, Alfie?

Alfie   Them stairs, they tek out of yer. I'll turn mi pacemekker up a couple of notches.

Stanley *opens the door quickly, knocking* **Alfie** *in the face and over, which turns into a roll, and he rolls backwards down the stairs, unseen by* **Stanley**.

Stanley   Where's that soup you had?

Francis   It was cold. I sent it back.

Stanley   Vichysois?

Francis   No. Back downstairs.

Stanley   Get me the wine list would you.

Stanley *returns to the Compton Room, closing the door.*

Enter **Gareth** *with a second soup tureen.*

Gareth   Rule number one, for a waiter. Don't eat the food. Soup for your other guvnor.

Francis   Smashing. And he wants a wine list.

Gareth *reaches out to a supply of wine lists.*

Gareth   No empties? Have you cleared that room?

Francis   Alright, alright!

Gareth   Next up is your quenelles de volaille

Francis   Ah! My favourite, my nan used to cook quenelles de volaille every bonfire night.

Gareth   Chicken balls! (*He exits with an imperious glare.*)

Francis   Chicken balls. Really? I didn't think chickens had . . . cockerels obviously. Never understood soup. You don't need a knife and fork to eat it, so it's not food, so it must be drink, in which case I'd rather have a pint.

He picks up the tureen and drinks the soup straight from the tureen. Enter **Rachel**. **Francis** *hides the empty tureen behind his back.*

Rachel   Francis!

Francis (*with mouthful of soup which he spits out*)   Yes, guv.

Rachel   Can you clear our table please of the soup, and we'd like to order some wine.

Exit **Rachel** *into Bradman followed by* **Francis**. *He closes the Bradman door.* **Stanley** *enters from the Compton Room and collects a wine menu from the table and returns.*

Stanley   Service! Henshall! I've had slicker service in a bamboo brothel!

Seeing no **Francis**, *he picks up the soup and wine list. Turns a page; it's a decent list.*

Mmm. Winerama!

He returns to the Compton. Enter **Francis** *from Bradman with their soup tureen and empty bowls. He closes the Bradman door.*

Francis   Yes! There's some soup left in here. I need someone to look after this soup for me. (*He goes into the front row, and hands the tureen to a planted actor.*) What's your name?

Christine   Christine Patterson.

Francis   Christine Patterson. Thanks for giving us all the info. Do you want to tell us your national insurance number? Will you look after this soup? Hide it under your seat. Don't let any of these bastards touch it. Thank you, Christine Patterson.

He goes back on stage. **Alfie** *arrives with the meatballs.*

Francis   What you got there, Alfie?

Alfie   Chicken balls.

Francis   At least they're not donkeys! How many have we got here?

Alfie   Twelve.

Francis   Right, three plates. (**Alfie** *gives him three plates.* **Francis** *dishes up four meatballs to each plate, then eats one meatball with each reasoning, leaving only one meatball on each of the plates.*) Three diners, so that's four each and none for me, or three each and three for me.

Alfie   'Kinell! He's eating the 'kin chicken balls!

Francis   Or two each and six for me.

Alfie   Eh! You can't do that son. They're not for you. What they like?

Francis   Beautiful. Or one each and nine for me. (*He picks up two plates.*) I'll give these to Roscoe and Charlie. Alfie! You get on that door. Don't let him open it!

Alfie *walks slowly to the Compton door.* **Francis** *sees this and carries* **Alfie** *to speed the process up.* **Francis** *heads for the Bradman with two plates.*

Francis   I love meatballs. Succulent. Meaty. Ballsy.

Stanley *enters from the Compton Room once again slamming* **Alfie** *in the face.*

Alfie   Sorry.

Stanley   What are you doing?

Francis   Bringing you your meatballs, guv.

Stanley   One at a time? This is the wonkiest meal I've ever had. I want a bottle of the Châteauneuf-du-Pape.

Francis   Right you are, guv.

Stanley *goes back into his room closing the door himself. Enter* **Gareth** *with a range of vegetables which he puts on the table.*

Gareth   Here's your veg.

Francis   He wants a bottle of the Châteauneuf-du-Pape.

Gareth   Certainly.

Rachel (*off*)   Francis!

Enter **Rachel**.

Francis   Chicken balls, guv.

Rachel   About time. (*To* **Gareth**.) Ah, are you the wine waiter?

Gareth   I can be.

Rachel   We'd like a bottle of the '58 claret please.

Gareth   So that's one bottle of Châteauneuf-du-Pape and a bottle of the claret.

*Francis, behind **Rachel**, gesticulates that **Gareth** shouldn't say anything about the other guvnor. **Rachel** catches him gesticulating, and **Francis** covers this with some ridiculous dance routine.*

Rachel   No. Just one bottle of claret. Alright?

Gareth   Ah yes, my mistake.

Rachel *closes the door.*

Francis   Gareth, a word. (**Francis** *knees him in the balls.* **Gareth** *collapses.*) You're lucky, I nearly had to kill you then.

Gareth   Sorry. Not easy is it. Having two bosses.

Francis   Thank you. (*Exit **Gareth**.*) Now, wow! Look at all these beautiful vegetables. I want some of these for later. (*He eats a few potatoes, etc.*) Christine Patterson!

*He goes into the audience to give the vegetables to **Christine**.*

Francis   I could do with some help up here. Come on.

Christine *goes up onstage.* **Francis** *puts vegetables into the tureen as soon as he can.*

Francis   Don't smile at the band, Christine. Seriously, they'll impregnate you in a second. Cor! That's a lovely dress, Christine Patterson! Is it made of soup-resistant material? Now don't be nervous. Just stand there, over the trap door.

He scrapes the vegetables into the tureen.

Let's get you and the tureen back down there.

Lloyd (*off*)   Service!

Christine *picks up the tureen.*

Francis   Hang on! (**Lloyd** *begins to climb the stairs in full chef gear.*) Oh bloody hell, Lloyd's coming. You're gonna have to hide, Christine! Get behind W.G. Grace.

Christine *steps up behind the W.G. Grace but her face fails to show through the hole, she is too short. Because she's got big hair it looks ridiculous as if Grace has hair growing out of his cap.* **Lloyd** *enters carrying a dish with three baked trout in almonds.*

Lloyd   This is my dish of the day. *Truit aux amandes. Truit?*

Francis   Fish.

Lloyd   Trout. *Aux?*

Francis (*musical theatre style*)   Trout oh?!

Lloyd   Trout *in. Amandes?*

Francis   I know this one. Germany. Trout in Germany.

Lloyd   Trout in . . . Germany is Allemanges. *Amandes* is almonds.

Francis   Trout in almonds! Yes!

Lloyd (*looking to the Compton*)   Where's Gareth?

He exits.

Francis   For in there? . . . I'll tell him. I want some of this. I want all of this. Christine! Christine!

Christine *comes forward. He cuts the head off one of the trout and puts the body in his stash. He does the same for the other two. He is left with three fish heads.*

Francis   I got it.

He puts each separated fish head on its own plate and puts some almonds on top.

Fish heads in Germany!

He cuts a second head off and puts it on a plate.

They'll think it's posh food won't they. Won't they? It's best you don't get involved. OK, Christine, I'm going to serve these to Roscoe and Charlie. You watch that door. Do not let him open it. (*He delivers two plates to the Bradman.*) Trout heads in Germany?!

Christine *is left onstage on her own.* **Francis** *rushes out, closes Bradman door, picks up a fish head.*

Francis   They like you, Christine! Say something funny!

He goes into the Compton suite with one plate. **Christine** *sees* **Alfie** *coming up the stairs.* **Francis** *enters from the Compton and sees* **Alfie***. He shepherds* **Christine** *back behind the cut-out cricketer.*

Francis   It's Alfie! Hide. Hide, Christine. Hide. Put your head through the hole this time, that's what it's there for.

A stage manager enters with a small wooden step, which **Christine** *steps on, and this time her face and eyes show through the hole.*

Alfie   Got yer wine here, son.

Francis   Lovely, can you open that one for me. I'm a bit busy.

He takes vegetables and wine into the Bradman.

Francis   Vegetables and wine, sir.

Alfie *looks around for a corkscrew.*

Alfie   Corkscrew?

He sees **Christine***. Double take. He finds a corkscrew, comes downstage and starts to open the wine but we see him not having the strength to pull open the cork. He eventually bends down, puts the bottle between his feet, and pulls up. Nothing. We hear him wheezing with the effort and he has another go. His next attempt is to hold the wings of the corkscrew between his two feet and pull up on the bottle. This time it gives suddenly and he bangs his head on the edge of the table, knocking himself out.* **Francis** *comes out of the Bradman, sees* **Alfie** *spark out on the floor.*

Francis   Christine! I leave you on your own for two minutes! What happened.

Christine   I think he banged his head.

Francis   Banged his head? Why don't you help, then?

Stanley *opens the door of the Compton and* **Christine** *hides back behind W.G. Grace.*

Stanley (*aside*)   Good God! Colonel Mustard in the ballroom with the lead pipe.

And there's my wine. That's grand cru. Can't spill that. What a waste. Is this one dead?

He picks the wine up, forcing it out of **Alfie***'s hand with his foot.*

Francis   He's got a pacemaker. I suppose I could just turn it up a notch see what happens.

He fiddles with the pacemaker dial. **Alfie** *leaps up and starts tearing around the room at an incredible pace.*

Francis   Stop him! Trip him up!

Alfie *bangs into the Bradman door and runs off.* **Rachel** *opens the Bradman and looks out.* **Francis** *runs to the door and pushes* **Rachel** *back in and slams the door shut.*

Rachel   Francis!

Stanley *picks an autographed cricket bat off the wall and whacks* **Alfie** *in the face. Which renders him unconscious again.* **Stanley** *exits into the Compton.* **Francis** *kneels beside* **Alfie***.* **Gareth** *is climbing the stairs carrying a crown of lamb which he sets on the carvery trolley.*

Gareth   What's happened to Alfie?

Francis   His pacemaker packed up I think.

Gareth   Let me have a go. (*He kneels and fiddles with the pacemaker.*) Should be set on three. How come he had it on nine?

Francis   For the stairs.

Gareth   That's *carré d'agneau*. Crown of lamb.

He grabs **Alfie** *by the legs and drags him down the stairs, his chin hitting each step.*

Francis   Lamb chops. My favourite! Come on, Christine!

Christine *appears with the tureen.* **Francis** *separates three chops and puts the remainder in the tureen.*

Rachel (*off*)   Francis!

Francis   Christine, get back behind the W.G. (**Rachel** *appears.*) Yes, guv . . . your lamb chops, à la trolley, carved at the table.

Rachel *goes back into the Bradman, as* **Francis** *heads for the Bradman with the trolley, just as* **Stanley** *opens the Compton door.* **Francis** *slams the Bradman door shut and spins around.*

Stanley   Henshall!

Francis   Yes, guv! Lamb on wheels, carved at the table.

Stanley *heads back into the Compton followed by* **Francis**. *On the threshold of the Compton* **Rachel** *opens the Bradman door.*

Rachel   Francis! I thought you were behind me.

Francis *kicks the Compton Room door closed, spins around with the lamb.*

Francis   Yes, guv! Where did you go?! I was right behind you and then . . .

Rachel *goes back into the Bradman quickly followed by* **Francis** *and the trolley.* **Rachel** *closes the door behind him.* **Stanley** *opens the Compton door as* **Alfie** *arrives at the top of the stairs.*

Stanley   Henshall! (*To* **Alfie**.) Where's he gone?

Alfie   Please don't hurt me.

Stanley, *bemused, walks back into the Compton Room, closing the door.* **Francis** *then comes out of the Bradman with the trolley.*

Francis   What you got there, Alfie?

Alfie   Roast potatoes.

Francis   Alright! I'm coming through!

Stanley   Food fight!

Francis *pushes the trolley towards the Compton picking up* **Alfie** *on the trolley as he goes.* **Stanley** *opens the door and they sweep past him into the room. Enter* **Gareth** *with the crêpe Suzette ingredients and equipment. Enter* **Francis** *with* **Alfie** *on his back, piggy back style.* **Francis** *unceremoniously dumps* **Alfie** *and he falls down the stairs.*

Gareth   Crêpes Suzette. When you were training in Ashby de la Zouch, did they teach you how to do a proper crêpe?

Francis   Yeah. Crêpe, liqueur, matches, what could possibly go wrong? (**Gareth** *exits downstairs.*) Christine. Now! Before you go, do you know how to do Crêpes Suzette?

Christine *giggles.*

Francis   Do you serve it and set fire to it or set fire to it and serve it as it were?

You haven't got a clue have you? Christine, you've been brilliant tonight, thank you, you can go back to your seat –

Stanley (*off*)   – Henshall!

Stanley *opens the door from the Compton.*

Francis   Hide! Get down!

He guides/persuades **Christine** *to hide under the table. This needs to take a little persuasion.* **Christine** *goes under the table.*

Stanley   Problem! This wine cannot be grand cru. Taste that. (*He gives* **Francis** *a glass which he downs in one.*) What do you reckon? Is it Pape?

Francis   No. Actually I think it's quite good.

Stanley   Ah! Crêpes Suzette. Go on then. I love to watch Grand Marnier burning.

Go on. You need more than that, man! (**Francis** *drops the bottle 'spilling' liquid onto the tray.*) Whoopsy daisy. (**Francis** *lights the liqueur, but it flashes up dangerously.*)

Stanley   Fire!

Christine *backs out from under the table, her hair smoking.* **Francis** *throws water over* **Christine**. **Stanley** *gets a fire extinguisher and drenches* **Christine** *from head to toe with foam. She stands there covered in foam like an iced cake. A stage manager leads her off the stage.*

Francis   Alright. Ladies and gentlemen! Don't worry. Nobody is injured.

(*Direct address.*) What I suggest we do is take a fifteen-minute interval here. You can have a drink. We're going to fill out health and safety forms. But I did it, didn't I! I served two guvnors, and they're still none the wiser, and most important of all, I get to eat! See you in fifteen minutes. Have a good interval!

Interval.

Act Two

Scene One

Round the back of **Charlie**'s *house. The trading sign reads 'SCRAP METALS' and a tag sign reads 'Ferrous and non-ferrous, copper and Yorkstone'.* **Alan** *arrives, determined. He takes out a knife. Enter* **Dangle**.

Alan   Destiny. Destiny. Destiny. What is destiny? If you're a bus, your destiny is the bus station. And if you talk to buses, as I do, they tell you that their destiny is writ deep in their bussy souls, it is inescapable, it is the timetable. Buses laugh at love. Love is fluff, very fluffy fluff, destiny is steel.

Dangle   Orlando?! What are you doing here?

Alan   I said I would return and take my revenge – *et voila*!

Dangle   Where did you get that knife?

Alan   Woolies. My honour has been fiddled with.

Dangle   Put it away, boy. We, the educated classes, have our own weapons: the law, contract and my particular specialism – *sesquipedalia verbis*.

Alan   Words?

Dangle   Not just words, words a foot and a half long.

Alan   If *sesquipedalia verbis* fails, if Charlie refuses to allow me to marry Pauline, tell him he will have this to deal with. (*He holds the knife out. He exits.* **Charlie** *opens his front door.*)

Charlie   What?

Dangle   Have the impediments before Alan's marriage to Pauline been removed as I demanded?

Charlie   No. And it ain't my fault. I thought Roscoe was dead.

During **Dangle**'s *next speech* **Charlie** *tries to interrupt but fails.*

Dangle   Your precocious contract with Roscoe was initiated in order to facilitate a relationship of mutual expediency and as such is antithetical to the Judeo/Christian and common law conception of marriage. The contract's legality is at best ephemeral and in resurrecting it, following Roscoe Crabbe's own miraculous resurrection, is a classic exemplar of breach of promise. *Post hoc ergo propter hoc*.

Charlie   What you trying to say?

Dangle   You're up shit creek without a paddle!

Charlie   In my world there's a code. It ain't written down, there's no books, but it's a code, like the law. I ain't got no choice, but to abide by it.

Dangle   On reflection I am not sure that I want my son to dive into the fetid pond that is your family.

Charlie   Yeah, yeah. Pauline's gonna marry Roscoe and that's that. And I'll give you some Latin for a change. *Que sera sera*! (*Exit* **Dangle**. **Charlie** *turns to go back indoors. Enter* **Alan**.) Bugger me, it's Errol Flynn!

Alan   Is it true?

Charlie   Yeah, it is true, yeah. What?

Alan   Is Pauline to marry Roscoe Crabbe?

Charlie   That's right. Wait here, I'll get you a presents list.

Alan *draws the knife, nervously, a little embarrassed by its reality.*

Alan   Do not torment me! I am no longer responsible for my actions, I am dangerous, unpredictable, like a wasp in a shop window.

Charlie   Where did you get that knife?

Alan   Woolies.

Charlie   What you gonna do with it, sunshine?

Alan   You've never shown me any respect! My first Chekhov, I got you a free ticket to see me give my Konstantin –

Charlie   – the Rottingdean Players?

Alan   – you didn't come! You went to play snooker!

Charlie   I live in Brighton. I don't need to drive to Rottingdean to watch someone shoot a bloody seagull.

Alan   Don't push me! I can do it.

Charlie   No, you can't. 'Cause this is real, it ain't a play.

Alan *lunges towards* **Charlie**. **Charlie** *parries the knife-bearing arm. They are in a clinch with* **Charlie** *holding the knife arm.* **Charlie** *falls on to his back.* **Charlie** *is at the mercy of* **Alan**, *who places the knife against his neck. Enter* **Rachel**.

Rachel   Alan?

Alan   Don't come any nearer, Roscoe! I will, I can!

Rachel   Where did you get that knife?

Alan   WOOLIES!

She takes out a flick knife and flicks it open. It's cool, it's gangland, it's the real thing. She walks up to **Alan** *and places the point of the knife under his chin.*

Rachel   It ain't the knife that's dangerous. It's the owner. Throw that away.

Alan   No. I came here to kill Charlie.

Rachel   You don't want to kill Charlie, you want to kill me. But you can't because, in the split second it would take to raise your arm, my knife will be sorting out your tonsils. Or have you had your tonsils removed?

Alan   No. I've still got them.

Enter **Pauline** *from the house.*

Pauline   Roscoe! Please, don't kill Alan, he don't mean no harm, he's only acting! Where'd yer . . . (*She ostentatiously looks at the knife.*)

Alan   Woolworths! On the high street. Hardware and kitchens! (*Distraught at his own failure to act he lets go of his knife.* **Rachel** *kicks it away.*)

Rachel   I'll spare him, for your sake, *my darling*.

Alan   Oh.

Rachel   And I expect you, in return, to do me a favour, that is to respect our secret.

Pauline   I do. I will.

Alan *stands, the action of which releases* **Charlie**, *who also stands.* **Dolly** *appears at the window. She's watching and listening.*

Charlie   Is that it, then? 'Cause I've got a cup of tea going cold in there.

Pauline   Yeah, go indoors, Dad.

Rachel   Charlie! It's gone three o'clock.

Charlie   What?! You're not telling me you ain't got your money yet? I don't believe it! I told Dolly to . . . agh! Cor! If you want anything done properly, you gotta do it yourself. Go indoors, Roscoe. I'll sort it for you.

He holds the door open for **Rachel**, *who enters.*

Charlie   Alan, son. A word.

Alan *turns to* **Charlie**. **Charlie** *nuts him and he collapses. Exit indoors* **Charlie**.

Pauline   Are you hurt, my love?

Alan   Have you been with him?

Pauline   Been where?

Alan   Bed!

Pauline   No! God! Alan. Really, absolutely no, not ever, never, no.

Alan   The lady doth protest too much methinks.

Pauline   I'm a virgin! Still. You know I am.

Alan   Don't I just.

Pauline   I'm saving myself for you, Alan, for when we're married, when we can do it two or three times a week legally.

She grabs him, he tosses her aside, and she falls near the knife.

Alan   No! I think your shared secret is that you've always loved him. You've bewitched him, like you've bewitched me, with your little prick teases. You play a man like a penny whistle. I loathe you.

Pauline   Don't talk like that, Alan! I'll die.

Alan   Do you think I care if you die?

Pauline   I'm gonna go do meself in then.

She sees the knife. She picks it up.

Alan   Go on then.

Pauline   How can you be so cruel?

Alan   I've had a good teacher.

She holds the knife in both hands and holds it against her heart. Because she's kneeling the idea is that she will fall forward on to the knife to kill herself. It looks as if she might do it.

Dolly   He's not worth it, love. He'd stand there and watch you do it, and not raise a finger. Look at him. You're not the great romantic lover are you? You're a bit of a twat. Let me give you some advice. Men, they'll do anything to get you into bed. Lie, cheat, buy you a bed. And the tragedy is once they've had you, they'll never want you quite as much ever again.

(*Aside.*) Don't take notes, girls, there's a handout at the end.

Pauline *throws the knife aside, takes* **Dolly***'s hand and stands.*

Pauline (*tearful*)   I can't believe you woulda let me kill meself. You're heartless. I'm gonna die anyway, 'cause I can't live with this pain. And when I'm dead I want you to know that it'll be you wot killed me. (*She exits into the house.*, **Dolly** *moves to follow but stays listening, surreptitiously.*)

Alan   Frailty, thy name is woman! Women are born actors. Whenever they want something, enter from stage left *the waterworks*.

Dolly   You want to watch your tongue, young man, slagging us women off. It's 1963, there's a revolution coming. I predict in twenty years' time there'll be a woman in 10 Downing Street, yeah, and she won't be doing the washing up. Then you'll see exactly what women can do. You'll see a more just and fair society. The feminine voice of compassion for the poor will be the guiding principle of government, and there'll be an end to foreign wars.

She closes the door and is gone.

Scene Two

The pub forecourt. Mid-morning. **Francis** *is sitting enjoying the sun, perhaps a post-food cigarette.*

Francis   So I've eaten. Now, after a lovely big meal there's a couple of things I just can't resist doing. One is having a little smoke – (*Drag on cigarette. Then he lifts a buttock and farts.*) And that's the other. Some of you out there, who understand your commedia dell'arte, your hummus eaters, might now be asking yourselves, 'If the Harlequin, that's me, has now eaten what will be his motivation in the second act?' Has anyone here said that? Perhaps in an attempt to impress a date. No. Good. Nice to know we don't have any dicks in tonight. My character, the Harlequin, now that he's eaten has to find some other base motivation to drive his actions in the second half. Your job is to try and work out what that might be.

Enter **Dolly**, *miniskirt, boobs, etc. She doesn't see* **Francis**. **Francis** *leches at her. Makes a mucky, lustful face for himself. Adjusts his tackle.*

Dolly   Pauline's written one letter to Alan today, and one letter for Roscoe.

Francis   Are we going then? Majorca?

Dolly (*aside*)   Oh it's him. I like him.

(*To* **Francis**.) I've got a letter here for your gaffer. Can I trust you with it?

Francis   'Confidential' is my middle name.

Dolly   What are your other names?

Francis   Francis . . . Henshall.

Dolly   So your full name is *Francis Confidential Henshall*?

Francis   At your service, gorgeous.

Dolly (*aside*)   Calling a woman 'gorgeous' is patronising and chauvinist, obviously, but since I fancy him rotten, and I haven't had a proper sorting out for a while, I'll forgive him.

(*To* **Francis**.) You've got honest eyes.

Francis   Thank you. Baby.

Dolly   No trouble. Big Boy.

Francis   A friend of mine likes you.

Dolly   What's his name?

Francis   Paddy.

Dolly   What's he look like?

Francis   He's a good-looking lad. He's er . . . big boned.

Dolly   And how did he get big bones?

Francis   The usual. Nature/nurture.

Dolly   Partly genetic, partly pies?

Francis   He likes his food, yeah.

Dolly   Does he prefer eating or making love?

Francis (*aside*)   Mmm. Tricky one that, innit.

Would you like to meet him?

Dolly   I wouldn't want to interrupt him if he's eating.

Francis   I'll go and get him. Stay there. Don't put your glasses on.

He enters the inn.

Dolly (*aside*)   I've done a lot worse. We've all done a lot worse haven't we, girls? We've all woken up 'the morning after the night' before, taken one look at the sorry state of the bloke lying next to us, and we've all leapt out of bed, sat down and written to Parliament demanding that tequila should be a controlled drug.

(*Only if no one laughs at the tequila joke.*) Just me then?

Francis *returns from the inn carrying a rose.*

Francis (*Irish accent*)   Now hello there! I'm Patrick. Me friends call me Paddy and I'm in love with you, I am so.

Dolly   Are you really?

Francis   Yes, I'm a hopeless case. I'm like a cork, tossed on an ocean of desire.

Dolly   Is that difficult?

Francis   It's exhausting. There's only so much tossing a man can endure. I grew this rose for you now, I did, so, aye. I watered it meself, and did the baby bio thing an' all, according to all them fancy instructions on the side of the packet there. Aye.

Dolly   That's very sweet of you.

Francis   Any chance of a kiss? (*They kiss.*) I'd better go now, I left me horse on a double yellow.

He exits.

Dolly   He's like a big kid. I've always liked that in a man, immaturity.

Francis *returns.*

Francis   What do you reckon to Paddy? D'yer like him?

Dolly   Why can't you, Francis, as Francis, just ask me out for a date?

Francis   I've asked you to go to Majorca.

Dolly   I can't just go to Majorca with you. We need to go on a date first.

Francis   Alright.

(*Aside, question direct to female audience member.*) What's a good first date from the girl's point of view?

Improvise on response along the lines of 'You slut!', 'Have you seen me eat?' etc.

NO! She's got to feel relaxed, secure, not under pressure. Er . . .?

(*To* **Dolly**.)   Dolly? How about me and you, you know, I was wondering, Saturday, Saturday afternoon, not evening, no pressure, would you like to go on a rabbit shoot?

Dolly   I think you should take me to the (*whatever the audience answer was*) . . . thank you . . . and we could go for a drink afterwards. We could give the relationship a go, see if it's got legs.

Francis   Excellent! And if it hasn't got legs and neither of us can stand up we'll have to find something that we can both do lying down.

Dolly   You've got everything worked out haven't you, Francis?

Francis   I'm a man. We plan. We don't just waddle into things with our eyes closed doing fluffy stuff because it feels right, like you women do.

Dolly *stands and moves away from him.*

Dolly   It's been nice knowing you, Francis.

Francis   What've I said now?

Dolly   It's not gonna work is it?

Francis   What? Me and you?

Dolly   Men and women!

Francis   That's a shame. 'Cause I really fancy you.

Dolly   Thank you. I've always wanted to be a sex object.

Francis   It's better than not being a sex object, innit?

Dolly   Uurgh!

Francis   We're supposed to be going to Majorca.

Dolly   You can't deliver Majorca, Francis. It's fifty quid a ticket.

Francis (*beat*)   Who's this letter for again?

Dolly   Your guvnor. (*He starts to open it.*) Don't open it!

Francis   I have to find out who it's for!

Dolly   Just give it to your boss.

Francis   IT'S NOT AS EASY AS THAT!

Dolly   I can't see what the problem –

Francis   LOOK! There's no name on the envelope.

Dolly   What do you need a name for?!

Francis   BECAUSE . . . BECAUSE . . . I CAN'T TELL YOU. IT'S VERY COMPLICATED AND REALLY YOU DON'T WANT TO KNOW!

He collapses onto the floor, and starts beating the floor and rocking catatonically. Enter **Rachel** *with* **Charlie***. They stand and view* **Francis** *rocking.*

Charlie   What's up, Dolly?

Dolly   No idea.

Rachel   Francis! What's that?!

Dolly   It's a letter. For you.

Francis *stops rocking suddenly and stands.*

Francis (*to* **Dolly**)   WHY DIDN'T YOU JUST SAY IT WAS FOR ROSCOE?!

Dolly *collapses dramatically onto the floor, and rocks catatonically. All an act mirroring* **Francis***'s reaction.*

Dolly   BECAUSE I'M A WOMAN AND I'M REALLY STUPID, AND I CAN'T BE TRUSTED TO DO ANYTHING PROPERLY! AAAAAGGHHH! (*She stops abruptly, stands, brushes herself down.*)

Men!

Rachel   This is the second private letter you've opened today. I have no choice, mate, you're sacked.

Dolly   No! I opened the letter.

Charlie   Come again?!

Dolly   I'm worried sick about Pauline. So I opened the letter. And I read it. And now I'm going home.

(*To* **Francis**.) Nice to see you, Francis. I like your friend, Paddy. He's not an idiot.

She exits.

Francis (*shouted after her*)   I'll get two tickets for Majorca, I promise.

Charlie   I'll go and see my mate Dino. Give me ten minutes. Carlotti's Amusements on the front.

He exits. **Rachel** *reads the whole of the letter.* **Francis** *tries to slowly sneak away.*

Rachel (*to* **Francis**, *without looking at him*)   Where are you going?

Francis   Me?

Rachel   Come here.

Francis *approaches* **Rachel**. *We see* **Stanley** *open a window.* **Rachel** *knees* **Francis** *in the testicles.*

Stanley (*aside*)   Who's that hitting my man?

Francis   What d'yer do that for?

Rachel   What's my name?

Francis   Roscoe Crabbe.

Rachel   And what have you heard about the Crabbes?

Francis (*aside*)   No, no. Don't worry, we're not going there.

You don't mess with them.

Rachel   If you need me, I'm in Carlotti's Amusement Arcade. On the front. What are you going to do?

Francis   I'm gonna do your ironing, then I'm gonna try and find Paddy on the pier, like you said.

Rachel   Who's Paddy?

A **Policeman** *enters and watches.*

Francis (*aside*)   Shit.

Francis   Paddy is a friend of mine who works as a kind of butler to someone in Brighton and he said he could teach me how to iron a shirt properly so that nobody gets seriously injured.

Rachel   Good man. Afternoon.

She exits.

Francis (*aside*)   My nerves!

Enter **Stanley**.

Stanley   Henshall?! What's going on? I swear I saw a chap kick you in the clementines?

Francis   Yeah, one of the locals.

Stanley   Soggy biscuits! What had you done?

Francis   I kissed his girlfriend.

Stanley   Out of the blue you just went up and kissed a chap's girl?

Francis   Yup.

Stanley   That's a bit Japanese. I'm sorry, I'm on his side. Come here.

Francis   Oh no please, guv.

Stanley *beats him up. The* **Policeman** *enters*.

Stanley   Morning.

Policeman   Afternoon.

Stanley   I'll give you one hour to finish my ironing that you never started, and then I want you to go to the pier and find Paddy.

He exits to the pub. Enter **Alfie**, *with a coat on and scarf.*

Francis   Alfie! Do you know where there's a Thomas Cook's?

Alfie   Of course I know her, she's my wife.

Francis HAS BRIGHTON GOT A TRAVEL AGENTS?

Alfie There's a Thomas Cook's opposite Brighton Pavilion.

Francis Pick us up a brochure for Majorca. I'll either be ironing indoors, or down on the pier.

Alfie *exits slowly.* **Francis** *sees this and turns up his pacemaker, and* **Alfie** *skips off manically.* **Francis** *sits.*

Francis (*aside*) So, do you see how this play works? In the first half I'm driven by my animal urges, hunger, but in this second half, because I've eaten, I am humanised, civilised, and I can embrace the potentiality of love. Which, in this version, is expressed as a leg-over in Majorca.

Scene Three

The corridor outside rooms 10 and 11. An ironing board and an iron. **Stanley**'s *trunk is set to stage right outside his room, room 10, and the trunk is open.* **Rachel**'s *trunk is outside room 11, and the trunk lid closed.*

Francis (*direct address*) Now, Mister Stubbers is asleep in number 10. Roscoe's chasing Charlie for the money. That's Mr Stubbers's shirts done. The plan is to do both sets of ironing and then go and look for Paddy on the pier. Yes, I know, Paddy doesn't exist, but that's the kind of insanity that makes perfect sense when you've got two jobs. (*He pulls out a pile of shirts from* **Rachel**'s *trunk and drops them on the ironing board. On top of the pile of shirts is a framed photograph.*) What's this? Bloody hell! It's a framed photograph of Mister Stubbers. These are Roscoe's shirts. What is my guvnor number one Roscoe doing with a framed photograph of my guvnor number two Mister Stubbers?

Stanley (*off*) Henshall! Is there a shirt ready yet?

Enter **Stanley** *naked from the waist up, but wearing trousers with braces hanging down. The great shock though is that he is extraordinarily hairy. His chest and up to his neck is totally covered* *in thick chest hair. It is extreme. He walks downstage of the ironing board and turns upstage showing his back, which is even worse, hairy like a gorilla.* **Francis** *is gobsmacked.*

Stanley   What are you gawping at, Henshall? Never seen a man naked from the waist up, eh? Don't tell me you're the kind of chap that didn't shower. That's how we won two world wars. The Germans had superior technology, but our officers showered together.

(*He picks up the framed photo.*) What's that?

Francis   Oh sorry, guv, that's mine.

Stanley (*aside*)   This is a framed photograph of me on graduation day, the very one I gave to Rachel.

Why do you have a framed photograph of me in your possession? Are you developing a thing for me?

Francis   No, guv. It's a nice frame.

Stanley   Where did you get it?

Francis (*aside*)   I've gotta be very careful what I say here.

I bought it off Paddy, who was given it by his previous employer in lieu of payment before . . . he died.

Silence.

Stanley   Before he did . . . before he did what?

Francis   Before he did . . . die.

Stanley   He did die did he?

Francis   He did.

Stanley   What did he die of?

Francis   He was diagnosed with diarrhoea but died of diabetes.

Stanley   He died of diabetes did he?

Francis   He did didn't he?

Stanley   Where you there?

Francis   When?

Stanley   When he was diagnosed with diarrhoea but died of diabetes.

Francis   No, I was in Didcot, and he was diagnosed with diarrhoea but died of diabetes in Dagenham.

Stanley   When did he die?

Francis   Of diabetes? Or of diarrhoea?

Stanley   He didn't die of diarrhoea he died of diabetes.

Francis   He did did he? Where?

Stanley   In Dagenham! Damn it! That's what you said!

Francis   Paddy told me it was a couple of days ago.

Stanley   Rachel is dead. But she is all I live for. Grief. Grief. My girl, my love, my life, is dead. Breathe, man, breathe. Everything. There is nothing without her.

He goes back into his room. The door closes.

Francis   That went quite well. (*He continues ironing.*)

Charlie (*off*)   I'm like you, I prefer cash –

Francis (*aside*)   Just my luck! It's my other guvnor, Roscoe, with Mister the Duck.

Enter **Rachel** *and* **Charlie**.

Charlie   It's not like Dino to let me down.

Rachel   Your failure to deliver means that I will have to change my plans.

Charlie   Give me the weekend. I'm playing golf Sunday with –

Rachel   – shut it! Francis, look in my trunk, find my diary.

Francis asks a female member of the audience on the front row for help identifying Roscoe's trunk.

Francis   Oh no! Can you remember which trunk is Roscoe's? This one? Thank you, madam. You are a life-saver . . . there you are, guv.

He reaches into **Stanley's** *trunk and takes out a diary with letters tucked inside, and he hands it over to her.* **Rachel** *is off.*

Francis (*to helpful audience member*)   Thank you, madam! Thank you! Brilliant!

Rachel (*off*)   This is not my diary!

Francis (*to audience member who 'helped' identify trunk*)   You stupid cow!

Threatens her with the iron. Enter **Rachel** *with diary.*

Francis   Ah! Yes, there it is! Cor! I've been looking for that! It's mine!

He tries to take it off **Rachel** *but she hangs on to it.*

Rachel   But you handed it to me, thinking it was mine.

Francis   The reason is . . . I haven't owned it for very long, so I don't yet recognise it that easily.

Rachel *moves downstage.*

Rachel (*aside*)   This diary is Stanley's. These are the letters in which I express my love for him. Letters and diagrams. It is a celebration of the most intimate details of our lovemaking. But how . . .

(*To* **Francis**.) Francis! How come this diary, and these private letters, are in your possession?

Francis (*aside*)   I've gotta be very careful what I say here.

(*To* **Rachel**.)   I bought it off Paddy.

Rachel   The ironing expert?

Francis   Yes. Who was given it in lieu of payment by my previous employer just before he died.

(*Aside.*) If it ain't broke, don't fix it.

Rachel *is stunned into silence.*

Rachel   He died did he?

Francis   He did.

Rachel   How did he die?

Francis   He died of disease.

Rachel   Where?

Francis   Where was the disease, or where did he die of disease?

Rachel   Where did he die of disease?

Francis   Dorking.

Rachel   And where was the disease?

Francis   In his diaphragm.

Rachel   So he died of a disease of the diaphragm in Dorking?

Francis   He did didn't he?

Rachel   Do you know Dorking?

Francis   I don't. Do you know Dorking Mister Duck?

Charlie   Indeed I do. Dorking is directly north of here.

Rachel   One might pass through Dorking on the way to Brighton?

Charlie   If you're daft and don't know what you're doing, definitely.

Rachel (*aside*)   Definitely Stanley.

(*Letting her disguise drop now.*) Stanley! Dead?! No! My love, dead?! No! This cannot be! Without Stanley my life is nothing. I do not want to live, here, on this earth, alone without him. I have given him my life, my love, my body.

Charlie and **Francis** *are confused.*

Francis (*aside*)   Bloody hell, he's a woman!

Charlie   Roscoe? You're not Roscoe, you're Rachel?

Rachel   Yes. I am in disguise as my twin brother. Who is also dead. I have lost a brother, and the love of my life both in the one week.

Charlie   You proper fooled us. I take my hat off to you. I guess it was easy enough 'cause you and Roscoe was identical twins.

Rachel   Roscoe was a man. I, as you can see, am a woman. So we cannot be identical twins.

Charlie   Why not?

Rachel   Excuse me, gentlemen. I am in mourning. For a brother, and a husband.

She exits to her room.

Charlie   I better go tell Harry Dangle this. His lad'll be chuffed to bits. Unless he's been and gone and done an 'amlet by now.

Francis   What's a Hamlet?

Charlie   A Hamlet is when you flip, kill everyone including yourself.

Francis   That's a bit rash.

Charlie   Not rash enough. The last time I saw it, it took him five hours.

He exits.

Scene Four

The pier. Enter **Stanley** *at pace. He jumps up on to the railing, hanging on to the lamp post. He takes a look at the ocean and jumps.*

Stanley   No! No! RACHEL!

Enter **Rachel**, *she climbs up on to the pier railing holding on to the lamp post stage right. Enter* **Lloyd** *at pace. He stops, believing that advancing might make* **Rachel** *jump.*

Rachel   STANLEY!

Lloyd   What you doin' girl?!

Rachel   I will, Lloyd! I will! Stanley is dead. I love him. He is everything. Without him this life has nothing to offer me.

Stanley *enters by climbing up.*

Stanley   Rachel?!

Rachel   Stanley?!

Lloyd   Mister Pubsign?!

Stanley   Rachel, my darling, I thought I'd lost you.

Rachel   I cried Stanley, you don't know how much I cried.

Still perilous on the pier railings.

Lloyd   Don't you think it might be a good idea if you both stepped down from off of that railing there.

Stanley   Good thinking! (*They both climb down. They hug.*) My little badger!

Rachel   My hairy bear!

Lloyd (*aside*)   My time to go!

He starts to leave.

Rachel   Lloyd! Wait. (*She comes downstage to talk to* **Lloyd**. *This is private from* **Stanley**.) I'm pretty certain Paddy is behind this.

Lloyd   Who the hell is Paddy?

Rachel   He's a friend of Francis, works for Stanley. I need to talk to Francis. Drag his arse down here would you, Lloyd?

Lloyd   My pleasure. I can't say no to you. You're like a daughter to me, girl!

Rachel   You're the very best of men, Lloyd. Has anyone ever told you that?

Lloyd   Yes. (*He looks to the audience with a wink, suggesting Parkhurst.*)

He exits. **Rachel** *and* **Stanley** *are alone. She runs to him.*

Stanley   What made you think I was dead, badgie?

Rachel   I was scared, after the fight, and I hired a minder for protection, and he had this – (*She shows* **Stanley**'s *diary and her letters.*)

Stanley   Bacon and eggs! That's my private diary!

Rachel   – and all the love letters I've ever sent you.

Stanley   No?!

Rachel   My minder said he'd bought your diary from a friend of his who had worked for you –

Stanley   – for me?!

Rachel   For you. But you'd died, and you'd given him the diary in lieu of payment.

Stanley (*aside/shocked*)   I don't remember doing any of this!

Did he read any of your love letters?

Rachel   I can't be sure.

Stanley   Let's hope not, eh, one or two of them have got some really good bits.

A **Policeman** *enters. He sees* **Rachel** *and* **Stanley** *and exits at pace.*

Rachel   But what made you think I was dead?

Stanley   My man had in his possession that framed photograph of me, the one I'd given you.

Rachel   But how come your man had my photograph of you?

Stanley   Paddy's story is that you gave it to him on your death bed, so I presumed that you must be Paddy's employer who died. But you're not dead.

Rachel   Did you feel terrible, hairy bear?

Stanley   I've never felt worse. I felt like a floral clock in the middle of winter.

Beat.

Rachel   That's exactly how I felt! All the flowers dead!

Stanley   And yet the mechanism of the clock is pointlessly turning?!

Rachel   The hour hand pointing to a dead geranium!

Stanley   The minute hand stuck on a long gone begonia.

They kiss. Two **Policemen** *loiter but leave them alone.*

Rachel   Stanley, I really don't want to go to Australia.

Stanley   Oh. Thank Christ! I never did. I can't stand bloody opera.

Rachel   What can we do?

Stanley   Could you marry a murderer?

Rachel   I guess, I'm already in love with a murderer.

Stanley   Who?!

Rachel   You.

Stanley   Oh God! Don't do that.

Enter **Lloyd** *dragging* **Francis** *along.*

Rachel   Here's one of the troublemakers now.

Stanley　Thank you, Lloyd, but in an ideal world we need them both here. It wouldn't be right to light a fire under one of them, and let the other one get away with it.

Lloyd　He's the only one I've seen.

Enter **Alfie** *carrying a Thomas Cook's travel brochure.*

Alfie　Here you go, son, here's your brochure.

Lloyd　Maybe Alfie would know.

Stanley　Alfie, have you seen the other gentleman?

Alfie　There's new toilets at the end of the pier.

Rachel　HAVE YOU SEEN PADDY?

Alfie　They had to put newspaper down 'cause I'd had a banana.

Francis　One minute, please?!

Francis *takes* **Alfie** *to one side, out of earshot.* **Stanley** *and* **Rachel** *talk together.* **Alfie** *hands over travel brochure to* **Francis** *who rapidly finds the section on Majorca.*

Francis　Now listen, there's a woman called Dolly works for Charlie Clench, the scrap metal dealer. Give her this Majorca page.

He gives the Majorca page from the brochure to **Alfie**.

Alfie　How will I recognise this Dolly?

Francis　Easy. (*He mimes big breasts with his hands.*)

Alfie　What? She's got arthritic hands?

Francis　No, she's a big girl. Tell Dolly that Paddy is dead, so she'll have to go to Majorca with me.

Alfie　You ain't got the money, son. It's fifty quid a ticket.

Francis　Not yet but I'm working on it.

Alfie *goes to leave but is accosted by* **Lloyd**.

Stanley   Henshall! I think this Paddy is the cause of all our problems.

Francis   Yes! And I have a completely brilliant plan which will punish him.

Stanley   Hit me.

Francis (*to* **Stanley**)   There's this sweet, shy, innocent girl called Dolly –

Stanley   – is she a virgin?

Francis   Definitely.

Stanley   Went out with a virgin once. Not for long, obviously, that'd be stupid.

Francis   Her Paddy has tricked Dolly into going for a dirty weekend in Margate.

Stanley   What a country life!

Francis   But she has this dream of going to Majorca, but she hasn't got the fifty quid for a ticket. If you could buy her a ticket to Spain then she won't want to go to Margate and we would have rescued her from Paddy's evil scheme and punished Paddy at the same time.

Stanley   Brilliant! Here's fifty sterling, go to the travel agent and get that poor girl a ticket.

Francis   Wait! Do you think we should let her go on her own?

Stanley   To Spain, no. Not with their men. I wouldn't trust a Spaniard alone with a Swiss roll. When's this dirty weekend?

Francis   Week after next.

Stanley   Here's another fifty, Henshall. You're just going to have to go with her. And if anything happens between you, at least the cherry was picked by an Englishman.

Stanley *heads upstage.*

Francis   Miss? A word.

Rachel *and* **Francis** *go downstage with* **Stanley**'s *nodded consent.*

Rachel   We need to punish Paddy. He nearly caused two suicides.

Francis   Mister Stubbers and I have a plan. Paddy has asked Dolly to go for a dirty weekend, but if I offer Dolly a week in Majorca, she's bound to prefer sunny Spain over forty-eight hours face down, handcuffed to a Margate four-poster.

Rachel   It would certainly be revenge on Paddy and much more satisfying than a punch in the face. What do you need?

Francis   Fifty quid and next week off.

Rachel   Brilliant, here's fifty.

She gets out a roll and gives **Francis** *fifty, and goes upstage to join* **Stanley**.

Francis (*aside*)   Yes! One hundred and fifty quid! That's two flights and fifty spenders! I'm a genius.

A police whistle blows offstage. Two uniformed **Policemen** *run on.*

Stanley   Rozzers!

Rachel   Oh my God! What do we do?

Lloyd   Split up! Meet at Charlie's! Alfie!

They all split up and run off in different directions. **Alfie** *beats the* **Policemen** *up. Or alternatively,* **Alfie** *diverts the* **Policemen** *but ends up crashing through the pier and falling into the sea.*

Scene Five

At **Charlie**'s *house. Same as Act One, Scene One. The living room.* **Charlie**, **Dolly**, **Dangle**, **Alan** *and* **Pauline**. **Alan** *is kneeling in the centre of the room.* **Pauline** *has her back turned against him, looking out the window.*

Dolly   How long's this gonna take? In an ideal world I'd be home by now, relaxing in a hot bath with a fireman.

Charlie (*to* **Pauline**)   Come on, Pauline, forgive the lad. He made a mistake.

Pauline (*with underlying tenderness*)   You've been really really horrible to me recently, Alan.

Dangle (*to* **Charlie**)   There is tenderness there.

Charlie (*to* **Dangle**)   She called him Alan.

Alan   I would cut myself and offer you my blood but first observe my tears.

He tries and succeeds in crying real tears.

Charlie   Cor! Look at that. He can turn it on like a tap! Turn around, girl, you can't miss this, he's actually crying real tears.

Pauline *turns around.* **Dangle** *and* **Charlie** *nod to each other hopefully.*

Pauline (*sigh*)   Don't cry, Alan.

Dangle (*under his breath*)   Excellent!

Charlie (*to* **Dangle**)   Them tears done the trick!

Alan   Pauline, will you share my life with me?

Pauline   I dunno, you said you loathed me.

Dangle/Charlie (*deflating*)   Oh!/Shit!

Alan   I did loathe you, yes. But that was in the distant past, this afternoon, when I was tossed on the ocean of love's vagaries.

Pauline   Eh?

Alan   I was deranged, aberrant, demented.

Pauline   I don't understand.

The doorbell sounds.

Alan   Do you forgive me, my love?

Pauline   Well . . .

Charlie *and* **Dangle** *are willing an affirmative.* **Dolly** *enters.*

Dolly   It's Lloyd, with a woman, and a man and Roscoe's minder.

Pauline   Let them in, Dad, please, I wanna know if Rachel's alright.

Alan   'If Rachel's alright'. What about me?!

Charlie/Dangle   No!/Ohhhh!

Pauline   I do forgive you, Alan. That's what love is, innit. Forgiving someone when they've been a right twat.

They kiss.

Charlie/Dangle   Yes!/Done!

Charlie *and* **Dangle** *shake hands. Enter* **Lloyd**, **Rachel**, **Stanley** *and* **Francis**. *Throughout the scene* **Francis** *winks and nods at* **Dolly**.

Lloyd   Charlie!

Charlie   I want a word with you, Lloydie? You're supposed to be my best china –

Lloyd   – I –

Charlie   – did you know about this!

Lloyd   Yessir, I did! What I did, I did for her. She's a great girl. She's like a daughter to me, man!

Rachel   I apologise, to you Alan, and to Charlie, for disguising myself as Roscoe.

Charlie   I guess it was the obvious thing to do, given you was identical twins.

Rachel   I'll do this once, Charlie, and once only. Identical twins, also known as monozygotic twins, develop when a single sperm fertilises a single egg to form a single zygote, hence *monozygote*, which then splits and forms two embryos which carry *identical* genetic material. Dizygotic twins are formed when two separate eggs are fertilised by two separate sperm forming two separate zygotes. Twins of different sexes must be dizygotic. They cannot be monozygotic, identical twins, because they would have to be, by definition, of the same sex.

Beat.

Charlie (*Beat.*)   What's your point?

Alan (*standing, taking his jacket off*)   Let me explain –

All   – No! Can we – Please! Listen!

Lloyd   Forget it! You're flogging a dead horse.

Rachel   Charlie. This is Stanley.

Pauline (*to* **Rachel**)   I'm so glad everything's worked out for you. I'm sorted with Alan now an' all.

Rachel   Stanley and I are going to get married.

Charlie   Congratulations.

Rachel   And we're going to the police, to face the music.

Lloyd   You do right! The police love you. You rid the East End of Roscoe Crabbe!

Stanley   I shall plead self-defence.

Charlie   What you need is a good solicitor. This is Harry Dangle. He's the best. He got the Mau Mau off.

Stanley   But in Kenya the Mau Mau killed a hundred thousand innocent men, women and children.

Dangle   Allegedly.

Gives his card to **Stanley**.

Dangle   I understand the only witness to the killing of Roscoe Crabbe was Rachel? Who is also your intended?

Stanley   Certainly.

Dangle   In England a wife cannot be made to give sworn evidence against her husband in a criminal trial.

Stanley   What does that mean?

Dangle   There are no witnesses to the crime.

Stanley   But I did actually kill him.

Charlie   No! You plead not guilty.

Stanley   But that would be lying.

Charlie   Lying ain't difficult. Here, give it a go. Did you kill Roscoe Crabbe?

Beat.

Stanley   No.

Pauline   Who did kill him then?

Alan (*aside to audience/defending her*)   Stupid, you cry?! I call it immaculate. Empty. Like a thermos.

Dangle   The prospect of two weddings, and a court case with fees. What a wonderful day!

Pauline *takes* **Dolly** *to one side.*

Pauline (*to all, but mainly* **Charlie**)   It's all very well us all having an happy ending dad, but you ain't done nothing for Dolly.

Charlie   What's Dolly got to do with anything?

Pauline   Rachel's minder has asked her to go on holiday. If you give her the time off, that's like three happy endings innit.

Stanley   Wait! No! Dolly, listen. (*To* **Dolly**.) Don't accept the first offer you get. You have a choice. Another man is in love with you and is offering a different kind of holiday.

Dolly   You spend your whole life waiting for one man, then two come along at once.

Alan (*aside*)   Like buses.

Dolly (*to* **Stanley** *and* **Rachel**)   What's the choice?

Stanley   A traditional British dirty weekend in Margate. That's forty-eight hours with only a sex pest for company.

Dolly   Oh yeah, sounds fantastic! (*Beat.*) Or?

Rachel   A romantic week abroad. Majorca.

Dolly   That's a clear choice, now what about the men?

Stanley   Paddy is offering Margate.

Rachel (*indicating* **Francis**)   Whereas with this man, next week, you'll be in Majorca in sunny Spain.

Stanley (*to* **Francis**)   I thought you said the week after next?

Francis   Let me try and explain.

Rachel   I agreed that he could have next week off.

Stanley   I've agreed that Henshall can have the week after next off, and I've paid him fifty pounds.

Rachel   I've paid him fifty pounds and given him next week off.

Dolly   Mmm. Two weeks in Majorca.

Together   What's going on?

Francis   It's all Paddy's fault –

Stanley   – where is Paddy?

Francis   I think he's outside.

Stanley   Go and get him.

Francis *exits.*

Charlie   Dolly? Have you met this Paddy character?

Dolly   Yeah. He's a bit of a charmer.

Enter **Francis***, no changes, except the accent.*

Francis (*bad Irish accent*)   Top of the morning to yous!
Where's the craic?

Rachel   Francis?

Francis   No, I'm Paddy. If you want me bro he's outside.

Charlie   I know what's going on here. Are you and Francis
monozygotic twins?

Francis   That's it, yes we are!

Stanley   Buzz-wham! That explains everything!

Doorbell.

Dolly   Except who that might be? I'll go.

She exits.

Charlie   So this must be Paddy trying to come back in.

Lloyd   No, man! This is Paddy.

Francis   I'm Paddy.

Dangle   Prove it?

Francis (*singing*)
    Oh Danny Boy, the pipes,
    the pipes are calling,
    From glen to glen, di da di da di da

Dangle   He's definitely an Irishman.

He draws a hanky to wipe away his tears. Enter **Dolly** *followed by*
Alfie*. He carries a Thomas Cook's travel brochure.*

Lloyd   Alfie! What are you doing here?

Alfie (*not seeing* **Francis**)   That lad Francis Henshall sent me
with a message for someone called Dolly.

Dolly   I'm Dolly.

Alfie   Don't apologise, love. Paddy has died! So you can go on holiday with Francis to Majorca.

Stanley (*accusingly at* **Francis**)   He died died, did he?

Alfie   He did.

Francis   Oh no.

Rachel (*at* **Francis**)   What did he die of?

All eyes on **Francis**.

Francis   Dermatitis.

Dangle   Dermatitis is a dermatological disease.

Lloyd   You don't die of dermatitis!

Francis   Dey do in Donegal. Dozens die daily.

Stanley   But you're Paddy and you're not dead.

Francis   Ah shit.

Lloyd   Man! What is it you don't understand?! Paddy never existed! Francis made Paddy up so's he could rip you both off for two salaries.

Stanley   You fabricating little communist.

He swings a punch at **Francis** *who ducks and the punch contacts with* **Alfie**, *knocking him clean out. He bounces back.*

Lloyd   Are you alright, Alfie?

Alfie   Yeah, I'm getting used to it.

Francis   Alright! I made Paddy up. I've been working for you, and simultaneously and at the same time for you. I'm only one man but I had two guvnors. I'm sorry you feel deceived, both of you, but I worked hard didn't I, I held down two jobs, and –

Rachel   – nearly caused a double suicide.

Francis   Both of you have deceived people today for love. You guvnor, and you guvnor, you can't criticise me for doing the same, for I too have fallen in love.

Pauline   With Alan?

Lloyd   He's right. There's no harm done.

Rachel   I forgive you. You can have next week off.

Stanley   I'd be a cad to complain. Take the week after next off too.

Francis   Dolly? What do you say?

Dolly   Charlie, can I have a fortnight holiday please? On full pay.

Charlie   Oh bloody hell. This happy ending's turning out expensive. Go on then.

Lloyd   Give her a kiss, man!

Stanley   Yummy!

Francis *kisses* **Dolly**. *Applause and ooohs.*

Song: 'Tomorrow Looks Good from Here'

Francis (*addressing the audience directly*)
    A bunk-up in Majorca.
    See sometimes, being a liar works.
    And with Dolly here – you have to say,
    There's gotta be some fireworks.
    I clocked on early, clocked off late.
    Didn't eat til two.
    I talked the talk and walked the walk.
    And then I fell for you . . .
    It's been a day of minor catastrophes

Dolly   It's been a day of sink or swim

Francis   I've done a lot of grovelling on my knees

Dolly
 I'd better go and shave my legs
 Because I'm off to Spain with him

Dolly/Francis
 Yesterday seems like last week
 Last week seems like last year
 But tomorrow looks good from here, oh yeah
 Tomorrow looks good from here

Stanley   I've been incognito and lying low

Rachel   I've been dressed up as a man

Stanley   There were times I thought you would never show

Rachel   I can't wait to rip your clothes off

Stanley/Rachel   Gonna sort you when I can

Stanley   Australia was looming dark

Rachel   Australia was near

All
 But tomorrow looks good from here, oh yeah
 Tomorrow looks good from here

Alan
 It's been a bus ride to hell and back again
 I felt like Mozart with just one hand
 But now she's mine I'm back on track again

Pauline
 A lot of stuff's been going on that I didn't understand
 Yesterday was lovely, yeah, today was nowhere near

All
 But tomorrow looks good from here, oh yeah
 Tomorrow looks good from here.

Dolly   I've got a package deal with one of these guvnors.

Francis   I'm only one man but I got two guvnors

All

Tomorrow looks good from here, oh yeah
Tomorrow looks good from here.

Tomorrow looks good from here, oh yeah
Tomorrow looks good from here – (*Claps.*)

Tomorrow looks good from here, oh yeah
Tomorrow looks good from here

Tomorrow looks good from hear oh yeah
Tomorrow looks good from here – (*Claps stop.*)

Tomorrow looks good, looks good, looks good from heeeeeeere.

The End.

Young Marx

Co-authored with Clive Coleman

Young Marx premiered at the Bridge Theatre, London on 26 October 2017 with the following cast in order of speaking:

Mr Fleece, Pawnbroker	**Duncan Wisbey**
Karl Marx	**Rory Kinnear**
Sergeant Savage	**Joseph Wilkins**
Jenny von Westphalen	**Nancy Carroll**
Friedrich Engels	**Oliver Chris**
Helene 'Nym' Demuth	**Laura Elphinstone**
Guido 'Fawksey' Marx	**Logan Clark**
	Rupert Turnbull
	Joseph Walker
Gert 'Doc' Schmidt	**Tony Jayawardena**
Konrad Schramm	**Eben Figueiredo**
Jenny Caroline 'Qui Qui' Marx	**Dixie Egerickx**
	Matilda Shapland
	Harriet Turnbull
Mr Grabiner, Bailiff	**Scott Karim**
Mrs Mullet, Whelk Seller	**Alana Ramsey**
Helmut, Prussian Spy	**Fode Simbo**
August von Willich	**Nicholas Burns**
Emmanuel Barthélemy	**Miltos Yerolemou**
Constable Crimp	**William Troughton**
Bearded Man in Library	**Duncan Wisbey**
Mrs Whitehead, Librarian	**Sophie Russell**
Constable Singe	**Scott Karim**
Pastor Flint	**Fode Simbo**

Other parts played by members of the Company.

Director Nicholas Hytner
Designer Mark Thompson
Lighting Designer Mark Henderson
Music Grant Olding
Sound Designer Paul Arditti
Fight Director Kate Waters
Assistant Director Sean Linnen

Characters

Karl Marx, *thirty-two*
Friedrich Engels, *twenty-nine*
Jenny von Westphalen, *thirty-six*
Jenny Caroline 'Qui Qui' Marx, *ten*
Guido 'Fawksey' Marx, *three*
Nym, *thirty*
August von Willich, *thirty-nine*
Emmanuel Barthélemy, *thirty*
Konrad Schramm, *twenty-one*
Gert 'Doc' Schmidt, *thirty-two*

And others, notably – Sergeant Savage, Constable Crimp, Mrs Mullet (Whelk Seller), Mr Fleece (Pawnbroker), Mr Grabiner (Bailiff), Helmut the spy, and émigrés, library staff, readers, traders, Londoners . . .

Setting

Soho 1850. Multi-location, Soho streets, rented apartment interior, Hampstead Heath, function room of Red Lion, pawnbroker's, graveyard.

Language Convention

When German characters are speaking to English characters their speech is accented. When in the company of Germans, it is not. The presumption being, amongst their own, they are all speaking German.

Act One

Scene One

1850. A pawnbroker's. On one end of the counter, **Mr Fleece** *is looking at paperwork. His assistant* **Jim** *is polishing a brass.* **Marx** *enters, produces the Argyll from under his coat and places it on the other end of the counter.*

Fleece (*without looking up*)   In a moment, I'm going to ask you to bring that item over here and tell me what it is.

Marx *picks up the Argyll.*

Fleece   Not yet!

He finally looks up from his papers.

Now, bring it over here, and tell me what it is.

Marx *delivers the Argyll to that bit of the counter before* **Fleece**.

Marx   Also, it's a gravy warmer, an Argyll, an original, invented by the eponymous Duke.

Mr Fleece   And what was he called?

Marx   Argyll.

Mr Fleece   Is that why it's called an Argyll?

Marx   Who knows?!

Mr Fleece   What's its value?

Beat.

Marx   Its use value or its exchange value?

Mr Fleece   What's the difference?

Marx   How long do you have? To fix an exchange value we would need to know the socially necessary labour time required to produce this commodity with the average degree of skill und intensity currently prevalent.

Fleece (*nods to* **Jim** *to leave*)   Jim!

Jim *leaves.*

Marx   Where is Jim going?

Fleece   There's always something. Love, money, duck eggs. (*Beat.*) So, is this a horse?

Marx   *Nein!*

Fleece   Good. That means we can take a butcher's at its arse.

He picks up the Argyll and turns it over to look at the hallmarks.

Let's see how much silver they reckon we got here.

Marx   The value of any commodity is an entirely social characteristic. The contribution of the silver is entirely arbitrary.

Fleece *puts the Argyll down.*

Fleece   Since it's entirely arbitrary, I'll give you one penny.

Marx   Is that all! It's a family heirloom.

Fleece   Are you Scottish then?

Marx   *Jawohl!*

Fleece   So what's your name then, son?

Marx   Karl Heinrich Marx.

Fleece   A Jew?

Marx   Yes, from a long line of rabbis, most of whom were also Jewish. It's my wife who's Scottish.

Fleece   And what's your wife's name?

Marx   Frau Jenny von Westphalen. She is the daughter of Baron Ludwig von Westphalen whose mother was Anne Wishart who was descended from the totally Scottish Earls of Argyll.

Fleece   Do you expect me to believe that a penniless German Jew married into the Scottish aristocracy?

Marx   I'm not saying they were happy about it. On the wedding day, I was only invited to the reception.

Fleece   Do you see what I did there? I picked it up and I put on the shelf. The stolen goods shelf. 'Cause you've half-inched this, ain't yer?!

Re-enter **Jim** *with a policeman,* **Sergeant Savage**.

Sgt Savage   Morning, Len. What we got here?

Fleece   Comedian.

Marx   We've met before, officer.

Sgt Savage   Maybe, maybe not. We policemen, we all dress the same.

Marx   *Mein* singular offence *ist* to be poor. Can you arrest me for that?

Sgt Savage   Dunno. Policing's new to us all.

Fleece   Says this Argyll is a family heirloom.

Marx   It is my wife's inheritance!

Sgt Savage   Does she know you've got it?

Marx   Does *mein* wife know that I'm pawning her inheritance?! Of course not!

Sgt Savage   My first volunteer. I'm gonna arrest you –

Marx *runs out of the shop.*

Sgt Savage   Stop thief!

Scene Two

Marx *runs from the pawnbroker's shop heading downstage. A police whistle sounds.*

Sgt Savage (*off*)   Stop thief! Thief!

Marx *heads upstage left and goes to buy something at a costermonger's cart.*

Marx   One carrot. On account.

Greengrocer   Oi! You're that German. You owe me!

Marx   Tomorrow!

Baker   Me an' all! Stop him!

The **Tobacconist** *has grabbed him by the coat, but* **Marx** *wriggles out of the coat, leaving the coat behind as he heads back downstage.* **Sgt Savage**, **Jim** *and* **Fleece** *run on and confront* **Marx**, *who stops in his tracks, and seeing a drainpipe he shimmies up it.* **Jim** *starts to follow but is stopped by* **Sgt Savage**.

Sgt Savage   No, son! It's not safe. He's a refugee, he ain't worth it!

You're under arrest! Come down!

Tobacconist   Bloody immigrants!

Baker   You'll get no more bread from me!

Greengrocer   He don't want your bread, he wants your bakery!

Marx *is on the roof by now.*

Tobacconist   You damage my tiles I'll have you!

Fleece   Bloody German tea leaves!

Sgt Savage   Anybody know where he lives?

Wine Merchant   Dean Street. Dunno the number.

Sgt Savage   D'yer have a name?

Wine Merchant   Monsieur Ramboz.

Fleece   No! They're German, Marx.

Marx   I'll pay you all. Tomorrow!

He falls through a skylight.

Scene Three

*The apartment in Soho. At all times the main door is bolted on the inside. Regular visitors and residents have their own coded knock. Pen and ink portraits of the spies who follow them hang from the dado rail. Two large suitcases are open on the floor, half-filled with superior dresses. There is a loud coded knock at the door – two short knocks, one long pause, two short knocks. **Jenny** enters from the upstage left bedroom with a dress which she drops into one of the cases. She opens the door. **Engels** enters, carrying a case and a package.*

Jenny   General!

*She bursts into tears and throws herself into **Engels**'s arms.*

Engels   Hey, Jenny, come on. What's all this?

Jenny   You got my letter?

Engels   I'm here.

Jenny   It's Karl, it's Moor!

Engels   Of course it's Moor. Everything's Moor. What a relief!

Jenny   Yes, Paris, you must be exhausted?

Engels   No, to be speaking German again. If I have to roll one more French 'r' I swear I'll spit my teeth out.

Jenny   You found us alright.

Engels   Strange place Soho. Churches and brothels side by side.

Nancy   They're both offering the same thing, heaven. One for eternity, the other for eight minutes.

Jenny *continues to pack.*

Engels   What are you doing?

Jenny   I'm leaving him.

Engels   You can't.

Jenny   I have to go.

Engels   He needs you.

Jenny   What about me? What do I need!

Engels   Yes, very well, to hell with the man you love.

Jenny   I didn't sign up for a life of bread and dripping, without the dripping, or the bread. I steal coal, I'm a bloody baroness and I steal coal.

Engels   I imagine you do it with great style.

Jenny   I can't live like this. The only reason the bailiff hasn't taken these dresses is because they were in hock until an hour ago. He as good as lives here.

Engels   The bailiff?

Jenny   Piece by piece, item by item, I am reduced. Soon I will be nothing.

Engels   You can't leave the children.

Jenny   Fawksey has Nym, he thinks she's his mother, and Qui Qui doesn't need me, she's at school.

Engels   You and Moor just need to –

Jenny   – we can't just do anything, we don't talk.

Engels   Alright. What's he done?

Jenny   He's given up.

Engels   On what?

Jenny   Everything. He's stopped going to League meetings.

Engels   He's stopped going to the League, which he runs?

Jenny   I've negotiated commissions for him, articles, that's money, and Meissner in Germany has signed for the book but he's not writing. And now, this.

She hands **Engels** *a letter.*

Engels   What's this?

Jenny   His letter applying for a job, on the railway.

Engels   It only takes one intellectual to bugger up a railway. No one's going to put him in charge of a train. He'll never get past the interview.

Jenny   Oh he'll have an answer for everything. Do you have a criminal record? Not in Canada. What was your first job? Rejecting Feuerbach, Hegel and God.

Engels   Na, he won't get an interview. They won't be able to read his handwriting.

Jenny   He knows that, he's asked me to scriven for him. I refused. I can't –

Engels   – be the wife of a railway worker?

A coded knock at the front door. Three knocks beat and one knock.

Engels   Whose knock is that?

Jenny   Nym.

Engels *unbolts the door.* **Nym** *enters.*

Engels   My dear Nym.

Nym   General.

Engels   The intellectual's housemaid of choice!

He grabs her by the waist.

How about a kiss?

Nym   I don't know where your lips have been.

Engels   On my face.

Nym   And where's your face been?

Engels   Paris.

Nym   Exactly.

Jenny   Yes, General, how is Mary?

Engels   Mary is in rude health, thank you.

Nym   And her sister, Lizzie?

Engels   Even ruder.

Jenny   Was it your life ambition to live, unmarried, with two Irish sisters in a worker's cottage in Manchester?

Engels   Not Manchester no. I'm never living up north again.

Nym   Packing?

Jenny   Did you get anything?

Nym   Flour, coal, sausages.

Engels   Sausages, without money?

Nym   There's a butcher in Camden has a thing for desperate lady émigrés.

Engels   A thing?

Nym   His penis.

She takes coal out of her pockets and drops it in the scuttle.

Jenny   Which one followed you?

Nym (*pointing at the portraits*)   Him. One eye, two chins, no neck.

Jenny   There are more spies in Dean Street than whores. Doc Schmidt sketches them

Engels   But they can't touch us? The spies.

Jenny   We're alright. We're political refugees, we're free.

Engels   Only in England, so thank God for England. Set foot in Germany and your brother would lock us up and throw away the door.

Jenny   Don't call him my brother.

Engels   What do we call him?

Nym   The Prussian Minister of the Interior, or the arsehole. Has Fawksey eaten?

Jenny   He wouldn't.

Nym   So is that a 'no'?

Jenny   He wouldn't eat anything.

Nym   That last drop of soup?

Jenny   I tried. My child would not eat.

Nym   Let me have a go.

Furious knocking at the door, Beethoven's fifth.

Moor.

Engels *unbolts the door.* **Marx** *bursts in.*

Engels   *Mon brave!*

Marx   General, this is not a good time for me to acknowledge how industrially overjoyed I am to see you, but I am.

Engels *throws open his arms, but* **Marx** *in haste climbs up the chimney. Banging on the door.*

Sgt Savage (*off*)   Open up! Police!

Jenny *opens the door.* **Sgt Savage** *comes in.*

Jenny   *Guten Morgen.*

Sgt Savage   Who lives here?

Jenny   *Ich spreche kein Englisch*, Constable.

Sgt Savage   Constable painted 'The Hay Wain'. Three stripes.

Engels   Sergeant?

Jenny   *Entshuldigan Sie, bitte.*

Sgt Savage   I'd love to but I don't drink on duty. What's your name ma'am?

Engels   *Dein Name.*

Jenny   Jenny von Westphalen.

Sgt Savage   And you, sir?

Engels   I'm her husband. Friedrich . . . Engels. I kept my maiden name when we got married.

Nym *comes in and lights the fire, putting some bread dough in the oven.*

Sgt Savage   And you, miss –

Nym   *Was weiß ich?!*

She leaves.

Sgt Savage   Are you all German in here?

Engels   *Ja*, what can we do for you, sergeant?

Sgt Savage   I don't have eyes in the back of my head, so maybe you can help.

Engels   I can't help with that. I don't have eyes in the back of my head either.

Marx *coughs.* **Sgt Savage** *turns to* **Engels** *who quickly coughs into a hanky.*

Jenny   *Was haben wir falsch gemacht?*

Engels   *Liebling, mach Dir keine Sorgen.*

Sgt Savage   Looking for a thief. This one's dark, hairy, talks gibberish.

Jenny   *Hat er einen Namen?*

Engels   Do you have a name?

Sgt Savage   Sergeant Savage.

Engels   For the thief?

Sgt Savage   Charles Marx or Monsieur Ramboz.

He walks the room sniffing out hidden bodies. By the piano he is sure someone is hiding inside, so he hits a key.

Middle C.

Nym *stokes the fire.* **Sgt Savage** *heads for one of the rooms.* **Jenny** *gets in his way.*

Jenny   *Liebling, was tut er jetzt!?*

Engels   *Mein* wife wants to know if you're licensed to search private property without a warrant.

Sgt Savage   I dunno. Law enforcement, early days, it's all up for grabs.

He inspects the rogues' gallery. **Engels** *pulls* **Nym** *away from the fire.* **Marx** *coughs from up the chimney.* **Engels** *takes out a hanky and coughs into it.*

Engels   It's a hobby of my wife's. They're hanging up to dry.

Sgt Savage   They're pencil.

Jenny   *Nasser Bleistift.*

Engels   Wet pencil.

Sgt Savage   What's in here?

Jenny   *Mein Sohn schlaeft da drin!*

Engels   Our son is asleep in there.

Sgt Savage   We'll see if that's true.

He opens the door and looks in without going in.

Yes, he's still asleep.

Closes the door loudly.

Fawksey (*off*)   Mamma.

Jenny   *Sie haben das Kind aufgeweckt!*

Nym   *Soll ich zu ihm gehen?* (*To* **Sgt Savage**.) *Idioten!*

Sergeant   What did she say?

Engels   She said maybe the idiot made it up to the roof?

Sergeant   This villain may be highly dangerous, so if you see him, approach him, knock his lights out, then come and get one of us. *Au revoir.*

He leaves. **Engels** *closes the door and laughs.*

Nym   Is Moor –?

Jenny   Up the chimney.

Nym   I didn't know!

She damps the fire down.

Engels   Monsieur Ramboz! You can come down.

Marx *clambers out, coughing and laughing.*

Marx   You utter bastardly bunch of bastards. That was such an unbelievably not very clever thing to do to a much loved friend, husband – *und* Hauptman!

He falls into **Engels**'s *arms. It's an extended embrace of genuine affection.* **Jenny** *looks on and then continues packing.* **Nym** *continues making the fire/bread.*

Engels   You didn't reply to my letter from last week.

Marx   So depressed was I by the industrial scale of the negativity –

Jenny   – industrial and all its cognates is this month's favourite word.

Marx   Jennychen, we're not supposed to be talking.

Jenny   I was talking to him.

Marx   She's packing again. Where's my damned wine?!

Engels   Bordeaux in my pocket.

He picks up a bottle from his overcoat and gives it to **Marx** *who opens it straight away.*

Marx   Chateaux Margaux '46?!

Engels   *D'accord!* Courtesy of the philistine, my father. I write a good letter, I cry in ink.

Marx   Drink before you go, darling? Wet the separation's head.

He blocks **Jenny** *on her way to the suitcase with more clothes.*

Engels   Moor, please –

Marx   – it's all for show.

Jenny *moves around* **Marx** *and deposits another pile of clothes into the suitcase.*

Marx   How was France?

Engels   It's one great big open-air asylum. But still, without French women life wouldn't be worth living. Present company –

Nym   – insulted!

Marx *blocks* **Jenny***'s path to the suitcases.*

Marx   Can we stop the cabaret? Woman has cried wolf before.

Jenny   I'm not crying wolf, I'm going.

She deposits more dresses in the suitcases.

Marx   She's not adapted at all well to abject poverty.

Jenny   Ha!

Marx   Back in Trier, in the von Westphalen mansion she had her own feathered four-poster. I shared a small double with three siblings. Never slept on my own until I married her.

Jenny   In his inward-looking universe, where every observation is fed by a prejudice in favour of the sole inhabitant, the needs and feelings of other human beings serve only to magnify and distort his bloated sense of personal torment.

Marx   She wanted to give that speech at our wedding. It was a traditional Prussian affair, military uniforms, guard of honour, firing squad. She's packing again because I didn't pay the doctor's bill. For Fawksey. I don't have any respect for prosaic imperative exigencies such as paying bourgeois tricksters like the specialist Doctor William Whitehead who, incidentally, is suing me. The Hippocratic Oath – 'don't give credit'. Thus I am seeking paid employment with the creator of the perforated ticket stub, Isambard Kingdom Brunel.

Engels   You're applying for a job?

Marx   I had a job in Berlin. Theatre critic.

Engels   You lasted three weeks.

Marx   At its best theatre criticism is the highest of the professions, combining intellect, spirit and compassion. At it's worst you're just a bit of a twat.

Engels   But Jenny tells me she's landed a contract with Meissner for the book.

Marx   So I'm a business now am I? A manufactory of words.

Jenny   And Polyakov in St Petersburg.

Marx   Russia?!

Engels   What's wrong with Russia wanting the book?

Marx   A book about capitalism?! Russia's never had capitalism! There's more chance of a proletarian revolution starting in Windsor.

Jenny   Polyakov will pay an advance.

Marx   She wants me to turn revolution into money?!

Engels   Does the book have a title yet?

Marx   *'Das Volkswirtschaft Schiesse'*.

Engels   'The Economic Shit'?

Marx   In English I'm inclined to drop the definite article.

Engels   'Economic Shit'?

Marx   Do you like it?

Engels   Five years, and all you've got is the title?! I've had some long craps in my time, but that takes the biscuit.

Jenny   You're wasting your time.

Engels   God –

Marx   – who?!

Engels   Although you killed him, God put you on earth to explain capitalism –

Marx   – I'll explain capitalism. The railway pays fifteen shillings a week, and the rent is only eight. What are the proletariat complaining about? We have a surplus of seven bob to spend on claret and cigars.

Jenny   Food!

Marx   I shall be a great railway clerk, maybe the greatest ever. When I'm gone they'll build a huge statue of me outside Paddington station.

Engels   The railway it is!

Fawksey *enters*.

Marx   Guido Fawksey Marx!

Fawksey   Daddy!

Marx   One day, son, all my debts will be yours! Say hello to Uncle Freddy.

Fawksey (*from behind* **Marx**'s *legs*)   Hello.

Engels   Hello, little fellah!

Fawksey (*flexing his muscles*)   I'm big and strong now. Can you be a horse, Daddy?

Marx   I am a horse!

*He gets down on all fours and puts **Fawksey** on his back.*

Marx   Hold on tight, Sir Fawksey, only you can tame this bucking stallion.

Fawksey   Fence! Neighhhhhhhh, neighhhhhh!

Marx *rears up like a horse.* **Fawksey** *holds on, yelping with delight.*

Marx   River!

Jenny   Careful. You'll make him ill.

Nym   His throat is red raw.

Nym *takes **Fawksey** from **Marx** and sits him down by the fire.*

Fawksey (*to **Engels***)   Daddy's going to drive a train.

Marx   Yes and then we'll have all the food, and all the doctors, we need, won't we, Fawksey!

Jenny   Doc Schmidt is coming to see him later.

Marx   Sorry, are you still here?

Jenny *moves towards **Fawksey**, a maternal hand outstretched.*

Marx   Fawksey, darling. Mummy's going away, just for a while.

As the stallion he rears up.

Say goodbye to Mummy.

Fawksey   I don't want Mamma to go!

Fawksey *starts crying.* **Nym** *steps in and comforts him.* **Jenny** *goes to look out of the window.*

Marx   Looking for someone?

Jenny   There's a hackney cab coming for me.

Marx   Is your lover stumping up the cash?

Engels   Excuse me?

Marx   Willich?

Engels   August Willich?

Jenny (*to* **Engels**)   August is not my lover. He's only doing what men do, pursuing the worm that lives in every marriage.

Marx   Johann August Ernst von Willich and Johanna Berthe Julie Jenny von Westphalen. They could have had the longest wedding invitations in Prussian history. Cigar?

He offers **Engels** *a cigar.*

Engels   Never known to refuse.

Marx   From a shyster Polak in Holborn, one and six a box, that's eight pence cheaper than my usuals, so every time I smoke a box, I'm saving eight pence. If I smoke three boxes a week I can live on my savings.

Engels   They're execrable!

Marx   I'm glad you like them!

Nym   There's a League meeting tonight and –

Engels   – tonight?!

Nym   He won't go. Will you?

Engels   He will go, he will speak.

Jenny *sits and takes* **Fawksey** *off* **Nym**.

Nym   Do you know Emmanuel Barthélemy? He's come over from France.

Engels   Loony Manny. Course I know him.

Marx   He's as mad as a spoon. As a child he was bitten by a dog.

Engels   He was alright but the dog died of rabies.

Marx   Marx and Engels!

Engels   Engels and Marx!

Marx   My wife's packing, she's travelling to Italy.

Engels   Genoa?

Marx   Of course I know her, she's my wife. Marx and Engels!

Engels   Engels and Marx!

Marx and **Engels** *dance around the room in a music hall routine, finding and donning hats and using pokers from the fire as canes.*

Marx/Engels (*scat*)   Da, da, da, dadadada, de da de da da, de da da, ta daaaa!

Fawksey   Daddy's silly!

Engels *looks to* **Jenny**. *She looks back, defiant, then rises from her chair and deliberately goes and retrieves her cases. She really is going.*

Nym   Barthélemy and Willich! That's the double act we should be worried about!

Marx   August Willich?! He couldn't start a revolution, he can't even schtup my wife, and he's been trying for ten years.

Jenny   Fifteen.

Marx   I gave him five off for appalling behaviour.

Nym   Is anyone listening to me?! Our people here, the refugees, are tolerated. Barthélemy, he's different, he's unstable, unpredictable –

Engels   – he's French.

Nym   And he's not on his own, he's brought the League of the Just with him.

Engels   Is this true?

Nym   Yes, those bloodthirsty fanatics. He will start an inferno. And then leave. And the English will blame us, and we will suffer the consequences.

Marx   Shall I be a train, Fawksey?

Fawksey   Yes!

Jenny   Though the train's the same as his horse.

Marx *takes* **Fawksey** *for a train ride around the room, clambering over chairs and tables, making train noises.* **Fawksey** *yelps with delight.*

Engels   Moor, you know you must speak at the meeting! The League of the Just are here because they can smell weakness.

Nym   They know you've stepped aside.

Marx   Excuse me, General. All aboard!

Fawksey   Bridge!

Marx   Tunnel!

Nym   Moor! He's not well! Stop it!

Marx   We don't stop till Doncaster!

Nym *plonks herself directly in* **Marx**'s *way, blocking him.*

Nym   Give him to me!

Marx   Prussian housemaid on the line!

He hands **Fawksey** *back to* **Nym** *who takes him back into the bedroom and then returns.*

Engels   Write something, for tonight. I'll read it.

Marx   I can't write! I can't sit down.

Jenny   Boils.

Engels   Boils?!

Marx   I have boils on my arse so big that they have arses of their own, with boils on.

He pulls his pants down and shows **Engels** *his arse.*

Jenny   He lances the boils himself with a razor.

Marx   Because my loving wife refused.

He demonstrates.

Hand-held mirror, razor arm through the legs, slit the bastard, clean the mirror, go again.

Nym   He has to stand at the British Museum, people think he's an exhibit.

Marx   General, go and flag her a hackney will you.

Engels   Enough! We're going to eat together, and we're going to talk. Is that agreed?

There is a knock at the door. **Gert 'Doc' Schmidt** *is admitted.*

Marx   Doc Schmidt. Our German doctor and comrade!

Schmidt   Moor. Frau Marx. Comrade Nym. Herr Engels! Good to see friendly faces. Good to see faces. I've administered three enemas today. I think I washed my hands.

Jenny   He's in the bedroom.

Schmidt   Why is every revolutionary émigré in London constipated? My theory is that they're all suffering under the sheer intellectual strain of understanding your prose, Herr Marx. How's your cock?

Engels   It's fine. Thanks for asking.

Schmidt   Cleared up?

Engels   Yes. It's like new again.

Schmidt   Ha! Your secret's safe with me. Coming to the meeting?

Engels   Certainly.

Schmidt   That arrogant bastard won't come.

Engels   I'm working on it.

Schmidt (*producing sketches*)   Three new spies. Uglier than the last lot. I had to sketch them at intervals just so I could keep my lunch down.

He places the new sketches on the dado rail alongside the existing 'rogues'.

(*To* **Jenny**.) I have a new theory, the Prussian Minister of the Interior –

Jenny   – my brother. Don't be polite, Gertie.

Schmidt   He wants his revenge on Moor for marrying you.

Marx   He calls it the 'Trier Incident'.

Schmidt   I sympathise. His sister decides to marry not just a penniless Jew, but a penniless Jew intent on destroying the Prussian monarchy.

Fawksey (*off*)   Mamma!

Schmidt   The patient calls! Think of the fees! Oh, but you don't pay.

He opens his valise and takes out his stethoscope, and puts it round his neck.

Any change in symptoms?

Jenny   The cough's harder.

Schmidt *and* **Jenny** *go into the bedroom.*

Nym   Moor! I need to speak to you. Alone.

Marx   He's not important.

Engels   I love you too.

There is a knock at the main door. **Marx** *and* **Nym** *look at each other with concern.*

Marx   No?

Nym   No.

Marx *goes in the cupboard.*

Nym   Who is it?

Schramm (*off*)   It's me!

Nym   Herr Schramm?!

Marx (*from the cupboard*)   Tell him I'm dead.

Nym *opens the door and* **Konrad Schramm** *enters.*

Schramm   A most felicitous day to you, comrade Nym.

Nym   Hello, Konrad.

Schramm   And Herr Engels, an additional pleasure of the most joyous kind.

Engels   Good to see you.

Schramm *goes to the cupboard.* **Engels** *laughs helplessly.*

Guten Tag, Herr Doktor Marx!

Beat.

Marx   I'm not in here!

Schramm   I apologise. Forgive my presumption, born as it is, of enthusiasm and warm fellowship.

Jenny *enters from the upstage left room.*

Jenny   He's stopped coughing. Doc Schmidt just picked him up.

Marx (*from within*)   The man's a genius!

Schramm   Madame Marx, radiance has found a new face, and calls itself Madame Marx.

Jenny   Konrad, how nice to see you. Doc Schmidt needs honey for the syrup.

Nym   I'll get it.

Jenny *goes back into the bedroom.*

Engels   What news of the *Zeitung*?

Schramm   Since Herr Marx did me the unfathomable honour of appointing me as his successor editor of the *New Rheinische Zeitung* I have been working ceaselessly on the relaunch.

Engels   And you have proofs, an edition to show us?

Marx   Which you can leave on the table.

Schramm   I have not yet an edition, sir, but I have made progress on the relaunch title.

Marx (*from within*)   I'm all ears.

Schramm   Indeed, sir, and I dare to hope that you will heartily approve. The organ, which I am honoured to edit, was named by you, in a stroke of unparalleled genius, as successor to the original *Rheinischer Zeitung*, the *New Rheinischer Zietung*! I have been touched, I hope, by my own muse, in humbly suggesting that the London edition should be relaunched –

Marx   – Schramm?! You are trespassing upon eternity!

Engels   What is your suggested title?

Schramm   The *New New Rheinischer Zeitung*!

Marx *kicks the cupboard door open violently.*

Marx   New new?! No no!

Schramm   Herr Doktor Marx, it is, as a title, a developing work in progress – there is more! I have six alternative suggestions –

Marx   No! Get out!

He manhandles him out of the door. Door slams.

If I had a choice to get rid of Schramm or my boils, I'd keep the boils. He worships me! I can't bear it!

Engels   You love it, worship, and you appointed him.

Marx   Never make editorial appointments when completely pissed.

Enter **Schmidt** *from the upstage left room.* **Jenny** *follows.* **Nym** *comes from the kitchen with the honey.*

Nym   How's Fawksey?

Schmidt   Croup. Continue with the borax.

Jenny   And the honey?

Schmidt   Coat the back of his throat, if he won't tolerate that, coat the tongue.

Nym   I'll try it now.

Jenny   No, let him sleep a little. Then I'll do it.

Marx   Ah, she's staying.

Jenny   I need to eat. And then I'm leaving.

Engels   Leg of lamb, potatoes, parsnips, butter. Any requests?

Marx   Bit of foie gras?

Engels   Or pâté de campagne.

Marx/Engels   Both!

Engels *leaves.* **Jenny** *hands* **Schmidt** *a glass.*

Schmidt   Thank you, Frau Marx. You know the League of the Just have sent a contingent over from Paris.

Marx   Let the lunatics run the asylum!

Schmidt   And allow these hotheads to take over?!

Nym   Will you do the door tonight?

Schmidt   Yes, of course, but I don't know the European membership.

Jenny   They're all members!

Nym   We have a list.

She leaves to the upstage right bedroom, and comes back with the lists.

Schmidt   They shot the King of Prussia two days ago.

Marx   We know. He survived.

Schmidt   And now they're here, with designs on Queen Victoria.

Nym   That would be the end for us, Moor.

Schmidt   What is it that is keeping you away?

Marx   I'm going to drink a pint in every pub on Tottenham Court Road.

Schmidt   Oh dear, you're an arsehole, and I know about arseholes.

Nym *gives* **Schmidt** *the lists.*

Nym   Each name has a number. If someone gives a name, ask them for their number.

Schmidt   Thank you. Moor, I beg of you, for those comrades who died in '48, please come. Cheerio.

He leaves. The door is bolted again by **Nym**.

Nym   You should be ashamed.

Marx   I have a far bigger task ahead of me. There are eighteen pubs on Tottenham Court Road.

Nym   Karl, we must talk!

Marx   All we ever do in this house is talk. What is it? (*Pause.*) What?

A knock on the door, coded.

Qui Qui! Everyone be upstanding for the Emperor of China!

Marx *lets in* **Qui Qui**.

Qui Qui   I saw Uncle Freddy in the street!

She kisses and hugs **Marx**, *and then* **Jenny**.

Jenny   Qui Qui!

Qui Qui   Is he staying?!

Marx   He'll stay for dinner. He's paying for it.

Qui Qui *goes straight to the piano.*

Qui Qui   I've learned a new piece by John Field.

Marx   Bloody English music!

Qui Qui   John Field is Irish, Daddy.

Marx   The Irish are English, Act of Union 1801.

They laugh. **Qui Qui** *plays Op. 51 Sehnsuchts-walzer. There is banging at the door.*

Jenny   No!

Nym   Keep playing!

Marx   I'm beginning to sympathise with cuckoos, the Swiss ones, that live in clocks.

He hides in the cupboard. **Qui Qui** *continues.*

Jenny   Who is it?

Grabiner (*off*)   Mister Grabiner!

Jenny *lets in* **Mr Grabiner**, *the bailiff, and two* **Porters**. **Nym** *is in the kitchen.*

Jenny   The bailiffs! Mister Grabiner.

Grabiner   I was only saying to my trouble and strife this morning that I spend more time with that Mrs Marx than I do with her.

Jenny   Take a seat.

Grabiner   Thank you.

He picks up a chair, hands it to a **Porter**, *and the* **Porter** *walks out the flat with it.*

Jenny   Who is it today?

Grabiner   Mrs Gertrude Price, the landlady. The rent never sleeps.

Jenny   Please, that's our one good chair.

Grabiner   What does your husband do all day? If you can't find work in London, you must be neither use nor ornament.

Jenny   The landlady, anyone else?

Grabiner   Mrs Eileen Wilson, piano lessons, unpaid.

Marx *opens the cupboard door and steps out.*

Marx   She teaches *mein* daughter Irish scrapings und then has the nerve to sue!

Grabiner   It won't happen again, 'cause the piano's going. Lads!

Qui Qui   Daddy!

The two **Porters** *approach the piano.* **Qui Qui** *cries and steps aside.* **Marx** *hits the keys with Beethoven's 5th.*

Grabiner   Piano, fifteen shillings.

Jenny   It's a Broadwood.

Grabiner   Fifteen shillings and sixpence. Take it away, lads.

Marx   You English can take the bread from out of our mouths, *aber nie*, you can't take our culture!

The lads wheel the piano out of the flat with **Marx** *still playing it. When they get to the door, he has to jump on the top of it in order to continue playing, which he does – Beethovern's 5th still. The piano, porters and* **Marx** *all leave but are heard off arguing/playing. The* **Porters** *come back in without* **Marx**, *who is now playing some Schubert out in the street.*

Porter One   Mozart?

Porter Two   Schubert. Opus 77.

*The **Porters** come out of the bedroom with a child's cot and place it before **Grabiner**.*

Fawksey   Mamma! My bed!

Jenny   *Bitte!* Leave the bed, he's not well. Take these dresses.

Grabiner   A shilling each. The bed two shillings.

Jenny   Do you not have a heart?

Grabiner   No. I'm a bailiff.

Jenny   I have a silver piece, an Argyll, very, very valuable.

She takes a screwdriver and starts desperately raising the floorboard.

Solid silver, and in here.

She lifts the floorboard. She lifts out a cloth, but no silver.

Nym! It's gone.

Nym   My God no.

Jenny   Where is it?

Moor?!

Grabiner   Take the bed, lads.

*The **Porters** take the cot, children's clothes and the linen out, passing **Marx** in the doorway. **Jenny** is on her knees and then lets out a scream.*

Jenny   Moor!

Scene Four

In a Soho Street. People go about their business, some émigrés in huddles. A spy is lurking on a street corner.

Landlady (*throwing **Marx** out*)   It's a pub. We give you beer, you give us money. We have, you haven't.

Mrs Mullet   Winkles, whelks and oysters!

Marx   Ah! Is this what you English call *ein* whelk stall?

Mrs Mullet   'appen as maybe.

Marx   Just that my brother-in-law is fond of saying that I couldn't run one.

Mrs Mullet   It's easy enough if you've got all your marbles.

Marx   So you own the cart obviously?

Mrs Mullet   Na, I rent the cart, shilling and six a week off my father-in-law; I got a lease on the pitch here, that's two shilling a month to the council –

Marx   – but *diese* whelks are yours? Your husband's *ein* fisherman?

Mrs Mullet   You're having a laugh, aincha?! Cowans of Barking, they give me thirty pints of whelks of a morning, and I get sixpence for every pint I sell, and a tuppeny penalty for every pint I don't sell. For the oysters –

Marx   – *nein, nein,* stop! It's already too complicated.

Enter **Engels** *followed by a spy.* **Engels** *grabs* **Marx**.

Engels   Moor! Come here!

Marx   No, I have an important and unfinished pub crawl to continue. See you there.

Engels   Who's that?

Marx   Let me introduce my personal spy.

(*Shouted.*) Evening, Helmut!

Helmut   Good evening, Herr Marx.

Marx   This is my tailor, Godfrey *Schnitzelgrueberleinchenlein*.

Helmut   Looks like Friedrich Engels to me.

Marx   So that explains the short sleeves!

Helmut   Red Lion League meeting tonight?

Marx   I've seen the light, given up revolution. Start work Monday, with Great Western.

Helmut   The railway?

Marx   I tried to change the world, I failed, but I will transform Paddington station. Tell your boss, my brother-in-law, that he needn't worry about me in future. He can focus fully on his halitosis. Off you pop.

Helmut *moves off.* **Marx** *starts walking.*

Engels   The Red Lion's that way.

Marx   But the King's Head is this way.

Engels   You've no money for drink, unless you got cash for the Argyll?

Marx   Not a penny from the pawnbroker.

Engels   You still have the Argyll, then?

Marx   I don't have money and I don't have the Argyll!

Engels   Do you know how pawnbroking works? She's furious!

Marx *starts walking off.*

Marx   Let me know what happens at the meeting.

Engels *walks off upstage towards the Red Lion.*

Mrs Mullet   Thames oysters! Surprise the wife!

Engels   Are they good oysters?

Mrs Mullet   Put it this way, my husband had five last night and three of them worked.

Enter **Nym** *and* **Jenny**.

Jenny I can threaten it, I can act it, but I can't leave, Fawksey's ill.

Nym Of course you can't leave.

Jenny What does Qui Qui think? She hears the arguments. Has she spoken to you?

Nym Qui Qui's not even listening. It's just shouting.

Jenny But Moor needs to be taught a lesson.

Nym Teach him one, then.

Jenny How?

Nym Would you be safe at Willich's?

Jenny It's August Willich. It's not one room, he has a suite.

Nym Then it could be one night? Moor's lesson.

Jenny Would that work?

Nym I think one night will be enough. You know I'll look after the children.

They laugh. **Willich** *appears.*

Willich Jenny.

Nym I'll see you in there.

She looks at **Willich** *and then moves off towards the Red Lion.*

Willich Why didn't you come?

Jenny The bailiffs took everything.

Willich I would take you with nothing. Where is he?

Jenny I don't know.

Willich He uses you.

Jenny For what?

Willich Money, from your family.

Jenny   They've stopped giving.

Willich   Is he coming? Tonight?

Jenny   He said not.

Willich   Then we can make progress. Are you with us?

Jenny   I don't know what you plan. But I will listen.

Willich   You could stay with me tonight.

Jenny   August –

Willich *gestures for her to stop.*

Willich   I exist on hope. That's how love works.

They head on to the Red Lion.

Scene Five

The upstairs function room of the Red Lion. Alive with émigrés of both sexes. Talk, shouting, drinking, laughter. **Schmidt** *is on the door.* **Schramm**, **Engels**, **Nym** *and others. A German workers' song.*

Engels   Comrades! Comrades!

Willich   Where is Marx?

Terrorists   Yes?! / Where is he?! / Is he with us?!

Engels   Comrade Marx told me he would be late.

Terrorists   Bourgeois coward / apologist! / He's in the museum!

Terrorist One   Is there something more urgent than the overthrow of the monarchy?!

Schmidt   Comrades! Let Engels speak!

Willich   Engels! Are you running the Marx party?!

Engels   Tonight we meet after the assassination attempt on the King of Prussia –

Cheers from the **Terrorists**.

Barthélemy   – Queen Victoria next!

Willich   Comrades! The Fox! Escaped from the galleys only last week. Emmanuel Barthélemy!

Some cheers. **Barthélemy** *kisses* **Willich**.

Willich   And he kisses like a horse!

Barthélemy   *Monsieurs, dames! Bon soir!* I am, how you say, *prêt?*

Willich   Ready.

Barthélemy   I am ready, *prêt*, ready. England is *prêt*, ready, for revolution. And our weapon, it is a *technique, technique?*

Willich   Technique.

Barthélemy   *Le technique* is *le terrorisme, c'es quoi?*

Willich   Terror.

Barthélemy   The Terror?!

Willich   Just terror, no definite article.

Barthélemy   Terror! We kill *au hasard?*

Willich   – at random.

Barthélemy   Soldiers, police, their wives, *dans la rue!* –

Willich   – in the street.

Barthélemy   – *dans la gare!*

Willich   In the stations.

Barthélemy   – *dans les etangs!*

Willich   – in the small lakes?!

Barthélemy   In the lakes, *en avant, encore, au hasard?*

Willich   At random.

Barthélemy   Kill at random, the terror, we kill *ici*, *voila*, *en face*!

Willich   Here, there and opposite.

Barthélemy   *Encore*, *au hasard?!*

Willich   At random!

Barthélemy   At random!

Terrorists *cheer*.

Schmidt   Helene Demuth. Nym.

Nym   There is a time for violence.

Barthélemy   A girl speaking?!

Jenny   A founder member of the League!

Nym   Kill Victoria and the English will turn against us. I am not against violence, and I will be there when that time comes, fighting beside you. But we are few, and the English workers love their Queen, they will not join us, they will hate us.

Terrorist Two   We can only win on the streets!

Jenny   – we are not ready! When we are ready! When!

Barthélemy   I am *prêt*! Now!

Willich   The English proletariat are ready but they need leadership, an act to fire this nation out of its complacency! A spark!

Barthélemy   Kill, *au hasard*!

Marx *enters unseen*.

Marx   You killed a policeman in Paris, *au haard*. What good did that do?

Barthélemy   Monsieur Marx?!

Marx   *Voila!* It got you ten years on the galleys. Comrades, do you know what ten years on the galleys is?! It's a fuck of a lot of rowing!

Willich   You're drunk!

Marx   But not insane. So August Willich, this is your big idea, to use this French attack dog as a spark?

Barthélemy   A match to fire Europe!

Marx   And we will all die in the fire.

Mumbles of discontent.

Have you seen the British army? They're a machine, a mindless, grinding machine that will crush us. Comrade Marx, have you spoken?

Beat.

Jenny   Comrades, we have an opportunity here. Fate has brought us to England. To this most advanced industrialised society with a vast city-living proletariat, oppressed, exploited, ripe to be educated which will bring them to us. Violence will turn them away.

Marx   '48 was a lesson and only idiots do not learn. And are we idiots?! Most of us are not. Time, which was invented just down the road here in Greenwich, only three years ago, is on our side. We use this time to prepare, to be ready –

Barthélemy   Ready?

Willich   *Prêt.*

Marx   Ready for power, because there will be a moment, in the future, a moment when the markets have crashed, the banks do not open their doors on this day, because they are bust. The money has eaten itself. And on this day there will be a beautiful void, and truth coalesces around a void, and that void will be filled by the universal truth that every man and every woman has the right not to be exploited by any other man or woman. And on this day the soldiers will not have been paid, the police will not have been paid, and without wages they will not defend capitalism, so we will not have to break down the doors, they'll give us the keys, and we'll walk in. And all class antagonisms will be swept aside, and the proletariat will become the ruling class, no, not the ruling class, there will be no classes, and all men and women will be equal, and we will have a socialist association in which the free development of each is the free development of all, and we will have a more honest and just way for our species to live.

Willich   Change cannot happen without violence!

Terrorist Three   When will the economic crash come?

Marx   Tomorrow, but not today!

Terrorist Four   We are sick of waiting?!

Marx   We are not waiting, we are making preparations for that day!

Barthélemy   But we are soldiers.

Willich   Your friend, the cotton lord, Herr Engels, was there on the barricade in '48. Where were you Marx? Where were you?!

Barthélemy   In the pissing room of the British Museum!

Marx   There are voices within our movement that want nothing more than to see Europe burn; these sirens offer you death, an abattoir, where you are the meat.

Barthélemy   Jewish coward!

Uproar. **Marx** *lunges at* **Barthélemy**. *The two are pulled apart.*

Engels   Coward, no! Jewish, yes, like Christ!

Barthélemy   You think he's Christ?! I have news for you, I am Christ!

He produces two pistols.

Willich   Marx is a coward!

Marx   Debatable, but I'm not an idiot.

Barthélemy   Are you calling Willich an idiot?

Marx   I said 'I'm not an idiot'.

Willich   Unlike me?!

Marx   Alright! If you insist! I'm not an idiot, unlike you!

Terrorist Five   Who's he calling an idiot!?

Willich   Are you calling me an idiot!

He lunges at **Marx**.

Marx   You are an uneducated, priapic Prussian prick of an idiot.

Barthélemy   Priapic?

Schmidt   Always er . . . *prêt*.

Barthélemy *resists disarmament but puts his pistols away.*

Willich   Do you accuse me of something, with this woman?!

Marx   I do.

Willich   What of my honour?!

Marx   What of my honour?! And she's not this woman, she's my wife!

The room hushes.

Jenny   I can speak for my own honour!

Marx   If your honour exists it has no blood, no substance, unlike the lives of the men and women in this room which you, with unbound profligacy, will piss away on your own vain, narcissistic fantasy of a peacock's death!

Willich   As a gentleman, I demand satisfaction! I shall await you at dawn, on Hampstead Heath –

All   No / stop this now / we are comrades (*etc.*).

Willich   A gentleman has a right to protect his honour.

Barthélemy   Choose your weapon, Marx!

Marx   The pen! Pens at dawn!

Barthélemy   What?!

Marx   Debate, ideas, argument!

Willich   I'm going to kill you! Be there, dog, or I will come for you!

Marx   I'll be there, likewise dog.

Jenny   Moor. Just go home.

Schramm   Herr Doktor Marx, please! Let us return to the business of the League.

Engels   Comrades, this is not intelligent.

Willich *and* **Barthélemy** *leave.* **Jenny** *turns to go with them.*

Willich   Jenny!

Marx   Ha!

Jenny   You stole from me.

Marx   What?! The Argyll, no, I can get that back.

Jenny (*to* **Nym**)   Don't let him go to the duel. He will be killed.

Marx   No!

Jenny *makes to leave.* **Marx** *stands to follow her.* **Engels** *and* **Schmidt** *hold him back.*

Schramm   Comrades! Remember, tickets for the German Workers' Educational Society ball on Saturday at the Huguenot Hall are selling fast! See me or Doc Schmidt!

Scene Six

Soho Square with St Patrick's Roman Catholic Church upstage with an opening where a door/gate should be, a hedge and then a pavement. Enter **Marx**, **Engels** *and* **Schmidt**, *all drunk.* **Marx** *and* **Engels** *are carrying a large outdoor door or gate.*

Marx   The illicit golden thread that bound Neanderthal man, through the earliest agrarian societies –

Engels *stops.*

Engels   – Moor! Stop talking! Write it down. Preferably in a book.

Marx   You wanted it explained, you bugger!

Engels   I wanted to know why we've stolen a gate.

Schmidt   It's metonymic, a symbol.

Engels   It's a bloody heavy symbol.

Marx   Society was stable, exchange and barter were the norm. Then the Phoenicians, sick of slipping a goat in your back pocket in order to buy a pint, introduced a commodity of universal exchange.

Engels   Garden gates?

Schmidt   Cash.

Marx   Money!

Engels   Yes, but WHY HAVE WE STOLEN THIS BASTARD GATE?!

Marx   Because there comes a time in every man's life when you've just got to nick a gate for a laugh.

They all laugh. And drop the gate.

Engels   What would that pawnbroker on Berwick Street give you for a gate like this?

Marx   Fuck-all.

Schmidt   Which is twice as much as he gave you for that silver Argyll.

Marx   How do you know about the Argyll?

Schmidt   I guessed! I'm going. I don't mind being arrested for sedition but drunk in charge of a gate, no.

Marx (*hugs him*)   Doc! You're the best of men.

Schmidt   Comrade.

Marx   I love you much more than that rich arsehole.

Schmidt *leaves.*

Engels   Who's a rich arsehole?

Marx   You! You fucking cotton lord. Ermen and Engels.

Engels   Oh I see, and which one of Ermen and Engels do you think is me?

Marx   Er . . . tough one. Engels?

Engels   No.

Marx   Ermen? You're Ermen?!

Engels   In Ermen and Engels I am neither Ermen nor Engels.

Marx   I don't understand.

Engels   I am not my father. When I worked in Manchester I was a wages clerk. The wages clerk does not get his name on the chimney.

Marx   Argh . . . don't give me that.

Engels   I drink good wine, yes, I hunt, I have my own hunter, yes, but only because I write begging letters to a father I detest, a philistine, and I pack every letter with lies and false affection.

Marx   I write him begging letters too.

Engels   My father?

Marx   Yes. Twice a week. I explain that I'm your best friend, and I tell him I love him.

Engels   Does he send you money?

Marx   No. Fucker.

Engels   You're taking the piss.

Marx   Piss! I knew there was something I had to do.

Marx *stands and goes for a piss.*

Engels   I hate Manchester. I'm never going back.

He joins **Marx** *for a piss.*

Marx   Marx and Engels!

Engels   Engels and Marx!

They piss.

Marx   You're pissing higher than me!

Engels   Because you're an intellectual, and I'm a machine for converting beer into piss.

Marx   Let me see your cock!

He turns his head to looks at **Engels***, ready to argue.*

Engels   Don't turn towards me! We can do this conversation in profile.

Marx   Freddy, I've known you since Paris 1844 and I've never seen it.

Engels   It's a perfectly normal Prussian penis –

Marx   – you're using two hands?! You've got a cock like a fucking horse!

A police officer, **Constable Crimp***, appears strolling his beat.*

Engels   Peeler!

Engels *and* **Marx** *hastily stop pissing.*

Constable Crimp   Evening, lads.

Engels   *Guten abent*, evening, constable.

Constable Crimp   What we got here?

Marx   *Ein* gate.

Engels   Officer, I can explain –

Marx   – *mein* gate.

Constable Crimp *examines the back of the gate, which* **Marx** *and* **Engels** *can't now see.*

Constable Crimp   And where do you live?

Marx   I live behind *diese* gate.

Constable Crimp   And when you go for a drink, you take your gate with you?

Marx   Doesn't everyone?

Engels   I apologise for my friend.

Marx *starts to move round to look at the address.* **Constable Crimp** *stops him.*

Constable Crimp   So this address here on the front is your address?

Marx   *Jawohl!*

Constable Crimp   What is it then?

Marx   Number one.

Constable Crimp   No.

He shakes his head after each number. **Engels** *sits it out giggling.*

Marx   Two? Three? Fifty-six?

Engels   Constable, we'll take the gate back.

Marx   Seventy-two.

Constable Crimp   St Patrick's Roman Catholic Church, Soho Square. That's this church, and that'll be the hole.

Engels   I bloody told you we were going round in circles!

Constable Crimp   Lads. I'll be back in half an hour.

Engels   Thank you. For using your discretion. And not hitting us.

Constable Crimp   I've been on a course.

He walks off. During the next dialogue **Marx** *and* **Engels** *put the door back on, possibly upside down.*

Engels   I will not let this duel happen.

Marx   No, I'm gonna kill him! My wife walked out of the Red Lion with him, in front of all of Europe.

Engels   Willich may love Jenny, but Jenny does not love Willich.

Marx   I've starved our marriage, killed it, every day with a thousand penurious indignities. She's a bloody princess! I can't expect her to live like this! She would've been better off with you.

Engels   Yes.

Marx   What?

Engels   Yes.

Marx   What was my question?

Engels   You said Jenny would've been better off with me, and I said 'yes'. I would've given her what she wants.

Marx   A pony.

Engels   But that wouldn't be enough.

Marx   Two ponies?

Engels   Willich is a cavalry officer, he's got loads of ponies.

Marx   And he smells of horses. I can't compete with that.

Engels   Jenny wants you.

Marx   But I'm a disaster area. I am the opposite of King Midas, everything I touch turns to debts. I have applied my mind to the analysis of political economy and I can see that history is determined by the economic relations between classes, and if I can communicate this to the world I know it will bring understanding and change, but I can't pay the fucking butcher. I am defeated, brutalised –

Engels   – brutalised?!

Marx   Brutalised. I can't –

Engels   – you're not fucking brutalised, you bourgeois prick.

Marx   Did you just call me a bourgeois prick?

Engels   Brutalised? Really, you can't use that word.

Marx   You're the word keeper now are you?

Engels   Go to Manchester. Then you'll see brutalised.

Marx   I'm sorry. I read your book. I couldn't put it down.

Engels   Fuck the book.

Marx   I apologise for reading your book.

Engels   I want you to smell it! And then to wretch it up.

Marx   I know –

Engels   – you don't know anything! A mile from where Mary lives there's a courtyard, I have never seen such a concentration of degradation, sickness and filth. Fifty families, one toilet between ten houses, the yard flows with piss and shit, human shit, and the kids play in this filth, barefoot. The parents of these children are not there, no, they're in the mill, all day every day, utterly consumed by a task which is regimented and repetitive, the noise is constant, they can't hear another human voice. An existence more unnatural cannot be imagined. They are brutalised, and unlike you, they have no choices, and no prospect of escape except death. And if you'd ever stepped inside a mill or a manufactory you wouldn't dare use the word brutalised to describe your own life.

Marx   You're right. I'm a dick.

Engels   Solipsistic, self-regarding prick. And if you don't write 'The Economic Shit', if you get a job, if you get shot in a duel, what about those people?! They need you. I can only observe, I write down what I see. I'm a beta plus. You're an alpha, a bona fide genius, you prick. You do that other thing, the analysis, the unlocking, the reveal.

He stands and makes to leave.

Marx   Alright, I'll make a research trip to Manchester.

Engels   Brutalised? Tch! What an arsehole.

He walks off.

Now, come on, help me put that gate back!

Scene Seven

*Later that same night. The flat in a low light, seemingly deserted. Various possessions are strewn around the floor as there are no cabinets or tables or chairs. A sleepy **Fawksey** enters from the bedroom trailing a blanket, stops in the centre of the room, looks around.*

Fawksey   Mamma?

Nym *in a nightdress comes from the bedroom.*

Nym   Little one.

Fawksey   Where's Mamma?

Nym *gathers **Fawksey** up.*

The sound of the door knob being turned and turned again in frustration when it is clear that the door is locked. Knocking on the door. Banging on the door.

Nym   You need to sleep. Then your mamma will be here.

Marx (*off*)   Nym! It's me. I'm really drunk. Nym! Open up! Come on! It's me who doesn't pay the rent. (*Laughs.*) Nym!

Nym *carries* **Fawksey** *back to bed.* **Marx** *is gone.* **Fawksey** *coughing, moaning.* **Nym** *comes out of the stage right room and goes into the stage left room, closing the door behind her.* **Fawksey***'s coughing eases.* **Marx** *climbs in the sash window, collapses onto the floor. He stands, closes the window, then starts to walk around the flat but stubs his toe on a book. Enter* **Nym**.

Marx   Nym, why are my things strewn all over the floor?

Nym   Because the bailiffs didn't take the floor.

Marx *sinks down on the floor with his back to the wall.*

Nym   Give me a cigar.

Marx   I've only got the Polish fireworks.

Nym   I like those. I like the smell.

Marx   We have so much in common, Nymchen.

Nym *lights the cigar skilfully. Puffs away and sits on the floor with her back to the wall.*

Nym   Where's the Argyll?

Marx   If you take Jenny's side in this I'll not have a friend left in the world.

Nym   I'm not going anywhere.

Marx   That is what I need. Unconditional love. In industrial quantities.

Nym   Where's the Argyll? If you die tomorrow –

Marx   – why would I die tomorrow?

Nym The duel.

Marx Forgot about that. I get it! If I die tomorrow, no one knows where the Argyll is

Nym Which pawnbroker's?! Mitchell's or Mr Fleece?

Marx I'll tell you where the Argyll is if you tell me where my wife is?

Nym That's childish.

Marx Yes.

Nym She's not here.

Marx Mr Fleece.

Nym Thank you.

Marx I want a glass of wine. On behalf of the Marx family, could I apologise. Most maidservants –

Nym – I'm not a maidservant.

Marx I didn't say you were, I said most maidservants. Most maidservants get a bed, time off, wages. Is it hell?

Nym To be a maid in Germany, that would be hell.

Marx I hate that you are suffering because of me. That I have influenced you at all. I'm an idiot! Everything I say and do causes pain, suffering, and yes, yes –

Nym – what?

Marx Death. Thousands of young men and women have died. And they were there because they'd read the manifesto. I killed them. And I'm killing you, and Jenny, and Qui Qui and Fawksey. Why don't these young people go out in the sun, and have picnics, and make love and drink at the well of their own serendipity, and stop thinking about the injustice and suffering of others. Live, laugh and bloody thrive! And they want the book in Russia. That's dangerous. The Russians, they eat pickled beetroot, and fuck their sisters. There's millions of them, we're not talking about Sussex. If I infect that lot with the virus of hope there will be perpetual conflict. I want to be ignored!

Nym   But the truth cannot be ignored.

Marx   You want to know the truth. The enemy is pliable, elastic, shape shifting. Greed is the most powerful elixir of all. Purified and strengthened in the hands of an elite, it commands not just banks and the markets, but governments, whole states, who must underpin and serve it. Capitalism is a seven-headed hydra that can't be killed. Kiss me.

Nym   Let me finish this cigar.

Marx   You wanted to tell me something earlier.

Nym   I can't tell you now.

Marx   We're alone.

Nym   You might die tomorrow.

Marx   You should marry. An attractive 'not a maidservant' like you.

Nym   This is my life, and I like it. And it's not because I love you, although I do, it's because I know who I am. It is a rich and purposeful life and it is you who said –

Marx   – no! Please do not quote me to me! Kiss me, Nymchen.

Nym   Don't call me Nymchen, you know what happened the last time.

Marx   Nymlein. Kiss me.

Nym *kisses him passionately, and then stops him.*

Marx   Jenny's not here.

Nym   She's not on a tour of Europe like last time.

Marx   I might take a bullet tomorrow.

Nym   Don't play that card, it's contemptible.

Marx   I know, I'm ashamed, but you know, come on, Nym. I might take a bullet tomorrow.

She kisses him, he responds, they fall into a deep embrace on the floor.

Scene Eight

On the way to Hampstead Heath. **Willich** *and* **Barthélemy**.

Barthélemy   *Mon brave*, 'ave you 'ad Marx's wife in your rooms?

Willich   I love her, she doesn't love me.

Barthélemy (*stops dead in his tracks*)   You took her to your rooms?! Go back and 'ave her now, in your rooms!

Willich   She doesn't love me.

Barthélemy   I do not wish to be the, 'ow you say, *deuxieme*?

Willich   – second.

Barthélemy   – the second to a man who 'as 'ad a beautiful woman in your rooms and 'as not 'ad her, one time, two time, three time, and 'ow you say, *quatre* –

Willich   – four.

Barthélemy   Four time. If you 'ave, in your rooms, *une noisette d'agneau*?

Willich   Noisette of lamb.

Barthélemy   Juicy, aromatic, cooked to perfection. Do you leave it on a plate, alone, in your rooms? No! You eat it!

Willich   Frau Marx is not a lamb chop. Now come on! The sun will not wait. I will kill Marx.

Barthélemy   You do not 'ave to kill Marx to 'ave his wife, she is in your rooms.

Willich   She doesn't love me.

Barthélemy   In France that doesn't matter, she is in your rooms, and you are a man, so you 'ave to 'ave her, in your rooms!

Scene Nine

The heath. **Schmidt** *is marking out the 'points' for the duel.* **Willich**, **Barthélemy**. **Engels** *and* **Marx** *arrive.*

Schmidt   Gentlemen!

Barthélemy   *Bonjour!* You 'ave arrived.

Willich   You look tired, Marx.

Marx   *Au contraire*, I slept like a log.

Willich   When I slay you, you will sleep to the end of eternity.

Marx   I have no wish to die a pedant, but eternity has no end, that's the unique and indeed defining quality of the concept of eternity.

Engels   Monsieur. It is the role of the seconds to explore an honourable resolution of the dispute.

Willich   I have been called one – an idiot; two – a fool; and three – a priapic Prussian prick.

Marx   If you're struggling with the maths, put your hand up!

Engels   A retraction can be made respectfully.

Willich   I have no quarrel with you, Engels.

Engels   Nor I with you. Comrades! Marx has simply confused friends and enemies, and for that he wishes to apologise.

Willich   From his mouth. The apology and retraction must come from his mouth, in supplication to me.

Marx   Where's my wife?

Barthélemy   She is in his rooms.

Marx   Is this true?

Willich   Yes, your wife is where she belongs.

Marx (*roars*)   You monstrous, moronic, cheating –

He charges towards **Willich**. **Barthélemy** *fells* **Engels** *with a vicious head-butt.*

Marx   I'll rip your throat out!

Schmidt *throws restraining arms around* **Marx**.

Schmidt   Restrain yourself, comrade.

Willich   I'll kill him with my bare hands if I have to.

Barthélemy   I will bite him!

Schmidt   Herr Willich, no! We came as gentlemen, and we will fight as gentlemen.

Marx   Hand me a pistol!

Schmidt *hands a pistol to* **Engels** *and* **Barthélemy**.

Schmidt   Gentlemen, to your points.

Marx *and the injured* **Engels**, *and* **Willich** *and* **Barthélemy** *walk to the points.*

Schmidt   Seconds prepare the weapons for those who duel. When you are ready, I will say 'Raise Your Pistols' and 'Fire'.

Out of the mists, **Schramm** *arrives and hurries to* **Marx**. *They comfort* **Engels**.

Schramm   Herr Marx!

Marx   What is it, Schramm?

Schramm   I am here sir, we are here, sir.

Marx   Who are 'we'?!

Schramm   We, the editorial board of the *New New Rheinische Zeitung*.

Marx   You've got a nose for a good story. I'll give you that.

Schramm   The second of March 1849, sir.

Marx   What?!

Schramm   A date etched on the heart of every revolutionary émigré who has ever put pen to paper, thought into word, word into voice, in the cause of the overthrow of repressive regimes.

Schmidt   Schramm, get out of the bloody way.

Schramm   Prussian soldiers came to your house, Herr Doktor Marx to arrest the writer Ernst Brauder. You held the threshold of your home and repelled the power of the state.

Marx   Schramm, you're in the firing line.

Schramm   You are the revolution, sir, its intellect, its spirit, its essence. The writers of the *New New Rheinische Zeitung* have come to save you, sir.

Marx *pushes* **Schramm** *to the ground.*

Engels   You're a damn fool, Schramm! Get out the way!

Schmidt   Raise your pistols.

Marx *and* **Willich** *take aim.* **Schramm** *struggles to his feet and wrestles the pistol from* **Marx** *who tries to wrestle it back.* **Schramm** *throws* **Marx** *to the ground and aims the pistol at* **Willich**.

Schramm   I am but one man. It is an honour.

Schmidt   Fire!

Two shots ring out. **Willich** *and* **Schramm** *remain standing for a couple of beats, and then* **Schramm** *touches his head.*

Schramm   Sweet mercy.

He falls to his knees. **Schmidt** *attends him. A peeler's whistle, and two policemen appear, everyone else runs.* **Schramm** *keels over.*

Interval.

Act Two

Scene One

The flat. The morning of the duel. **Nym**, *in a nightdress, enters from the women's bedroom sobbing. Enter* **Qui Qui** *from the same room, also in a nightdress.*

Qui Qui   Is my father dead?

Nym   No.

Qui Qui   Then why are you crying?

Nym   I'm allergic to a lack of furniture. The General would never let a duel happen. Come on! School!

Qui Qui   Is Mamma with Herr Willich?

Nym *starts brushing* **Qui Qui***'s hair.*

Nym   No, no. What a tangle! Look! An owl's nest!

Qui Qui   Will I go to prison?

Nym   For what?

Qui Qui   We're his children. We're terrorists.

Nym   It is not a crime to be his child.

Qui Qui   Without Daddy, how will we live?

Nym   By breathing.

There is a noise on the stairs.

Engels (*off*)   To me! To you!

Qui Qui *unbolts the door, and in comes* **Engels** *and* **Marx** *pulling a piano, on top of which is a table and chairs.* **Qui Qui** *throws himself into* **Marx***'s arms.*

Qui Qui   Dadda!

Engels   Aargh! Do you know this incredibly expensive piano is resting on my foot?

Marx   You hum it and I'll play it. Marx and Engels!

Engels   Engels and Marx!

Marx   Princess, for you, the finest piano in Austria. How it got to London I do not know.

Engels   I pushed it from Vienna.

Qui Qui *is still hanging on to* **Marx** *and now crying.*

Marx   Hey, stop this! Come on, your very own Bösendorfer, and next year, when you're a little older –

Qui Qui   – a year older.

Marx   We'll hold a soirée and invite lots of young Englishmen and when they hear you play that little Mozart sonata the richest and most handsome one will fall hopelessly in love with you and ask me if he can marry you, and take you away to his castle on the Isle of Dogs.

Engels   Isle of Wight.

Qui Qui   But I'll only be eleven!

Marx   Eleven years old, and still bumming off your parents!

Marx *picks up* **Qui Qui**. *She giggles and screams.*

Nym   Stop teasing! She thought you were dead!

Marx *sings to the tune of Beethoven's 'Ode to Joy', maybe at the piano.* **Engels** *joins in.*

Marx/Engels
  Hegel, Hess and Feuerbach are stupider than Fichte is,
  In a competition you could not tell who the victor is.
  Kant Kant Kant could rave and rant, but none of his
    ravings can detract

> From the brilliant Marx and Engels, Europe's favourite double act.

Engels   I'll pay the carter, shall I? It's amazing how much ready cash one needs visiting the Marxes.

He exits to pay the carter. **Marx** *puts* **Qui Qui** *down and she runs to the piano and starts playing.*

Engels *returns.*

Engels   Now that you're not dead, saved indeed, might this be seen as a sign that you have a purpose? 'The Economic Shit'.

Marx   No definite article!

Engels   'Economic Shit'. What are the chances of you passing the economic stool, sit down, or stand up, and write the damn thing!

Marx   Breakfast! We need breakfast!

Engels   You are the emperor of procrastination!

A knock at the door.

Nym   Doc Schmidt.

She opens the door. And **Schmidt** *enters carrying the lists.*

Engels   Doc? What news of Schramm?

Marx   Is he dead?

Schmidt   I can't say. They arrested me, and carried him away.

Marx   You don't look arrested.

Schmidt   I convinced them that I was taking my morning constitutional and not a party to events. But I do have bad news. Schapper has been arrested in Cologne. We have an informer in our midst.

Marx   Was Willich arrested with you?

Schmidt   Willich was not arrested, indeed he walked down the road with the police, chatting and laughing.

Marx   Willich is Judas?

Schmidt   Aristocracy, Prussian, Cologne, a military background, and he knows your wife's brother.

Marx   Are you implicating my wife?

Schmidt   Is she here?

Marx   You are!

Schmidt   Someone has to speak out.

Jenny*'s knock at the door.*

Marx   The spy, my wife.

He unbolts the door and **Jenny** *enters.* **Qui Qui** *hugs her.*

Jenny   Is Willich dead?

Marx   You ask about your lover before your husband?

Jenny   I can see you're alive.

Engels   Willich lives, unfortunately. The police turned up. We all ran.

Schmidt (*goes to leave*)   Excuse me.

Qui Qui   Mamma!

Jenny   How's my boy?

Schmidt   I didn't come here for Fawksey. Comrades.

He leaves.

Nym   Fawksey is restless.

Jenny   Temperature?

Nym   It was high, but it's come down.

Marx   Jenny? Do you have something to tell me?

Jenny   Yes. Change your shirt. You've had it on for three days now.

Marx   Did you sleep with that Prussian flagpole of yours?

Nym   Qui Qui, come with me –

Marx   – no! She needs to know what her mother is.

Jenny   I'm here, am I not. (*To* **Engels**.) Did Schramm find you?

Engels   He was hit.

Jenny   Hit?!

Engels   In the head.

Jenny   You let that boy –

Marx   – she'd rather I was dead!

Jenny   He worshipped you, and you let him –

Marx   – he took the pistol off me! The boy's a fully paid-up half-wit. There's more brains in a large saveloy.

Jenny   My God you can be heartless.

Marx (*to* **Engels**)   The frozen waste that is my wife.

Nym   Qui Qui.

Marx   She's not stupid! Are you, princess? Play your mother the funeral march, cheer her up.

Qui Qui   I know 'Für Elise'.

Marx   Perfect! 'Für Elise'! A frivolous bagatelle!

Qui Qui *starts playing*.

Jenny   I liked Schramm.

Nym   He is dead then?

Engels   It looks that way.

Marx   Let's not mourn the death of dunces. Schramm is dead, and forgotten. But every cloud, silver lining, the *New New Rheinische Zeitung* will have a new new editor!

Jenny (*to* **Engels**)   Have you seen this side of him? It's ugly.

Marx   Isn't the truth always.

Jenny   He didn't go to his father's funeral.

Marx   Snitch!

Engels   My father is a Calvinist, Prussian, tit on a horse, but I'll still be there at his funeral.

Marx   Nym! Lard! Qui Qui! Play one of Mendelssohn's breakfast overtures.

Fawksey *cries out.* **Jenny** *goes into the bedroom closing the door behind her.*

Nym (*sotto*)   I need to speak with you. Alone.

Marx   General! We need bacon, black pudding.

Engels   You want me to go out and buy bacon so you can talk about something with Nym?

Marx   Yes.

Marx   Qui Qui! Go to the shops and help the General –

Engels   – carry the bacon?

Qui Qui   What?

Engels   I'll buy you some sherbet.

He and **Qui Qui** *leave.* **Nym** *and* **Marx** *are alone.*

Marx   Alone. What is it?

Nym   I'm sorry but you'll –

Jenny *opens the bedroom door and comes out.*

Jenny   Where's the honey?

Nym   He's had it all.

(*Shouting out the window.*) General, we need honey!

Jenny *looks between* **Nym** *and* **Marx**. *Then goes back into the room.*

Nym   I'm pregnant.

Marx   You're pregnant?

Nym   Yes.

Marx   It was only last night.

Nym   Two months ago. Greenwich Park. Remember?

Marx   And are you saying –

Jenny *opens the door to the bedroom.*

Jenny   He says he'll eat something.

She closes the door. **Marx** *puts a pan on the stove and rakes the coals.*

Marx   It can't be anyone else?

Nym   No.

Marx   Are you sure?

Nym   I've never slept with anyone else.

Marx   How do you know that?

Nym   Because I would have had to have been there when it happened.

Marx   And you would have remembered something like that?

Nym   Yes.

Jenny *comes out of the kitchen with a cup of water.*

Jenny   Remembered something like what?

Marx   Nym says she's only ever been to Greenwich with us.

Jenny   I've never been to Greenwich.

Marx   But she exists outside of us. She could've gone to any number of exotic destinations that we wouldn't know about.

Jenny *has gone back into the bedroom.*

Marx   Alright. I'm the father, but are you sure you're the mother?

Nym   What will happen?

Marx   Here? You, me, Engels, Jenny, Fawksey, Qui Qui, and your baby?

Nym   Do I need to leave? What are we going to do?

Marx   Two options. I can kill myself, or I could sit in a corner and rock like a Bedlamite.

Jenny *comes out, checks the pan, stokes the fire, puts on more coal.*

Jenny   Every time I open that door you two stop talking.

Fawksey (*off*)   Daddy! Daddy!

Jenny   I'm many things, but I'm not Daddy.

Marx *goes into the bedroom.*

Nym   Are you alright?

Jenny   No, but I'm back.

Nym   For good?

Jenny   For now. I had to do it. To bring him to his senses.

Nym   He was prepared to die for you.

Jenny   How was he last night?

Nym   He was Moor.

Jenny   Drunk?

Nym   Thoughtful. Do you still love him?

Jenny   I'm caught between a rock and a hard place. My wedding vows and murder.

Qui Qui *knocks.* **Nym** *opens the door. Enter* **Engels** *and* **Qui Qui** *with bacon and sherbert.*

Engels   Half a pound of streaky, with a hint of sherbert lemon.

Marx *enters.*

Marx   Excellent! I loathe the English, but they do understand one thing, the best things in life are fried!

He starts the process of cooking a fried breakfast.

Jenny   Sweets before breakfast!?

Marx   Leave her alone! Her father survived a duel. Princess pianoforte! Eggs! When I say 'egg' you throw. Egg!

Qui Qui *throws an egg to* **Marx** *who cracks it and starts to cook.* **Jenny** *exits.*

Marx   Qui Qui, at breakfast, there's a fundamental difference in motivation between the chicken and the pig. Egg!

Qui Qui   What do you mean, Daddy?

Marx   Vis à vis breakfast – the chicken is reasonably motivated – egg! – involved, happy to be asked –

Qui Qui   – eggs.

Marx   Yes! But the pig is committed. Bacon, throw!

Qui Qui *laughs and throws her father the bacon.*

Engels   This all smells good. Thank you, Mister Engels.

Marx   Thank you, Mister Engels, for the bacon.

Engels   And the table and chairs.

Qui Qui   And the piano.

Engels   That's all I need, a little love.

Marx   A little love? Ha! If Uncle Freddy doesn't have a different woman every couple of days he'll explode.

Qui Qui   What do you do with them, Uncle Freddy?

Laughter.

Engels   Tea. I like to have tea with different women, in the afternoons, because I need tea, and they like tea.

Marx   Or his cock falls off.

Jenny *comes in.*

Jenny   Qui Qui, it's a school day.

Qui Qui   But Mamma?!

An unsteady **Fawksey** *staggers out of his room.*

Fawksey   I'm hungry, Daddy.

Marx   Cuddle with squeeze, or cuddle with tickle?

Fawksey   Squeeze, don't tickle.

Marx *cuddles* **Fawksey** *but tickles him. He giggles.*

Fawksey   No, no, don't tickle!

Jenny   Mind his breathing.

Marx *puts him down.*

Engels   I could eat a horse, but this is not France.

Fawksey   Do they eat horses in France?

Engels   Continental breakfast, croissant, two hooves and jam.

Qui Qui *laughs, then maternally takes* **Fawksey** *into her arms.*

Marx   Look at it, before us.

Nym   What?

Marx   Breakfast. Look at that egg.

Jenny   Another epiphany.

Marx *holds his plate in the air, showing them his fried egg.*

Marx   I don't know who laid this egg.

Qui Qui   Chickens lay eggs, Daddy, not people.

Marx   You wait, capitalism'll soon have a manufactory churning out eggs by the thousands.

Marx   My point is that in earlier times, in say the feudal era –

Engels   – in worse times then?

Marx   At least I knew who I was! Before capitalism I could see my brother's hand in the labour content of my breakfast. This sausage was metonymic of the social relations prevalent at that time.

Engels   This is good, but write it down.

Marx   A sausage could explain my life.

Engels   Your species essence.

Marx   In its offal lies the explanation of who I am.

Engels   It maps your social relations.

Marx   And reminds me that I am connected to my fellow man. But then came capitalism and its trusty dog, the money commodity –

Engels   – woof, woof!

Marx   – which destroyed all social relations allowing no other point of contact other than cash.

Engels   But cash –

Marx   – unlike sausages.

Engels   Can't tell us who we are.

Jenny   Cash does allow one to live with some dignity.

Marx   It alienates me, utterly.

Engels   Alienates? Good word.

Marx   Money prevents me seeing the labour of my brother, and if I can't see his labour, I can't see his life! All relations are commodified. Capitalism will even commodify the bones of the saints, and render religion obsolete. Christmas will disappear into capitalism's foul, gaping maw, and will be sicked up again, utterly commodified.

Fawksey/Qui Qui   We love Christmas!

Marx   In ten years' time Christmas will no longer be a day to celebrate Christ's birth, it will be a week-long festival of commodification, a whole week, and so universal and meaningless that even Rabbis'll be scoffing mince pies, and snogging under the mistletoe.

There is a loud knocking at the door.

Jenny   No.

Marx *is already in the cupboard.* **Jenny** *goes to the door.*

Jenny   Who is it?

Schramm (*off*)   It's me!

Jenny   Schramm!

She opens the door. **Schramm** *enters. Bandaged.*

Jenny   Konrad!

She holds him.

Schramm   Agh!

Nym   We thought you were dead!

Engels   *Mon brave!*

He hugs **Schramm**. **Schramm** *approaches the cupboard.*

Schramm   Herr Doktor Marx! I am dead and then reborn, like Dionysus, son of Zeus, I am torn to pieces and eaten by Titans, but I have faced down Thanatos, and Rhea has brought me back to life to live, write, talk, debate and go on and on for ever!

Marx (*from the cupboard*)   He's bloody worse than before!

Schramm   Thank you, sir.

Engels   Come on, give him a kiss.

Marx (*opening the cupboard*)   You selfish bastard!

Schramm   I am alive!

Marx   Why?!

Schramm   Fate!

Marx   Sweet mercy!

Schramm *lustily embraces* **Marx**.

Schramm   Your wit, sir, I am overjoyed to find, is mercifully undiminished by your ordeal.

Marx   Why aren't you dead?

Schramm   The bullet only grazed my temple.

Marx (*to* **Engels**)   You told me Willich was a crack shot?

Schramm   His aim, I confess myself modestly grateful to report, on this singular occasion, fell somewhat below his customary standard of deadly perfection.

Marx   Maybe, but I've lined up a new new editor for the *Zeitung*.

Schramm (*laughs*)   If I may pick up on the elegant coat-tails of your epigram, might I perhaps presume to apologise profusely for not being dead.

Marx   Apology not accepted.

Schramm   I am bested in wit once again by a master of that specialised craft.

Marx (*to* **Engels**)   You piss in his face and he thanks you for the baptism.

Jenny   I was beside myself with worry.

Schramm   Madam Marx, you do me, by a very considerable degree, too great a kindness.

Jenny   Have you eaten?

Marx   No!

Schramm   I would not presume to impose upon your generous hospitality, but no I haven't, thank you.

He sits and picks up a knife and fork.

Marx   You have the impertinence not to die, and then you eat my breakfast. I shall be in the Reading Room of the British Museum if you wish to send a written apology. Do not deliver it yourself!

He leaves.

Engels   He's working! He's gone to work. He's writing. Finally. Schramm you are a genius!

*He kisses **Schramm** on the forehead.*

Transition

*In the street. **Marx** walking along, he realises that **Helmut** is following him. **Marx** stops, **Helmut** stops.*

Marx   Helmut. Why are you following me?

Helmut   Because the Prussian Minister of the Interior pays me.

Marx   But you know where I'm going.

Helmut   I'd guess the British Museum Reading Room where you will read a very big, very heavy, difficult book, standing up, on account of your boils.

Marx   You told them about my boils?

Helmut   Couple of sentences in the report, yeah. They like detail.

Marx   Who is betraying me?

Helmut   I can't tell you, that'd be silly.

Marx   Willich? Is it Willich? Engels? Nym? Jenny? Doc Schmidt? Konrad Schramm?

Helmut *coughs.*

Marx   Konrad?!

Helmut   No. I just coughed.

Marx   But he took a bullet for me, it can't be Konrad.

Helmut   I have a cold. And excuse me, I'm going to sneeze.

He sneezes. **Marx** *exits.*

Marx (*off*)   *Gesundheit!*

Helmut   Herr Marx! Wait for me! Why do you insist on making this difficult for me?

Scene Two

The Reading Room of the British Museum. A man of about sixty sits reading/writing upstage centre of a large study table. Behind him there are three other smaller study tables – each has a male 'reader' with their head down in books or specimens. The sixty-year-old looks exactly like the iconic figure of **Marx** *we know from the headstone.* **Marx** *walks in and sees him, double takes, turns and stands at a table (he can't sit because of the boils), but can't help being impressed by the bearded figure. The man catches* **Marx** *looking at him. They both work.* **Marx** *looks up at him. The man looks up, and catches* **Marx** *looking at him again.*

Bearded Man   Can I help?

Marx   Do I know you?

Bearded Man   Are you interested in barnacles?

Marx   As in stuck to a ship barnacles?

Bearded Man   Yes.

Marx   *Nie.* I have never been diverted from my life's purpose *mit* barnacles.

Bearded Man   Then you're a fool. Because you are a barnacle.

Marx   Absolutely foolish, yes, *aber* a barnacle?

Bearded Man   We're all barnacles.

Marx   Metaphorically?

Bearded Man   Literally. Are you not driven to understand who you are? I'm talking about the foundations of life, of –

Marx   – the origin of species?

Beat.

Bearded Man   That's good. Can I have that?

Marx   *Ich habe* no use for it.

The **Bearded Man** *writes something down.*

Marx   Do the barnacle *und* man share *ein mutter*?

Bearded Man   The barnacles took the low road, we took the high the road.

Marx   *Also, ich bin ein* barnacle! Every day *ist ein* school day.

Mrs Whitehead   Shh!

Enter **Engels**.

Engels   Moor?!

Reader One   Shh!

Marx   Yes.

Reader Two   Shh!

Engels   Where?

Reader One   Shh!

Marx   Here.

Reader Two   Shh!

Engels   Crisis. News from Cologne.

Marx   From where?

Reader Two   Cologne.

Engels   Shh! The committee are arrested.

Marx   Moll?

Engels   Moll, Anneke, the whole committee!

A **Reader** *stands and exits leaving his book/samples on the desk.*

Marx   After Schapper, we knew that would happen. I have a domestic problem.

Engels   The entire central committee are in prison!

Marx   And Nym has got a bun in the oven. And I'm the baker.

Engels   You fucked the maid?!

All   Shush!

Mrs Whitehead   I cannot endorse this! Leave. Now!

Marx   I'm really incredibly sorry, Mrs Whitehead.

Engels   I apologise.

Mrs Whitehead *walks away.*

Engels   You fucked the maid!

Everyone looks up again. One **Reader** *picks up his books and leaves in disgust.*

Reader One   This is a place of learning!

Engels   Sorry!

Marx   You know what this means?

Engels   Nine months' gestation and then a baby?

Marx   *Mon brave*, you're going to have to take responsibility.

Engels   For what?

Marx   I need you to say you're the father.

Engels   You want everyone to think that I fucked the maid?!

Reader Two   Shh!

Engels   You shush!

Marx   For my marriage, for Jenny, for the movement.

Engels   Are you insane?!

Marx   My enemies will destroy me with this. My reputation –

Engels   – what of my reputation?

Marx   You do not have a reputation to defend. Fucking maids is your metier.

Reader Two   Woah!

Engels *stands suddenly, kicking a chair over which causes a chain reaction domino style of destruction which causes other readers to protect their books and specimens.* **Mrs Whitehead** *returns with a man in a beige work coat.*

Engels   I will never agree to this! Never!

Mrs Whitehead   That's enough, out, both of you!

Mrs Whitehead's *assistant grabs* **Engels**. **Engels** *nuts him. A* **Reader** *punches* **Engels**. **Marx** *punches the* **Reader** *who punched*

Engels. *Another* **Reader** *rugby tackles* **Engels** *onto the big table. Samples go all over. A bookcase goes over followed by screams and the other* **Readers** *join in Wild West style, using large books like chairs in a saloon brawl to smash each other over the heads. Think Alan Ladd in* Shane. **Engels** *is dragged off.*

Mrs Whitehead   Who do you think you are? You come over here, you live off the soup, and you spend all day every day in my reading room just because I've got a fire going, and I wouldn't mind that but it's the superiority, the arrogance, 'we're Prussian', 'we're Austrian', 'we're Bavarian' as if I care, and no we don't have this book in German, no, and we don't have a translation service, why would we have translation service? If you want it translated, learn English and translate it yourself you leather-bound, pompous, sausage-eating, pissed twenty-four hours a day, humourless, militaristic, bloodsucking, arse out the back of your rags begging waste of space.

She is prostrate, possibly injured.

Bearded Man   Mrs Whitehead? Has the Reverend Klinkard finished with DeLacy's *Almanack of Molluscs*?

Mrs Whitehead   When I get a moment, I'll go and look.

Bearded Man   Thank you.

Scene Three

The Dean Street flat. **Marx**, **Engels** *and* **Nym**. **Marx** *and* **Engels** *are both sporting bandages.*

Nym   A fight in a library?

Marx   It was a typical library brawl. Somebody threw a punch at my friend, so, as you do, I went in.

Nym   But you wanted to talk to me?

Marx   The thing is . . . and it is not entirely straightforward, this thing, but it is a thing that can be managed, wonderfully successfully in fact, with other things being part of it. And those things will fall into place as things happen, making the thing itself a more than passable thing.

Nym My baby.

Marx Is the thing we are talking about.

Engels You bastard.

Nym (*to* **Engels**) You know?

Marx He knows.

Nym I never wanted to cause pain between you and Jenny.

Marx No, no, yes, no, I understand –

Nym I love Jenny like a sister, but I cannot deny my feelings. Is that wrong?

Marx It's a valid question, full of validity, and I'm glad you –

Nym – my love is not illegitimate –

Engels – unlike the baby.

Marx You must have the child.

Nym Our child!

Marx General here has agreed, with unselfish altruism, to be the, um, you know, to the, er, child.

Nym Godfather! Thank you.

Engels You bastard.

Marx The father.

Nym What?

Marx He's always quite liked you.

Engels You absolute bastard.

Marx This might not be exactly what you had in mind, Nym.

Nym   What extraordinary insight into womankind you have.

Marx   Are my political enemies to be given the gift of my social ignominy?

Nym   Is that is what our child means to you? Social ignominy?

Marx   Ignominy, scandal, humiliation, let's not split hairs! The movement, the revolution, these are our true children.

Engels   I just threw up a bit in my mouth.

Marx   The child will officially be the General's. He will make provision for the foster parents, and we'll find good people.

Nym   You bastard.

Marx   I'm married! The public revelation of a child born out of wedlock would ruin me.

Engels   You absolute bastard.

Nym   But no one will believe that the General is father to my child?

Marx   They will! You have been seduced by the great seducer!

Engels *grabs him by the lapels.*

Engels   *Du bist wirklich ein total dreck-kotzgefullter-hosenscheisse-arschklarsch-wanzsphilitische-Feigling!*

Marx   That's all agreed then.

Jenny's *knock.*

Marx   Jenny! You two, into the bedroom.

He ushers **Nym** *and* **Engels** *into the bedroom.* **Jenny** *knocks.*

Marx   I'm coming!

He lets her in.

You're on your own?

Jenny   They're at the Gilbert's.

Marx   Qui Qui's friend's?

Jenny   Yes. Fawksey loves Mrs Gilbert, and she feeds them up.

Marx   But –

Jenny   – he's not coughing. I wouldn't have left them if –

Marx   – alright, I trust you.

A look.

Guess who's been round.

Jenny   Who?

Marx   The General.

Jenny   Where is he?

Marx   Do you need to ask?

Jenny   Are you going to tell me?

Marx   Do I really have to?

Jenny   Do you really want to?

Marx   He came round, like a love-struck teenager, powered by a heady mixture of infatuation and anticipation.

Engels (*off*)   I do not deny it!

Jenny   Mary Burns is here?

Marx   No, no, no. I hardly need to tell you the identity of the wholly reciprocating recipient of his amour?

Engels (*off*)   What else could I bloody do?!

Nym *has kicked or punched a cupboard door.*

Marx   Ooh! This one really does seem to be '*la grande passion*'.

Jenny   Who has he got in there?

Marx   Nym.

Jenny   Nym? And him?

Marx   Him and Nym.

Jenny   He –

Marx   – and Ny. When you think about it it's obvious.

Jenny   No! It isn't. They don't particularly like each other.

Marx   I know, I was shocked, initially. I thought Nym with him, no. Maybe more him with Nym, to begin, but no, Nym was as into him as he into Ny.

Jenny   And they're?

Marx   In there. Took the opportunity, with the kids out the house. Couldn't stop them. Like two young lovebirds, or rabbits, or in season mink.

Engels (*off*)   Alright! I don't care anymore, hit me, go on, hit me!

Nym (*off*)   What makes you think you'll get away with this?!

Engels (*off*)   Put that down. No, don't!

Noise of something being thrown, and smashed, an actual breakage.

Marx   Mmm. Lively. It's a little presumptious, in our place, but I guess we're all adults.

Another smash.

They're really good together.

Engels *and* **Nym** *enter about as far apart as is possible.*

Marx   You two, tch! Welcome back.

Nym *and* **Engels** *sit, separately.*

Jenny   Hello, Nym.

Nym   Hello, Jenny.

Jenny   Hello, General.

Engels   Hello, Jenny.

Silence.

Marx   This is nice. Drink? Bit early in the day, but I think I have some quite acceptable Scotch the General bought.

Jenny   Moor was just saying –

Marx   – that, um, you two, both of you, were, as a couple, both together, and wasn't it a bit of a surprise, but also very lovely for both of the two of you lovely people to be together as a lovely couple.

Jenny   I had no idea.

Nym *and* **Engels** *can barely look at each other.*

Marx   It was obvious to me!

Engels   What?

Jenny   When did you two first . . .

Marx   General? Ladies first I know, but Freddy? It was definitely more than eight weeks ago?

Engels   I'd say eight weeks and two days ago.

Jenny   And you felt the same, Nym?

Nym   No.

Marx   What?!

Nym   My feelings went back further. I was attracted to a man I had admired for more than ten years.

Jenny   Oh sweet. And General, you found yourself feeling the same way?

Engels   Similar. Along those lines.

Marx (*with glass*)   What more joyous than celebrating love between two people. What more? Unless there was something more, or additional, to celebrate on top of it. Or with it, or connected in some way, or as a result.

Nym   I'm pregnant?

Marx   Now I did not expect that!

Jenny   Nym!

She embraces **Nym**.

Marx   This is wonderful news indeed.

Engels *downs his second large whisky in one, and pours himself another.*

Jenny   Nymchen?! How are you feeling?

Nym   Terrible.

Jenny *holds her closer.*

Engels   Me too.

Jenny (*to* **Nym**)   Morning sickness?

Engels   Yes.

Marx   Sympathetic pains. A true mark of love.

Jenny   How long now?

Nym   Eight weeks.

Jenny   And two days?

Nym *cries.*

Jenny   Don't cry. This is happy news.

Nym   Yes, I am very happy.

Engels   We both are.

Nym   I'd like to lie down.

Jenny   Yes. Come to the bedroom.

She takes **Nym** *to the bedroom.* **Marx** *pours another drink.*

Engels   Happy, Daddy?

Marx   Thanks a lot. I mean you really entered into the spirit of that.

Engels   You bastard.

Marx   You know, there's a really cynical side to you.

Jenny *comes back out of the bedroom.*

Jenny   She's completely wrung-out. The emotion. But she's settled now.

Marx   Some women would have been pretty annoyed their maid had become pregnant. But not this woman, General. Wife, mother – not my mother – secretary, amanuensis.

Jenny *knees him hard in the balls.*

Jenny   You bastard. I am disappointed in you, General.

Engels *protects his groin.*

Engels   I am disappointed in myself!

Loud banging on the front door.

Sgt Savage   Police! Unlock the door!

Marx *walks on his knees into the cupboard.* **Jenny** *opens the front door.*

Sgt Savage   Ah yes, I thought I'd been here already. Mister Engels.

Engels   It's good to see you again, sergeant.

Sgt Savage   Where is he? Charles Marx.

Engels   Jenny *hasst du –*

Jenny   *Ja.*

Jenny *opens the cupboard door.*

Sgt Savage   Mister Marx. Er . . . never know what to say at this point.

Marx   You are arresting me on suspicion of the theft of an Argyll?

Sgt Savage   I like that wording.

Marx   Will it harm my defence if I fail to mention something, when questioned, which I later rely on in court?

Sgt Savage   What are you on about?

Marx   Then I shall assume that anything I do say may be given in evidence.

Sgt Savage   I wouldn't worry about that, it's all down to whether the beak don't like the look of you.

Marx   *Das* Argyll *ist* a family heirloom. *Ein* wedding present. Ergo, it is mine *und* hers!

Sgt Savage   Is this true, madam?

Jenny   *Mein* Argyll is missing. *Und* I do not know this man.

Sgt Savage *cuffs* **Marx**.

Scene Four

Marx *is at the cell door in discussion with a sceptical gaoler,* **Constable Singe**, *who is reading to him.*

Constable Singe (*reading*)   'Hegel's argument is essentially mystical and idealistic, whereas my dialectic is the antithesis, rooted in a materialistic view of man's situation. So, as a man, without economic autonomy, utterly alienated from my brother worker, and suffering grinding poverty, I decided to nick a solid silver gravy warmer.'

Marx   I'm happy *mit* that.

Constable Singe   Sign here.

He passes the statement through the bars and **Marx** *signs it. A door is heard opening, off. Enter* **Constable Crimp** *with* **Willich** *and* **Barthélemy**.

Comstable Crimp   Right, come on, lads. Hurry up. None of us are getting any younger.

Constable Singe   The beak'll have fun with that.

Constable Crimp   Stand there.

Constable Singe   What are these two in for?

Constable Crimp   Duelling. Yesterday morning. On the Heath. Arrested at Charing Cross today, trying to leg it.

Constable Singe   Name?

Barthélemy   *Je suis Français!*

Constable Singe   How do you spell that?

Willich   I am French.

Constable Crimp (*to* **Willich**)   You're French?

Willich   No.

Constable Crimp   Don't lie to the police then, son.

Willich   He's French.

Constable Crimp (*to* **Barthélemy**)   Good, you'll be impressed by the plumbing.

He thrusts a bucket into **Barthélemy**'s *hands.*

Marx   August Willich.

Willich   Marx? What are you doing here?

Marx   Discussing dialectical materialism with Constable Singe.

Willich   I am arrested for duelling.

Marx   I don't believe a word of it.

Constable Singe   Cell eleven at the end.

Constable Crimp   Come on, lads. Follow me.

Barthélemy   Eleven?

Willich   *Onze.*

Marx   You can count to eleven, Willich. Five fingers on each hand makes ten, and then you get your cock out.

Willich   Why do you not believe my word, that I am arrested?

Marx   Because Schapper is arrested in Cologne! And you –

Willich   – you think I am the informer?! You do not know yourself Marx! You need your rival in love to be your Judas. Life would be simpler that way, but unfortunately for you, I am a man of honour, true to our cause, and I am arrested!

Barthélemy   *Moi aussi!*

Marx   Doc Schmidt told me you –

Willich   Schmidt! You never see the lies you believe!

Enter **Engels** *led by* **Sgt Savage**.

Sgt Savage   Miladdo's bailed.

Barthélemy   I will dig a tunnel *comme un blaireau!*

Willich   I will build a tunnel like a shaving brush.

Barthélemy   Then I will escape ! *Pendant votre petit dejeuner.*

Willich   I will escape into your breakfast.

Constable Crimp   That's it! I've had enough of this babble! Chop, chop!

Barthélemy   You need to know, I don't eat shellfish.

Constable Crimp *takes them to the cells.*

Constable Singe   Rich friends, eh?

He unlocks the cell and opens the gate.

Marx   How did you arrange bail?

Engels   Circumstances.

Marx   Circumstances?

Engels   Fawksey.

Marx   What's happened?

Engels   He's gone. I'm sorry.

Marx   What 'gone'? Gone? No, not 'gone'. No, no, no.

Engels   He didn't wake this morning. He died during the night.

Marx *moans quietly and holds his own head in his hands. Then he comes out of it quickly.*

Marx   Was Doc Schmidt there when Fawksey died?

Engels   No.

Marx   You remember when we nicked the gate?

Engels   Moor?! Fawksey is dead.

Marx   Doc Schmidt was with us, wasn't he?

Engels   What –

Marx   He knew about the Argyll.

Engels   What are you talking about?!

Marx   It's Doc Schmidt!

He is on his feet and out of the cell.

Engels (*grabbing him*)   You must bury your son! Jenny needs you!

Marx   I will not take a lecture in family from you.

Engels   Moor!

Scene Five

Berwick Street. **Marx** *enters, sits on a step and waits. A door opens and* **Schmidt** *exits carrying a suitcase, wearing a hat and great coat.*

Marx   Give it back, Schmidt.

Schmidt   Moor, good to see you.

Marx   Give it back!

Schmidt   You have me at a disadvantage –   '

Marx   – I should kill you.

Schmidt   Kill me later! Let's have a whisky –

Marx   Give me the Argyll.

Schmidt   Even if I have what you say I have, which I don't admit, I have to return it to its rightful owner.

Marx   Fawksey's dead.

Schmidt   I'm sorry.

Marx   Are you?

Schmidt   I am a doctor. I treated his symptoms correctly, with borax administered with honey. It wasn't me that killed him.

Marx *runs at* **Schmidt**, *knocks him down, pins him to the ground and picks up a loose cobble.*

Marx   You were a friend.

Schmidt   I serve Prussia.

He fumbles inside his greatcoat and produces the Argyll. **Marx** *takes it.*

Marx   Who controls you? Jenny's brother?

Schmidt   Minister von Westphalen's sent me to break the League and rescue the family silver.

Marx   And destroy my family?!

Schmidt   You've got the Argyll, let me go.

Marx *raises his arm again, poised to bring the cobble down on* **Schmidt**'s *head.*

Marx   You killed Fawksey!

Schmidt   You can't do it, Marx, you're not a soldier.

Marx *pauses, then brings the stone down hard on* **Schmidt**'s *head. The bystanders wade in and break them up.*

Scene Six

A graveyard and a hole in the ground, with fresh earth around. A gravedigger sits smoking a pipe. Enter a procession made up of a **Lutheran Pastor**, **Jenny** *and* **Engels** *carrying a small wooden coffin.* **Qui Qui**, *then* **Nym**. *They put the box by the hole.* **Jenny** *looks around.*

Pastor   Frau Marx?

Jenny *ignores him.*

Pastor   I have a baptism at –

Jenny   – please, my husband is not yet here.

Pastor   But –

Engels   – Pastor Flint, please, may we just wait another minute?

The **Pastor** *stands five yards away.* **Qui Qui** *sits on a bench away from the grave.*

Nym   He'll come.

Jenny   You don't know him. He considers the dead lucky.

Nym *takes this as some kind of rebuke, and slopes off to sit on the bench with* **Qui Qui**.

Engels   His own son's funeral!

Jenny   He doesn't do funerals. He won't even go to his own.

Pastor   We really need to begin.

Jenny   *Ja*, I apologise, it appears that my husband is indisposed.

Jenny, **Engels** *and the* **Pastor**, *with the help of the gravedigger, lower the coffin into the ground.* **Qui Qui** *and* **Nym** *step forward. They all throw some soil in.*

Pastor   You may speak to the child before I give the dedication.

Engels   Do you want me to say something?

Jenny   I'll try.

Beat. And then **Jenny** *speaks.*

Jenny   Born on Guy Fawkes Night 1847 my son Guido Fawksey Marx, I shall live your life for you so that you suffer no more. Bronchitis, measles, the croup, the colic –

She starts to cry. **Engels** *comforts her.*

Engels   – the dens in the woods, the horses, the fights, games, dances, er . . .

Nym   – swimming in the sea –

Engels   – roast dinners –

Qui Qui   – sandcastles –

Jenny   – picnics –

Nym   – snowball fights –

Qui Qui   – cycling –

Jenny   – camp fires –

Qui Qui   – tree houses –

Engels   – girls.

They laugh.

Nym   Love.

Jenny   Love.

Engels   That he had.

Schramm *arrives at pace.*

Schramm   Frau Doktor Marx –

Engels   – not now, Schramm.

Engels *marshals* **Schramm** *away from the grave.*

Schramm   – I wished to pay my respects to one who knew too little of the world, one robbed by untimely time of his place at life's feast –

Engels   – Schramm?!

Schramm   Yes, sir. I know, sir, that I am prone to prolixity. My life has become a quest for brevity.

Engels   This is a child's funeral!

Schramm   So I will convey my secondary purpose in attending upon this ceremony with uncharacteristic economy.

Engels   What's happened?!

Schramm   Herr Doctor Marx has curtailed the egregious and nefarious machinations of a traitor.

Pastor   Frau Marx, please, I must complete the service.

Jenny   Yes, yes.

Schramm   Doc Schmidt is the informer! Herr Doktor Marx wounded the cur, and it was whilst the dog was in hospital that we found about his person plans to arrest a further twenty comrades across Europe. They have been forewarned! And that, that is why Doctor Marx is not here!

Enter **Marx**.

Pastor   Are you the father? May we continue?

Marx   *Ja.* (*To the* **Gravedigger**.) Did you dig *diese* grave?

Gravedigger   Aye, sir.

Marx   *Danke. Und* a fine grave it is.

Marx *hugs him.*

Join us.

Gravedigger   Sir?

Marx   No one should be ashamed of their working clothes.

The **Gravedigger** *stays.*

Pastor   We give thanks to God for the deceased, and commend the remains to God's care. Nothing can separate us from the love of God in Christ Jesus our Lord, not even death, and –

Marx   – enough! My son doesn't need your stories. The only truth here is our pain. Please, leave us with that. Jenny, have you spoken?

Jenny   Yes.

Engels   But he needs to hear your voice.

Marx   Yes. (*Beat.*) Fawksey! Son! I'm here. It's your father. Late, yes, but you knew I'd be late. And for that, I ask for your forgiveness. You were my son and an Englishman, and we bury you today in the soil of your mother country, and you take your rightful place with their great men. Wat Tyler, Henry Hunt, Thomas Paine, Oliver Cromwell and William Shakespeare.

(*To the* **Gravedigger**.) Comrade, *deine Schaufel*, please?

The **Gravedigger** *gives him his spade.*

Marx   I should've dug your grave, as a penance, punishment for the pain I caused you, but that would've been easy, and selfish. I'll fill it in, and this labour is the gift I give you.

He fills in the grave, and gives the spade back to the **Gravedigger**.

Marx   Thank you.

General?

Engels   Qui Qui, come with me.

Marx *and* **Jenny** *are left alone.*

Marx   I killed him.

Jenny   Stop it.

Marx   If I'd –

Jenny   – stop it!

Marx   I could've got a job –

Jenny   – the railway?

Marx   Yes! Why not?

Jenny   That was never an option.

Marx   It's good enough for everyone else. And those people, they don't have to sacrifice their children.

Jenny   Everything we've ever done, we've done together.

Marx   We haven't done anything yet. (*Beat.*) Do you forgive me? For me and Nym.

Jenny   No.

Marx   Good. That's good. It's clear. We know where we are on that one. (*Beat.*) I forgive you.

Jenny   For what?

Marx   You're right. I'm sorry. You haven't done anything have you. I don't forgive you.

Jenny   Moor, don't try to make me laugh.

Marx   Sorry.

He reaches out and takes her hand.

Fawksey? What can we do? Me and your mother. To honour you. Carry on?

Scene Seven

The flat. Seven months later. Evening. **Marx** *is stood writing.*
Jenny *is sat to one side transcribing* **Marx**'s *scribble into legible*
handwriting. **Engels** *has a glass of wine and alternates between*
tending the fire and reading. **Nym** *is organising filing cards.* **Qui**
Qui *is playing the piano, sotto. The Argyll is there on* **Jenny**'s *table.*

Jenny (*with papers in hand*)   General?

Engels   That's me, I'm still here. For which I apologise.

Marx   Stay for dinner. You're family.

Jenny   We love you.

Engels   Nym?

Nym   I didn't say anything.

They laugh. **Engels** *pours wine for* **Nym**.

Engels   Have some more wine.

Jenny (*with papers in hand*)   – what –

Marx   – you put the wine in the gravy warmer?!

Engels   Someone had to find a use for it.

Nym *drinks it without thanking or looking at* **Engels**. **Engels** *taps*
his glass with a fork or similar.

Jenny   An official announcement.

Engels   I've decided to abandon you. I'm going back to
Manchester.

Marx   You hate Manchester.

Engels   I wrote to my father.

Marx   Please can I have my job back?

Jenny   But you've just got rooms in Soho.

Marx   You're properly going to be a cotton lord?

Engels   I will send you a five pound note every week.

Jenny   And where will you get this five pound note?

Engels   I shall steal it from the cash box at Ermen and Engels, risking dismissal by either Ermen or Engels.

Nym   You're Engels.

Engels   Which is why I might get away with it. And I will do this partly because I believe his writing will contribute to the progress of mankind, but more importantly because there is another soul out there more in need of the job of railway clerk at Paddington.

Marx *stands and embraces him.*

Marx   Marx and Engels.

Engels   Engels and Marx.

Marx   Thank you, Freddy.

Engels   Now, I'm sorry, Jenny, you wanted to ask me a question.

Jenny   Yes. As a cotton lord yourself –

Nym   – capitalist.

Jenny (*reading*)   Capital is dead labour, that, vampire-like, only lives by sucking living labour –

Marx   – and lives the more, the more labour it sucks.

Engels   This is meant to be a book about political economy not a penny dreadful. And two sucks in one sentence.

Jenny   One sucking, and one suck.

Engels   It's a bit bloody bloodthirsty.

Nym   It's an accurate metaphor. The capitalist is vampiric, a blood sucker.

Marx   You pay the worker a shilling, but he creates three shillings value.

Nym   You've vampire-sucked two shillings surplus value.

Marx   Labour is different from other commodities, it has the capacity to create a value greater than its own value.

Engels   That's the only reason to buy it!

Marx   That is where capitalism is antithetical to natural justice!

Engels   The capitalist pays a shilling for something he knows to be worth three shillings.

Jenny   And you give no share in the surplus created.

Nym   You're a vampire.

Engels   I don't start till Monday.

Jenny   But why does the worker agree to this unjust exchange?

Engels   He has to eat.

Jenny   And pay the rent.

Marx   No!

Nym   Because there's someone who will work for less.

Marx   Thank you, Nym. Surplus value is the modern battleground. Collective capital versus collective labour. This battle will write the history of man in the next century. Where's my wine then?

Engels   Is he allowed to drink and bring down capitalism at the same time?

Marx   Yes! *L'chaim!*

Engels   *Zum Wohl!*

They drink. **Engels** *pours* **Marx** *a glass and looks over his shoulder.*

Engels   Are we sticking with sucking vampires then?

Marx   Yes.

Engels   This isn't work!

Marx   Piss off.

Engels   He's hiding something Jenny.

Marx   A private letter.

Engels   There's nothing private in here. We're communists!

Qui Qui *stops playing and looks for a new piece of sheet music.*

Qui Qui   Chopin?

Marx   Polish!

Qui Qui   Liszt?

Engels   Hungarian!?

Qui Qui   Schumann?

All   German!

Qui Qui *looks for her sheet music and during the next she plays Kinderzenen Op. 15, No. 1.* **Engels** *kisses* **Jenny** *on the forehead.*

Engels *tends the fire.* **Qui Qui** *starts playing the Schumann again.* **Marx** *finishes the letter and puts it down on the table next to* **Jenny**.

Engels   *Attention! C'est fini!* The secret letter thing.

Nym *takes the baby.* **Jenny** *picks up the letter.*

Marx   Read it.

Jenny   Out loud?

Marx   Please.

Qui Qui *stops playing.*

Jenny (*reading*) 'My dearest Jenny, I shall be martyred for my philosophy. Traduced, vilified, defamed. I care little, because my purpose on this earth is to love you. There have been poets, braggards all, who, facetiously, have rhymed a greater love, but they were ignorant of my heart. Had they looked inside it, they would have stepped aside, and handed me the quill. Of course, I failed you. I looked away, to another. You took me back, and embraced her, without judgement. That is why I shall always be unworthy of you. But if there is anything good and pure in me, it is yours. Your loving husband, Moor.'

A baby cries.

Jenny   I'll get him for you.

Qui Qui *starts playing again.* **Jenny** *goes into the bedroom, and returns with the baby. She rocks the baby gently.*

Marx   'It becomes the unique job of the money commodity' –

Nym   – I don't like 'unique job'.

Engels   It's not a job is it?

Nym   Special social function.

Engels   How about she writes *Das Kapital* and we just put your name on it?

Marx   'It becomes the special social function of the money commodity, and consequently its social monopoly, to play within the world of commodities the part of the general substitute.'

Jenny   I don't like 'general substitute'.

Nym   Universal exchange?

Engels   Universal substitute?

Marx   Universal equivalent. Money as the universal equivalent! Excellent. Thank you! Thank you. Thank you.

Qui Qui *plays on.*

The End.

The Hypocrite

The Hypocrite was co-produced by the Royal Shakespeare Company, Hull Truck Theatre and Hull UK City of Culture 2017. It was first performed at Hull Truck Theatre on 24 February 2017. The production transferred to the Swan Theatre, Stratford-upon-Avon on 31 March 2017. It featured the following cast and crew:

Sir John Hotham	**Mark Addy**
Lord Mayor Barnard	**Martin Barrass**
Drudge Scullion	**Danielle Bird**
Messenger/Soldier/Local	**Rachel Dale**
Peregrine Pelham MP	**Neil D'Souza**
Connie	**Laura Elsworthy**
King Charles I/Ghost	**Ben Goffe**
Sweet Lips/Mademoiselle Frottage	**Danielle Henry**
Executioner/Captain Moyer	**Adrian Hood**
Captain Jack	**Asif Khan**
Hugh Peters/Messenger/Soldier	**Andrew Langtree**
James, Duke of York	**Jordan Metcalfe**
Frances Hotham	**Sarah Middleton**
Durand Hotham	**Pierro Niel-Mee**
Prince Rupert of the Rhine	**Rowan Polonski**
Albert Calvert	**Paul Popplewell**
Lady Sarah Hotham	**Caroline Quentin**
The Ranter	**Josh Sneesby**
John Saltmarsh	**Matt Sutton**

All other parts played by members of the Company.

Director   Phillip Breen
Designer   Max Jones
Lighting Designer   Tina MacHugh
Music and Lyrics   Grant Olding
Sound Designer   Andrea J. Cox
Stunts and Movement   Annie Lees-Jones
Fight Director   Renny Krupinski
Illusionist   Chris Fisher
Text and Voice Work   Michaela Kennen
Assistant Director   Becky Hope-Palmer

Music Director   Phill Ward
RSC Casting Directors   Helena Palmer, Matthew Dewsbury
Dramaturg   Pippa Hill
Production Manager   Jacqui Leigh
Production Manager   Carl Root
Costume Supervisor   Sian Thomas
Props Supervisor   Beckie May
Company Stage Manager   Paul Sawtell
Deputy Stage Manager   Bryony Rutter
Assistant Stage Manager   Amy Hawthorne
Rehearsal Musical Director   Paul Frankish
Hull Truck Theatre Producer   Rowan Rutter
RSC Producer   Kevin Fitzmaurice
Musicians   Guitar/mandolin/percussion/voice Phill Ward,
double bass Adam Jarvis

Set

An open stage that can become indoor rooms and outdoor street
scenes, both London and Hull.

Props

Some props need to be engineered: the vase, the trunk, the collapsing
bed, the 'walk through the wall' ghost panel, etc.

Characters

Sir John Hotham, *fifty-three*
Lady Sarah Hotham, *late thirties/early forties*
Durand, *son, early twenties*
Frances, *daughter, late twenties*
Captain Jack, *twenty-five*
Connie, *maid/cook, forty*
Drudge Scullion, *108, no one's entirely sure*
Captain Moyer, *thirties*
Sweet Lips/Mademoiselle Frottage, *thirties/forties*
John Saltmarsh, *thirties*
Lord Mayor Barnard, *fifties*
Albert Calvert, *money lender, forties*
Peregrine Pelham MP, *fifty-six*
Duke of York, *eighteen*
Prince Rupert, *twenty-one*
Charles I, *forty-two*
Ghost, *double with Charles I*
The Ranter, *a lone punk songsmith, male or female*

Ensemble to play all other parts.

Prologue

London, 1645. Before the Tower of London. An execution block and basket on a plinth. The mob mill and wait for the execution. Costermongers, cutpurses, beggars, soldiers. Chuggers try to collect money and signatures for the Ranters, Seekers, Anabaptists, Familists, Levellers, Diggers from the audience. Each actor is knowledgeable about their movement and has pamphlets. Entrepreneurs try and sell souvenir block and axe carvings.

Costermonger One   Thames oysters! Surprise the wife!

Costermonger Two   Sea coals?! Come on, muvver, sort it out! (*etc. throughout pre-show*)

Enter **Connie**, *speaking with a Hull accent.*

Connie
    In a world turned upside down
    Our story starts at the end.
    The epilogue usurps the prologue
    And is by a woman penned.

She passes a **Chugger**, *with waistcoat, quill and pamphlet, representing the Levellers.*

Chugger One   Good mornin, ma'am, could you spare a minute for the Levellers –

Connie   – sorry, luv, I'm late.

    Our play begins in London, unfortunately,
    A terrible place, unlike mi cultured 'ull.
    The English revolution is full blown,
    Parliament's king, and the King's annulled.

An aristocrat fallen on hard times pleads with her.

Lord Beggar   For a lord now emulated. Spare change please?!

Connie   I'm from Yorkshire, love, we don't have spare change.

Lords beg and the beggars are all on horse,
Charles Stuart slips from shire to fen
Like poor Tom, in plays of old,
Searching for a hearth and the hearts of men.

Drunken Ranter   I, aye me, I am the Lord your God!

Connie

God's a shattered Baptist, Ranter, Quaker,
And if He lives in this new republic
He's in the book, in the stocks, or in His grave
God's now owt you like, 'cept Catholic.

A **Diggers' Chugger** *approaches* **Connie**.

Chugger Two   Spare a couple of minutes for the
Diggers?

Connie   I signed up yesterday, love!

In accord with the discord of the age,
When traditions burn up like parchment in the fire,
We'll begin our comedy at the end,
With the tragic execution of a friend.

*Drums. Enter a dwarf executioner with a small axe, followed
by a medium executioner with a medium axe, then a huge
executioner with a huge axe. Then* **Sir John Hotham**. *Also*
Hugh Peters, *the executing officer, and* **Durand Hotham**.
The **Mob** *boo.*

Peters   Sir John Hotham, Governor of Hull –

Mob One   Hypocrite!

Mob Two   We needed Hull, you damned feculent shit
breech!

Peters   – guilty of betrayal of trust to Parliament and
adherence to the king.

Mob Three   Traitor!

Whore   You wanna last kiss, love?!

Mob One   He's a right mutton monger!

Peters   Guilty of refusing to supply Lord Fairfax with powder –

Mob Two   – I got snuff! Who wants snuff?!

Peters   – guilty of intent to betray Hull.

Mob (*furious*)   Turncoat / Papist / Renegade / Dog!

Mob Three   Wanker.

Peters   To the block.

Sir John   May I speak to London?

Peters   The prisoner is not to speak!

Sir John *is led to the block.*

Durand   Why shan't my father speak?

Peters   The prisoner commends to the people his terrestrial life, namely, the mask of honour –

Mob One   – woah!

Peters   – the emptiness of words

Mob Two   – woah!

Peters   – and the betrayal of friends. All else is vanity!

Laughter.

Connie   Lord Fairfax is behind this!

Peters   Silence! Do the deed.

Executioner   Come on! Chop, chop!

Sir John *takes off his coat and gives it to* **Durand**. *He places his head back on the block. The* **Executioner** *swings the axe and with one blow* **Sir John**'s *head is separated from his body. The mob gasp, but then are respectfully silent. The* **Executioner** *picks the head out, shows it to the mob and hands it to* **Durand**. **Durand** *puts his father's head on his coffin downstage.*

Peters   Next execution, noon tomorrow. Monsieur André Picq, for papism and being a bit French.

Executioner   The fun's over! Move on!

The **Mob** *disperse. The bloodied, separated head speaks:*

Sir John   I am called traitor, changeling, ambidexter, yet I have been constant to Parliament, but also unfortunately constant to the king. Honour is contained in motive. I never gave a thought to saving my own skin, or the fate of my vast estates across Holderness. I will miss East Yorkshire, most of which I own.

I leave a pack of hounds, a pet snake and seventeen children. My first wife, Catherine, awaits me in heaven. My second wife, the fragrant Anne, will be sat beside her. My third wife, Jane, (*spits blood*) is in hell, probably running it. My fourth wife, Catherine, whom I married because she reminded me of my first wife, Catherine, I shall woo again. My fifth wife, Sarah Anlaby, survives me, and for her, life will be perilous, but at least she has a road in West Hull named after her. Connie, my cook –

Connie   – I'm here, John!

Sir John   Connie?! I bequeath to you and your like, the common people, (*spits*) a new politic, constitutional parliamentary democracy.

(*To the audience.*) And to you, the audience, I give the torments of my life as light entertainment.

Song – 'World Turned Upside Down'

The king is now a beggar and the beggar's now a god.
The bishop's in the gutter and his staff's a cattle prod.
The Digger wants more knowledge and the Ranter wants
    the crown
The peasant wants for nothing in a world turned upside
    down.

We're living in a world turned upside down
We're living in a time turned inside out.
We're living in a world turned upside down.
How did this come about?

The layman is the expert and the many rule the few
We're levelling the land to build our albion anew.
The shoots of green will soon emerge out of the fields of
    brown
By standing on your head you see the world turned upside
    down.

We're living in a world turned upside down
We're living in a time turned inside out.
We're living in a world turned upside down.
How did this come about?

No idols for to worship and no royalty to serve,
To live and love as freeborn men's no more than we deserve.
The king is now a rover, and a knave is now a king.
The world turned upside is such an edifying thing.

We're living in a world turned upside down
We're living in a time turned inside out.
We're living in a world turned upside down.
How did this come about?

We're living in a world turned upside down
We're living in a time turned inside out.
We're living in a world turned upside down.
How'd it all come about?

Act One

Scene One

*Indoors at the **Hotham** estate just outside Beverley. The servant*
***Drudge Scullion** is revealed to be hanging from a hook on the*
fireplace. On the floor beneath him is the animal head he has
replaced. He seems to be asleep. There is a pool of urine on the
*boards beneath him. Enter **Connie**, the cook.*

Connie
That was the end, but where do we begin?
Hotham Hall, Beverley, ten mile from Hull, and home of
    his kin,
Eleven times passed from *Hotham* father to *Hotham* son,
1642, the English Civil War is brewing, but has not begun.

*Enter **Sir John** followed by **Lady Sarah**.*

Lady Sarah   Whose side are we on?!

Sir John   You, as my wife, are on my side!

Lady Sarah   The servants need to know.

Sir John   The servants will be told when I have decided!

Lady Sarah   You'll take the side of Parliament.

Sir John   Will I?

Lady Sarah   Because they have promised to make you
commander of all Yorkshire.

Sir John   If I decide to affiliate with Parliament it will be a
decision born of principle and unrelated to the possibility of
being made commander of all Yorkshire.

Lady Sarah   With a stipend of three thousand a year.

Sir John   I am loyal to the Stuarts –

Lady Sarah   – because they gave you a knighthood!

Sir John   Do you honestly believe that three thousand pounds would turn me to Parliament?

Lady Sarah   In our present financial predicament, yes, absolutely.

Sir John   Anyway, what's it got to do with you, you overbosomed prune?!

Lady Sarah   Urgh! Why did I marry such a pompous, half-wiped arse!

Sir John   Why did I marry such a prick-shrinking, scrotum-breathed, dried-up vale of nothing!

Lady Sarah   For the two pig farms that made up the dowry!

Enter **Connie**.

Sir John   A marvellous lunch, Connie.

Lady Sarah   What name do you give to that heinous crime?

Connie   Mutton casserole.

Lady Sarah   The meat was off!

Connie   I got it in fresh, for your return from London.

Lady Sarah   I was delayed a week!

Connie   Not my fault, then, is it.

Lady Sarah   Insolence! The air may be thick with revolution but there'll be no innovations in this house.

Connie   Are we for Parliament?

Lady Sarah   Sir John will decide and if you don't approve you can hawk your mutton elsewhere.

Connie   Aye, I might. My own baker's shop.

Lady Sarah   It's two shillings to incorporate into the guild, if you're a man. You'd need a thousand pounds to grease their palms.

Connie   I'll get mesen a new dream then.

She leaves.

Lady Sarah   Drudge! (*To* **Sir John**.) Why did you put Drudge on his hook?

Sir John   To teach him not to be old and incontinent.

Lady Sarah   Why don't you shoot him?

Sir John   That would be murder.

Lady Sarah   He's one hundred and eight. It would be an act of compassion.

Sir John *unhooks* **Drudge**.

Lady Sarah   Go and fetch my satchel from the haystack.

Drudge *exits staggering*.

Lady Sarah   And what kind of week have you had?

Sir John   Without you around? A peaceful, productive week, unplagued by thoughts of suicide. You were late.

Lady Sarah   My horse fell lame, near Doncaster. I had to stay at your cousin's.

Sir John   Very convenient.

Lady Sarah   He was generous, in his hospitality.

Enter **John Saltmarsh**, *a louche- looking individual.* **Lady Sarah** *and he touch, unseen by* **Sir John**.

Lady Sarah   And he accompanied me on the road.

Sir John   Reverend cousin?! What brings you to East Yorkshire? We have no virgins.

Saltmarsh   I escorted your wife from Doncaster.

Sir John   I am told that she was delayed a week at your house.

Lady Sarah *mimes first a horse, and then a lame horse.*

Saltmarsh   Yes, her horse . . . I taught her horse some dressage.

Sir John   Lame. Her horse fell lame.

Saltmarsh   Yes! A lame horse. No matter, your wife is pleasant company.

Sir John   Is she? I'm surprised you managed to find the time given the demands of your congregation. How many wives do you have now?

Saltmarsh   The Family of Love continues to flourish.

Sir John   How come everyone else makes do with one wife at a time but you –

Lady Sarah   – your reverend cousin needs a thousand a year to continue his work with the congregation.

Sir John   I was told Lord Selby has issued an eviction order on your human menagerie.

Saltmarsh   The first of May.

Sir John   I don't give alms. And I don't believe you've paid your ship money.

Saltmarsh   I'll not pay that tax to the king.

Sir John   As sherriff I am charged by the king to collect.

Saltmarsh   Have you paid your ship money?

Lady Sarah   He's not paid.

Sir John   It's a punitive, unjust tax, and I've no intention of paying! But! It is my duty to collect it!

Lady Sarah   John wishes to impress Pym and Parliament by not paying, but maintain good relations with the king by collecting.

Saltmarsh   How can one soul minister to such varied agendas?

Sir John   As you satisfy your various wives, cuz, with sweet words, vigorously, and one at a time. Doncaster's that way!

Saltmarsh *leaves.*

Sir John   Lame horse indeed.

Enter **Frances**, *reading a book of poetry. She reads in a frenzy of passion.*

Lady Sarah   She has discovered Shakespeare.

Sir John   Oh no! Not that acrimonious, wormy scrote?! Why did you teach her to read?! To what purpose?! A girl?!

Lady Sarah   So that she might read your will to me as I grieve, at leisure, in my bath.

Sir John   I sent you to London to find that damned giglet a rich husband!

She shows him a small framed woodcut of **Peregrine Pelham MP**.

Lady Sarah   And here he is.

Sir John   He's covered in scars.

Lady Sarah   It's a woodcut.

Sir John   Do I know him?

Lady Sarah   Peregrine Pelham. The Member for Hull.

Sir John   He's a damned Puritan zealot! He won't approve of my billiards, my snuff, my drinking. I'll have to stop shitting off the bridge.

Lady Sarah   We'd all like that.

Sir John   It's my bridge and it's my river!

Lady Sarah   Pelham is favoured by John Pym, the leader of the House!

Sir John   Is he? Excellent. Well done.

Lady Sarah   He's a gold merchant and keeper of running cash.

Sir John   The kind of son-in-law who could mortgage these estates?!

Lady Sarah   Two problems. He is demanding a dowry of two thousand and Frances is refusing.

Sir John   Horses refuse, not daughters! Why is she reluctant?

Lady Sarah   She met him. (*Beat.*) Do we have two thousand?

Sir John   Argh, money, money, money! Ten years of bad harvests and every day I'm working to keep the wolf from the door! One of these days I'm tempted just to let the bastard in!

Lady Sarah   I'll tell him no then.

Sir John   No! We have to mortgage. And I want her out the house. Frances! Your mother has found you a suitable husband.

Frances   He may suit you father, but I do not love him.

Sir John   The aristocracy do not marry for love.

Lady Sarah   If it's passion you want, go and kill a fox.

Frances   Peregrine Pelham is fifty-six.

Sir John   And he'll be fifty-seven next year so the sooner you marry him the better!

Frances   I want a lover who, unaided, can climb the stairs!

Lady Sarah   There are advantages to an elderly husband. Financial security, property, and an early death.

Frances   I don't want to die early!

Lady Sarah   *His* early death.

Frances   If I had love I would want for nothing!

Lady Sarah   Have you ever tried living in a hedge?

Frances   It would be an abundant, prolific and opulent hedge if it were furnished with love! Every thorn would be a caress and –

Sir John   – if I choose a damned feculent windmill you will marry a damned feculent windmill!

Enter **Durand**.

Frances   My brother can marry for love, but not I!

Frances *bursts into tears.*

Durand   Love, I'm told, arrives, uninvited, like a storm, everybody gets wet, and then it passes painfully, like a stubborn stool.

Lady Sarah (*aside*)   Merton College, Oxford.

Sir John   Be warned, that brief, thrilling hurricane can turn into forty years of drizzle.

Durand   I love what the minds of learned men have distilled into perfection over generations, namely the law.

Sir John   Your sweetheart, the law, will be of no use in this coming conflict.

Durand   On which side of the dichotomy in the body politic do we fall?

Sir John   Eh?

Lady Sarah   Which of the two sides are we on?!

Sir John   I know what dichotomy means!

Lady Sarah   Then think on, for my life, all our lives depend on your decision.

She leaves.

Durand   Surely Parliament. You represent Beverley.

Sir John   I didn't lose an eye in the Thirty Years' War
fighting for the Stuarts to sign up for the other side in
a civil war.

Durand   You didn't lose an eye *fighting*. It was a drunken,
camp-fire jape which involved half an ounce of gunpowder
and a live hedgehog.

Sir John   In extremis men will always blow up hedgehogs
for a laugh. And, the Thirty Years' War did have the odd lull.

Durand   Has John Pym made you commander of all
Yorkshire?

Sir John   Not yet. But who is better qualified?

Durand   Fairfax.

The hounds bark, go crazy. They wait, reluctantly, resigned.

Sir John   Fairfax is not a lord!

The hounds bark again.

He . . . bought a title like I'd buy a kipper.

*He sits at his desk, and prepares to write, but gets his finger stuck in
the ink well.*

Connie! Durand, leave us a moment.

Durand *leaves.* **Connie** *comforts* **Sir John**.

Sir John   Connie. I need to choose between the king or
Parliament. Between the right and moral thing to do, and
cowardly, expedient and self-serving. It's not easy. And I've
got my finger stuck in an ink well.

Connie   Calm yourself, my sweet.

She extracts his thumb and rubs his finger.

Sir John   Ah, Connie! To be common as muck, like you,
must be really awful, but the blessing is you're free and have
no responsibilities.

Connie   Who are we for in these upturned times?

Sir John   I have no feculent idea.

Connie   It's vital that you're on the winning side at the end of the war.

Sir John   Yes! But –

Connie   – declare for Parliament then.

Sir John   Because they'll win?

Connie   No. Because Parliament is the instrument of the king. If you declare for the king's instrument, then you are also declaring for the king.

Sir John   So we're on both sides? The king, and his instrument, Parliament. Brilliant! Such wisdom. Such buzwams. Connie, have you bathed?

Connie   Not this year.

Sir John   Tonight.

She kisses him and turns to leave. Enter **Drudge** *followed by a messenger.*

Drudge *mimes having found a* **Messenger** *on the road.*

Sir John   You found this man on the road, a messenger.

Enter **Frances**. *She swoons at the sight of a man.*

Frances   Oh! A young man!

Sir John   Sirrah, in whose employ do you serve as a messenger?

Messenger (*utterly unintelligible Irish*)   I've come two days on foot from the north of the county in the employ there of the Earl of Newcastle, as you well know one of the king's loyal men, aye, I have, so, aye.

Sir John   Are you Irish?

Messenger (*unintelligible*)   County Offaly.

Sir John   Sarah, your mother was Irish.

Lady Sarah (*equally unintelligible*)   Now come on there, young fellah, who sent you, and what's the message or give us a letter. There. So.

Messenger (*unintelligible*)   The Earl of Newcastle commands you to take Hull and the arsenal for the king.

Lady Sarah   He's a messenger from the Earl of Newcastle who commands you to take Hull for the king working under Newcastle's authority.

Sir John   *Moi?* Serve *under*?! Beneath? *Au de sous de.* The Earl of Newcastle?! The man's a poet and, which is worse, a playwright. Drudge! My sword!

Drudge *goes off to get a huge sword, which he drags along the floor.*

Sir John   Sirrah, honour prevents me from serving under a lyricist. And my honour is like a maiden's honesty, not to be repaired, once broken.

Frances   I don't understand.

Sir John   My honour is like a maiden's honesty, not to be repaired, once broken.

Frances   Her honesty, once broken?

Durand   *Her honesty* is a euphemism.

Frances   For what?

Lady Sarah   Her damned hymen!

Frances (*slips into a pleasurable swooning faint*)   Ooooh!

Sir John   Newcastle cannot give law unto those from whom he should be receiving law! Leave, or die!

He lifts the sword with difficulty. The **Messenger** *throws down a thousand pounds in coin.*

Messenger (*unintelligible*)   A thousand pounds, there, you know, aye, so there is.

Lady Sarah (*intelligible*)   A thousand pounds, there, you know, aye, so there is.

Sir John *looks at* **Frances**.

Frances   No, father, it's not enough. Pelham demands two thousand.

Silence as **Sir John** *thinks*.

Sir John   It's half way there. Sirrah, I accept this weighty calling, without hesitation. Go north with news of my willing service, do not falter.

The **Messenger** *leaves*.

Durand   Are we now, because of this turn, for the king?

Lady Sarah   John, do not be rash! Today is not a good time to make profound decisions. Mars is in opposition to Venus.

Sir John   Mars? Venus? I'm the member for Beverley!

Lady Sarah   The heavens are in tumult.

Sir John   I've got enough troubles without you dragging in the firmament!

Enter **Captain Jack** *at a burst. He's in military uniform with sword.* **Connie** *trails in his wake*.

Sir John   Jack. My eldest son!

Frances   My big brother!

Connie (*aside*)   Is that all clear?

Jack   Father!

He throws his saddle at **Drudge**, *then embraces his father*.

Sarah   What news from London, Jack?

Jack   London is a dog in the slips! The king launched the first cannonade and Pym, Haslerig, Holles, Hampden and William Strode are blown away.

Sir John   He's executed five members by cannon fire?!

Jack   No, that was a metaphor.

Sir John   Oh! Can you please not use metaphor, Jack, it's too exciting.

Lady Sarah   We weren't there, we just want to know what happened.

Jack   Similes?

Lady Sarah   If you must!

Jack   The king, like Hercules in a bad mood, with troop, entered the House intent on arresting the five but seeing that they were like absent he said, 'I see the birds have flown'.

Durand   That's a metaphor.

Sir John   Why would he have them arrested?

Jack   He believed the unstoppable tide –

Durand   – metaphor.

Jack   The king thought the members had colluded with the London mob, encouraging them to rise against him *like* an unstoppable tide.

Sir John   That has been the constant fear of his queen.

Jack   The Catholic Queen Henrietta is a stoat in the henhouse.

Durand   No!

Jack   Like a stoat in the, like, henhouse, in the night, in search of eggs, she has stolen the crown jewels!

All   What! / No?! / good Lord!

Jack   The masked stoat queen, like, a masked stoat in, like, disguise, has fled to Holland intent on selling the eggs –

Sir John   – what eggs?!

Lady Sarah   – the jewels.

Durand   Metaphor.

Jack   To expedite the raising of ten thousand foot.

Frances   What use are ten thousand feet?

Durand   The metonym foot is used to signify an infantryman.

Frances   Is ten thousand foot, five thousand soldiers?

Lady Sarah   With two feet each.

Durand   Ten thousand foot is ten thousand soldiers.

Frances   Only if they're one legged.

Lady Sarah   Jack! You've been to military school. If an enemy has ten thousand foot –

Frances   – and all their soldiers had two legs –

Lady Sarah   – how many soldiers would you be facing?

Jack (*thinks hard*)   Either five or ten thousand.

Sir John   Out! Now! All the women out!

Jack   The king has flown.

Durand   He can fly can he?

Jack   Like a hawk the king has, like, flown to York, where he prowls.

Durand   Hawks don't prowl.

Jack   Like a cat he prowls, ready to swoop like a hawk, on Hull. Cat/hawk/hawk/cat.

Sir John (*to* **Connie**)   Connie, what is the meaning of this penny theatre?

Connie   Whoever secures the arsenal at Hull wins the war.

Jack *throws his sword to* **Drudge** *who catches it, falling over backwards with the weight.*

Durand   Who have Parliament appointed as commander of all of Yorkshire?

Jack   My father's enemy.

Sir John   Not . . .?

Jack   Yes. Fairfax.

The dogs bark, go crazy.

But I have orders for you too, father. This letter from Pym commissions you to take Hull, secure the arsenal, and lock out the Royalist wolves, who might devour the munitions like wolves, if wolves liked gunpowder.

Frances   Yes! I want to go to Hull! Out here there are no boys or shops!

Jack   Pym requires you and three hundred horse to take Hull.

Frances   How can my father, alone, with only three hundred stupid horses take Hull? Or are they vicious siege attack horses?

Durand   *Horse* for *horse and rider*, cavalry.

Frances   Oh.

Sir John   But I cannot serve under the self-raising Lord Fairfax.

The hounds bark, go crazy.

Lady Sarah   From now on Lord – you know – we call Black Tom.

One lone dog barks – the only one that knows he's also called Black Tom.

Jack   John Pym is financing you!

Jack *throws a bag of coins onto the floor.*

Sir John   That poodle can't buy my reputation! I am committed to the king.

Jack   One thousand for the billeting of the troops.

Sir John   Another thousand?! One thousand plus another thousand, that's . . .

Connie   – two thousand.

Frances   No! No! No!

She runs out.

Lady Sarah   John, that money is from Parliament to secure Hull.

Sir John   We need Pelham to secure the estates, and I can't live for one more day with that incessant, febrile inamorata.

Lady Sarah   It cannot be used as her dowry!

Sir John   Watch me. Prepare for Hull! Durand! A letter, to John Pym.

Durand   Dear John.

Sir John   Noble sir, supreme authority of this nation, leader of Parliament, trust that I shall serve you until the death of time, without sway, sans bending, sans – what's another word for bend?

Durand   Er . . . stoop, lean, squat.

Sir John   Sans squatting.

Durand   Unswerving.

Sir John   Good. I accept your commission, and shall tomorrow, for there is no day sooner, secure Hull for Parliament.

Lady Sarah   So we're for Parliament now?

Sir John   We're on both sides, you witless sphincter shrinker! Get out! Everybody!

Connie *remains. She knows that 'everybody' doesn't include her.*

Sir John   Sweet chestnut, what have I done?

Connie   You have betrayed the king, and betrayed Parliament.

Sir John   Yes, it's been a full day.

Connie   Best make sure we end up on the winning side.

She leaves.

Act Two

Scene One

Hull, inside the walls. Busy with soldiers, and trained band members, traders, costermongers, prostitutes, fish wives. The **Ranter** *sings.*

Song: 'Enfranchise Me'

When Adam delved and Eve span
Where was then the gentleman?
From where did the entitled start to crawl?
These landed men that got no shame,
The long and short – not in my name
Their parliament don't stand for me at all.

Oh oh enfranchise me
Oh oh give me a choice
Oh oh enfranchise me
All I want's a voice.

For years we battle flood and drought,
The bastards leave us less than nowt.
They take our land and then they ask for rent.
The better part decide what's what
The greater part accept their lot
The ninety-nine ruled by the one per cent.

Oh oh enfranchise me
Oh oh give me a choice
Oh oh enfranchise me
All I want's a voice

To say 'enough, no more state tricks.'
Reject the villains' politics.
To serve no one but him i choose.
I've little left but life to lose.

Enfranchise me

Oh oh give me a choice
Oh oh enfranchise me
All I want's a voice
All I want's a voice
All I want's a voice

Sweet Lips *is soliciting and propositioning* **Soldiers**.

Sweet Lips   Eh, soldier boy, d'yer want me to polish your weapon?

Soldier   How much?

Sweet Lips   By hand, a farthing; lips, an 'apenny; full fanny horizontal, three farthings; anal, a penny.

Soldier   By hand will suffice.

He gives her the gun.

Sweet Lips   Why have you given me the gun?

Soldier   Sorry, I think there's been a misunderstanding.

Enter **Sir John** *with* **Durand**.

Sir John   They're a funny-looking lot, Hull folk. Bald, tattooed, unshaven. I couldn't commend the men either.

Enter **Jack** *at pace with* **Captain Moyer**.

Jack   Father! Meet Achilles.

Sir John   Congratulations on slaying Hector.

Moyer   Captain Moyer, sir. The arsenal is secure and well defended.

Sir John   Do you know of any arsenals anywhere where you can just wander in and take what you like?

Moyer   No, sir.

Sir John   Well, don't look so pleased with yourself then.

Moyer   Sir, there were four soldiers on each watch, and I've increased that number twofold.

Sir John   Not enough. Each watch needs at least eight men.

Durand   Father, twofold four is eight.

Sir John   In Oxford maybe, but this is Hull. Tell me, with what ease can we defend this town, Captain Moyer?

Moyer   'ull is defended by the 'umber on the south and by the river to the east.

Sir John   What's the river called?

Moyer   The River 'ull.

Sir John   Bit fancy.

Moyer   I've stationed batteries before the Myton, Beverley and North Gates, and the forts on the east of the river are all armed with cannon.

Sir John   Good, well done, take the week off.

Jack   No, father, there is no respite! There is a cuckoo in the nest.

Sir John   A cuckoo?

Jack   The king's feared and bloodthirsty cavalry officer, Prince Rupert, the Royalist commander of horse, is in town, somewhere, hiding.

Sir John   Hide and seek, and the other fellah's got a horse. Shouldn't be too difficult.

Moyer   They say he can kill a man with his bare feet.

Jack   During the Thirty Years' War, abandoned and starving in a dungeon, he ate a human liver to survive.

Sir John   His own or someone else's?

Moyer   His first priority is to capture the arsenal; failing that, destroy it by fire.

Sir John   What would happen to eighteen tons of gunpowder in a fire?

Moyer   We'd all be blown to hell and back, sir.

Sir John   You can come back, I'm not.

Moyer   The English Civil War could start today, in Hull. If Rupert –

Sir John   – what does he look like?

Moyer   He's German, sir, bit of a dandy, wears feathers.

Sir John   Just feathers? Nothing else?

Moyer   Feathers as decoration.

Jack   Can I kill him, father?!

Durand   We are not at war.

Sir John   Secure him.

Jack   But if he resists, can I kill him?

Sir John   Alright yes! If you must! Just don't tell your mother.

Jack *heads off in search of* **Prince Rupert**.

Durand (*to* **Moyer**)   Where's Newcastle?

Sir John   It's a small failing port on the River Tyne.

Moyer   The Royalist Earl of Newcastle with six hundred horse and a thousand foot is camped twenty miles north of Hull.

Durand   Between the king and Parliament how does the town incline?

Moyer   Seven thousand citizens, a dangerous number of masterless men, thrown off common land, ignited by the ideas of the age. All of Hull is in a wild humour. Ranters, Levellers, Millenarians.

Sir John   We all need hats.

Moyer   In any dozen men, nine will be for the king.

Sir John   What about the other four?

Durand   Three.

Sir John   The other three are villains are they?

Moyer   Villains, sir? They're for Parliament. Like you and I.

Sir John   Forgive me, Captain Moyer, a trap to test your loyalty.

Moyer   The town objects to the billeting of our Parliament troops.

Durand   Father, it would serve us if we invented an outside threat, a rumour, to encourage the people to house the soldiers willingly.

Sir John   Who do Hull folk hate most?

Moyer   People coming in from Beverley telling them what to do.

Sir John   What else?

Moyer   The pope, Spain and buggery.

Sir John   You! Come here.

A local comes over. **Sir John** *slips him a coin.*

The king's papist wife approaches from Beverley with three thousand *Spanish* rape attack monks intent on sodomising any who objects to the quartering of Parliament troops. Pass it on.

He pushes him/her off. **Sweet Lips** *approaches* **Sir John.**

Sweet Lips   D'yer wanna girl?

Sir John   No thank you.

Sweet Lips   Two girls?

Sir John   No.

Sweet Lips   A boy?

Sir John   What happened to three girls?

Moyer   This is Sweet Lips.

Sweet Lips   You're Sir John Hot Hams aren't yer?

Moyer   You can't talk to the governor like that.

Sweet Lips   Oh I can! The world's turned upside down. There's plots against you!

Sir John   A Royalist bounty on my head?

Sweet Lips   I were pleasing a Lord Cavalier, last night, outside the walls.

Sir John   One of Newcastle's men? What was he like?

Sweet Lips   Very quick.

She slopes off.

Moyer   Should I have her thrown out of the town, sir?

Sir John   Heavens no, man! She is magnificent!

Moyer   These are Puritan times, sir. The London theatres are closed.

Sir John   She is what theatre could be. She reaches out into the community, satisfying the real needs of her diverse clients. She's not an expensive building open six times a week and twice on Wednesdays.

Moyer   You're not of like mind then with John Pym on matters of godliness?

Sir John   The damned Puritans are madmen and fanatics! Can you think of anything more dangerous than everyone being able to read the Bible?!

Moyer   Out of uniform, I'm a Puritan lay preacher.

Sir John   As am I. The very instigator of the Protestant Reformation, John Calvin, is a close personal friend of mine.

Moyer   He's dead.

Sir John   And on his death bed he gave me this.

He pulls a biscuit out of his pocket.

Moyer   A biscuit?

Sir John   His *personal* biscuit. Can you see, look, the face of the Virgin Mary.

Moyer   A relic? But Calvin was against the worship of icons.

Beat.

Sir John   Which is why he gave it to me.

Two trained bandsmen drag a Cavalier along beating him furiously.

Moyer   Who is he?

Soldier   Spy for the king. Armed by the Beverley Gate.

Moyer   Put him on the rack. We need to find Prince Rupert.

The soldiers drag the Cavalier off roughly.

Cavalier   Not the face!

Enter **Lady Sarah** *and* **Saltmarsh**. **Lady Sarah**, *seeing* **Sir John**, *holds back* **Saltmarsh**.

Sir John   So, if you're Achilles, and Hull is Troy, who am I?

Durand   Helen.

Sir John   What happened to her?

Durand   Raped by Paris. I hope to find a bookshop.

He goes off on his own.

Moyer   Would you like a tour of the defences?

Sir John   Excellent!

He and **Moyer** *exit.*

Saltmarsh   What is the sum of his commissions?

Lady Sarah   A thousand from each, in coin. In two bags.

Saltmarsh   Sarah, two thousand could save my community and give you a new life with me, as an equal in the Family of Love.

Lady Sarah   As your wife?

Saltmarsh   As one of my wives, yes. Women are brethren and saints in my church.

Lady Sarah   I don't want to be a wife of any kind ever again.

Saltmarsh   Then be a lover, and take other men as lovers in the Family. England is in flux. Together we can create that state of innocence before Adam's fall.

Lady Sarah   But the money is promised to Pelham as a dowry for Frances.

Saltmarsh   But Pelham warmed to you more than your daughter?

Lady Sarah   Around me his passion is unfettered.

Saltmarsh   His eagerness is manifest, in his hose?

Lady Sarah   I might be wrong, it could be a ferret.

Saltmarsh   This is excellent. Tempt Pelham further, and his indiscretion might cause the marriage to founder, and the dowry will be our flotsam.

Lady Sarah   Seduce and steal?!

Saltmarsh   Sin did not exist before Adam's fall! Men and women were equal and all property was held in common and that is how we shall live!

Enter **Lord Mayor Barnard**, *searching*.

Watch out! The Mayor! He's threatened to bar me from the within the walls.

They scatter. **Barnard** *approaches* **Sweet Lips**.

Sweet Lips   Percy!

Barnard　Don't call me Percy in public, I'm the 'kin mayor. Sweet Lips, 'ave yer seen two o' king's men? Military men, fearsome looking. They wan't where I arranged to meet 'em, undercover.

Sweet Lips　They've not been under my covers.

Enter **Prince Rupert** *and the* **Duke of York**. *They are a pair of dandies essentially, with no trace of any military threat.*

York　Lord Mayor Barnard?

Barnard　Aye. What do you lads want? I'm busy.

York　James, Duke of York.

Barnard　'kinnell! Your majesty. I were expecting, you know, soldiers, not . . . I mean I wouldn't wear that 'at in 'ull. And who –

Rupert　– Ruprecht Pfalzgraf bei Rhein, Herzog von Bayern!

Barnard　And you're the terrifying Cavalier general of horse?

Rupert　With the right horse, I am very scary.

This volley attracts the interest of a few local Parliament trained band members.

Barnard　Keep yer cake 'ole buttoned when –

Rupert　– 'cake 'ole'?

York　Mouth?

Barnard　Aye! (*Finger to his lips.*) . . . when yer on the rerd.

Rupert/York　The rerd?

Barnard　The rerd!

York　Oh, the road!

Barnard　Aye! And why wan't yer in the tenfoot as arranged?

York   We didn't know what a tenfoot was.

Barnard   The alley down back o' the houses, usually ten foot wide.

Rupert/York   Oh!

Barnard   And 'ave yer worked out 'ow the two of yer, on yer tod, are gonna capture an arsenal guarded by eight 'undred men?

York   The strategy I explained in my letter. Which is dependent on the loyalty of the citizens.

Rupert   We storm the garrison, *unter* cover of dark, supported by the people, and invite the night watch to obey their king.

York   Have you informed the aldermen of this plan?

Barnard   Aye, I terldamerl.

Rupert   *Was?!*

Barnard   I terldermerl!

York   I told them all?

Barnard   Aye.

(*Aggressively.*) Oi! Are you lads fer the perp?

Rupert/York   The perp?

Barnard   The 'ead o' Catholic church.

York   No! Papist scum. Boo.

Rupert   *Ja!* We pass urine on Catholics.

Barnard   Yer gonna have to lern yersen some 'ull and hide yersens an'all.

York   Disguises?

Barnard   This is the English Civil War not a ruddy London masque!

He exits. Enter **Frances**. *She is running, carrying letters, looking lost.*

York   Miss! You look lost?! Can we help?

Frances   Eurgh! We've just got here, and . . . there's no messenger service!

York (*giving a card*)   This messenger is a shilling a month.

Frances (*aside*)   Oh! He's gorgeous!

Rupert   Unlimited letters.

Frances (*aside*)   And his friend is gorgeous too. And a bit bigger! Frances Hotham.

York   Are you Hotham's daughter?

Frances   Yes, I'm the middle child. Ninth out of seventeen.

York   Is that a Shakespeare quarto you're reading?

Frances   Yes. *Romeo*.

York   *And Juliet?*

Frances   I don't know, I've just started it.

She looks at the cover.

Oh yes.

York   They both die.

Frances   Deurgghhh!

York   Don't read it. It would be a tragedy for such a fair lily to fear love. Read one of his comedies.

Frances   Is love nothing, sir?

York   To me, love is everything.

Frances (*aside*)   Ohhh!

York   Do you write letters?

Frances   Yeah.

York   Here's my address.

Frances   James at Mayor's House, Hull.

Rupert   Rupert at Mayor's House, Hull.

Frances   All upper case?

Rupert   I'm German.

Frances (*offers her card*)   Frances Hotham, at Governor's House, Hull.

York (*to* **Frances**)   Do you ride?

Frances   Yeah. Mainly horses.

York   Tomorrow?

Frances   Ohhh. Yes.

Durand *approaches.*

Durand   Sister! Alone? Out here?! The streets are teeming with soldiers.

Frances   I know.

York   We mean your sister no harm, we are innocently debating the merits of *Romeo and Juliet*.

Durand   A ridiculous play. Two wholly unsuitable *children*, both fantastically shallow and ignorant – both of each other, and how the world works – utterly selfish, choose to throw themselves under the cart of love.

Rupert   You have never met the right girl.

Durand   I have met several girls in Beverley and found them all ridiculous.

York   Are you never transported by a woman's beauty?

Durand   Beauty does not exist. It is culturally defined, a series of learned constructs.

York (*aside*)   I shall stake this cold raisonneur's heart and then tup his sister.

First you dismiss love. Then you banish love's first lieutenant, beauty.

Durand   A small nose is admired. Why not condemn it as weak? It only needs society to decide that large noses are the height of loveliness and then a nose the size of St Paul's would delight everyone.

York   What of your own heart? Does it never leap?

Durand   The circulationists tell us that the heart is a muscle and its function is to deliver blood to the extremities of the body. The heart has no amorous vocation. It is a pump.

York   Then, sir, I hope you have a long and rational life and that you never suffer a broken pump.

Durand *exits*.

Rupert   If we are to wear disguises, can I be *ein mädchen*? Please.

York   Yes. We will make a fine pair of wenches.

Enter, upstage, **Jack**.

Rupert   *Achtung!* A Parliament officer!

York   I'll send you a letter.

Rupert   *Ich auch!*

Frances (*aside*)   I am struck! Twice! Opened by the softness and charm of one, and hopelessly pinned by the bigger man's uniform.

Jack   Sister! What are you doing? Alone in the streets with all these soldiers about? A lone mouse amongst a thousand hungry hawks.

Frances   If only.

She runs off. Enter **Moyer** *and* **Sir John**.

Moyer   You and your family will be safe here at the governor's house. I'll post a mariner on the door.

Sir John   It's a fine house, it would make a good pub.

Moyer   It's very secure as it also houses the strong boxes for the town. Do you believe in ghosts?

Sir John   I'm a rational man, Captain Moyer. I do not fear the supernatural.

Moyer   They say it is a child, murdered by her father for breaking a vase. She wanders the stairs at night.

Sir John   Is there nowhere else we can stay?

Beat of a drum and in come the Family of Love singing.

Song: 'The Power of Love'

Family
  The power of love is truly awesome
  Truly awesome, truly awesome,
  The power of love is truly awesome
  And he gave us sin to save our souls

  Did you know sinners that sin can make you happy
  Sin can make you happy, sin can make you happy
  Did you know sinners that sin can make you happy
  And you don't have to go to church

Local   Don't you mean 'he gave *his son* to save our souls'?

Saltmarsh   No. He gave *us sin*. Judgement is finished and sin is victorious! Only the libertine can achieve heaven! And who can judge the libertine?

Family Member   God?

Saltmarsh   No! Not God, for God created sin! Sin is God's work! So sin some! And sin some more! And sin again!

Sir John   If Jesus Christ had preached that kind of doctrine they'd have crucified him.

Moyer   They did.

Sir John   Well, there you go then.

He goes in, shutting out **Moyer**. **Saltmarsh** *stands on a milking stool.*

Moyer   What say you of adultery?

Saltmarsh   Adultery is the path to enlightenment! Join the Family of Love, and together we can build a new Eden here on the Humber. Bring your wives!

Local   Where exactly is this new paradise?

Saltmarsh   North Ferriby.

Moyer   Where is God in all of this?

Saltmarsh   God is in the wood of your pipe, Captain, and in the brass of your corset, ma'am.

Local   Why don't I have to go to church no more?

Saltmarsh   Because the horn you wake with on a Sunday, that is your steeple! Do not baptise your children, do not pay your tithes, reject war!

Local   What about drinking?

Saltmarsh   One drink is good, two saintly, three divine, but getting absolutely shit faced every night, that is the true path to the Lord!

Local   Where do we sign up?

Saltmarsh   Come with us, and give your love freely. The light of God has risen on the Humber!

Family
  Jesus loves you if you go round thieving
  Go round nicking stuff, go round thieving
  Jesus loves you if you go round thieving
  And God helps those who help themselves

Scene Two

Hull. Inside the governor's house. Baskets of linen. A trunk set downstage. A hatch/trap to the coal cellar downstage. On the fireplace, either side a knight's helmet and broad sword. Enter **Connie** *from the coal cellar. A vase set on a low table.*

Lady Sarah   Are you happy sleeping in the coal cellar, Connie?

Connie *mumbles at length her inaudible discontent.*

Lady Sarah   Don't mumble!

Connie *mumbles more.*

Lady Sarah   I asked you a question!

Connie (*loud*)   I'm as happy as a flea on a nun's muff!

Lady Sarah   Have you seen Drudge?

Connie   No! He's so lazy he wouldn't pull a soldier off his own mother.

Lady Sarah   Take this linen into the master bedroom. But don't look at the bed.

Connie   Don't look at the bed?

Lady Sarah   A creation by the theatre designer Inigo Jones, it is . . . affecting.

Connie   Oh, he's built a theatre of loving has he?

Lady Sarah   Indeed.

Connie *exits to the bedroom leaving the door open.*

Connie (*off*)   Bloody 'ell!

Lady Sarah   Drudge!

Drudge *opens the trunk with the vase on it, and climbs out. The vase hits the floor but does not break.*

Lady Sarah   Must be unbreakable stoneware.

Drudge *tries to break it.* **Frances** *opens the door to the bedroom stage right.*

Frances   Please, Mummy! Could I have this room overlooking the street! There's a quarterlight and if I stand on a chair I can see men!

She closes the door. Enter **Sir John**.

Sir John   There's a plot against my life!

Lady Sarah   I've never made a secret of it.

Sir John   Royalists. Connie, a glass of porter!

Connie *organises the porter.*

Sir John   Drudge?! Listen! Someone may try to poison my food or drink so you have to taste it before I do. That way you die not me, which is better for everyone, because I'm a gentleman and you're an idiot. Understand?

Connie *delivers the glass of porter to* **Sir John**. **Drudge** *takes it out of his hand and drinks it down in one leaving nothing, then gives it back to him.* **Connie** *tops it up, and* **Drudge** *drinks it all again. And throughout the scene where possible.*

Lady Sarah   Mr Pelham will arrive shortly to collect his dowry. Where is it?

Sir John   I've locked it in a safe box in the master bedroom.

Lady Sarah   You have the key?

Sir John   Around my neck.

Knock at the door. **Sir John** *opens the door.*

Barnard   Percy Barnard.

Sir John   Who are you and what do you want?

Barnard   I'm the rightly elected Lord Mayor of 'ull.

Sir John   By influence, nepotism, favours. I am Sir John Hotham, appointed Governor of Hull by Parliament, ergo, you're a pint pot of piss and I'm the ocean.

Barnard   Parliament dun't mean nowt to the 'ull mob, none of them gorra vote.

Sir John   You love the king –

Barnard   – aye.

Sir John   As do I.

Barnard   Grand! Burr I were told, you was appointed by John Pym to secure the arsenal for Parliament.

Sir John   Correct, but at an opportune time, I will hand it over to the king to further his cause, which is my cause, which is your cause, which is his cause.

Lady Sarah   My husband was knighted by Charles's father, James, and is loyal to the Stuarts.

Sir John   Sarah? What are you doing?

Lady Sarah   Participating –

Sir John   – in matters of state?! Find some women's work. Wash a pony or shave your back!

Lady Sarah *exits*.

Sir John   I apologise for my wife's exaggerated opinion of her own abilities.

Barnard   I wanna see yer orders!

Sir John (*to* **Durand**)   The letter from John Pym.

Durand *opens the letter and reads*.

Durand   'Sir John Hotham, knight, –

Sir John   – that's me.

Durand   – 'shall secure Hull and ensure that no English or other forces whatsoever be suffered to enter. In the doing whereof the mayor' –

Sir John   – that's you.

Durand   – 'is commanded to assist the governor' –

Sir John   – that's me.

Durand   – 'or he' –

Barnard   – me?

Sir John   No, I think that's me again.

Durand   – 'will answer to the governor' –

Barnard   – no! That me was me not you!

Durand   – 'and Parliament at his peril.'

Sir John   That's your peril.

Barnard   My peril?

Sir John   Yes! And peril can mean anything up to and including execution.

Barnard   I ant done owt yit!

Sir John   I shall protect you.

Barnard   Are yer gonna welcome Charles into the town then?

Sir John   Charles who?

Barnard   Charles Stuart, the king! He's coming to 'ull.

Sir John   What?!

Durand   The king comes to Hull?!

Barnard   At first light!

Sir John (*aside*)   Sodom and tomorrow!

To comply with my orders I shall have to bar the king.

Barnard   Bugger me! I'll go t' foot of our stairs! No man has ever denied an English king and kept his 'ead! Right then! I'm gonna send his son round. Yer can explain to the prince why yer might choose to bar his father.

Sir John   The king's son is here in Hull?

Barnard   The Duke of York, aye. Now I have summat to thrash out wi' you.

Sir John   We both have concerns.

Barnard   Bags foggy!

Sir John   Eh?!

Barnard   I'll go fost. Where's the thousand pound what John Pym give yer for the billeting o' these bastard roundheads?

Sir John   The money is being weighed. In London. It arrives tomorrow.

Barnard   Pay the mob or I fear for your life. They're west Hull lads. Everything's, you know, black and white.

Sir John   Consider it done. Now my concern. My duplicity must remain a strict confidence, or Captain Moyer and Parliament will have my head.

Barnard *hugs* **Sir John**.

Barnard   We're brothers! Long live the king!

Sir John   Long live the king!

Barnard *leaves*. **Sir John** *slams the door on him*.

Sir John   Charles comes to Hull tomorrow!

Lady Sarah *enters*.

Lady Sarah   Why did you say we could pay for the billeting? We've promised that money to Pelham for the dowry!

Sir John   Thank you for reminding me! Where would I be without you, you barren, Sapphic aspirant.

Lady Sarah   In hell, prick for brains.

Sir John   Cavern fadged, dildo breaker.

Lady Sarah   Wanker.

She exits.

Durand (*aside*)   All I know of love, I know from these two.

Sir John (*aside*)   My king comes to Hull, to take the arsenal, his arsenal. And I am aligned against him, opposed, antagonistic, ornery. A mortal man versus God's agent. Am I thus antithetical to God? Oh dear, what have I done.

Knock at door. **Lady Sarah** *returns but* **Frances** *runs out, opens it and takes two letters off a messenger and gives back two more before returning to her room.*

Durand   Father, it might be prudent to use the Parliament money for the billeting and delay Frances's marriage.

Sir John   No!

Durand   I fear the mob.

Lady Sarah   No!

Sir John   We only have to raise a thousand.

(*To* **Lady Sarah**.) Give me your jewellery!

Grabbing the necklace around her throat.

Lady Sarah   You'll have to kill me first.

Sir John   Drudge! Knife!

Drudge *produces a knife.* **Lady Sarah** *knees* **Sir John** *in the balls. He collapses.* **Lady Sarah** *exits to the main bedroom.*

Connie   Stay calm, my sweet.

Sir John   I can't cope.

Connie   You can. You've got me.

Sir John   I would swap everything for a commoner's cottage and you.

Connie   Aye well, enclosure's done for that.

Enter **Lady Sarah**.

Lady Sarah   There's a moneylender across the road. Connie, get him to visit Sir John.

Connie *exits*.

Sir John   Oh brilliant! I'm going to be in hock to Shylock of Hull!

Lady Sarah   He's called Albert Calvert.

Durand   He doesn't sound Jewish.

Sir John   Did Jesus?

Lady Sarah   Did Jesus what?

Sir John   Sound Jewish.

Lady Sarah   Jesus Christ?

Sir John   Doesn't sound Jewish does it? They change their names to fit in. Fischman/Fisher; Herschel/Hurst; Ashkenazi/Albert Calvert.

Lady Sarah   What are you saying?

Sir John   That Jesus Christ was probably called Moshe Cohen before he moved to Jerusalem!

Knock at the door.

Argh!

Durand   That might be the Duke of York.

Lady Sarah *opens it to* **Pelham**. *He is carrying books and some meat wrapped in bloodied paper.*

Lady Sarah   Mister Pelham!

She offers her hand to kiss.

Pelham   I must divert my eyes from your perfect hand. All the sins can make use of a woman's fingers.

Lady Sarah   I could wear a glove.

He hands over the bloodied meat wrapper.

Pelham   For you madam, a gift.

Lady Sarah   What lovely wrapping. What is it?

Pelham   Pork.

Lady Sarah   Loin.

Pelham   Shoulder.

Lady Sarah   Bone in.

Pelham   Are you offended? I could take it out.

Lady Sarah   No, no I like a bone in.

Drudge *attacks the vase.*

Sir John   Drudge! Stop that. Come here!

He picks **Drudge** *up and drops him down the cellar steps, then kicks the hatch closed.*

Lady Sarah   And you have brought your library with you, sir?

Pelham   Reading, for your daughter's improvement. *Foxe's Book of Martyrs*; *The Practice of Piety*; *A Way in Prayer*; and my favourite, *Sin*.

Sir John   My favourite sin? Lust. Every time. What's yours?

Pelham   My favourite book, *Sin*.

Sir John   Ah!

Lady Sarah   Be assured sir, this is a Puritan house.

Sir John   Of which John Pym would approve. Our only recreation is the mortification of the flesh, and on Tuesdays self-flagellation.

Lady Sarah   Sir John and I abstain from all physical pleasures.

Sir John   Seeking that pure state of misery known as marriage.

Enter **Frances** *from the master bedroom.*

Frances   Oooh. I've just seen the bed! Have you seen the bed?! Oooh.

Lady Sarah   Frances! Come and sit with your future husband.

Frances   Eeurgh yuk!

She runs up to her room.

Sir John   When she really likes someone she goes yuk and locks herself in her room.

Durand *offers his hand as introduction.*

Sir John   My son, Durand. He's a lawyer, and tedious with it.

Durand   The marriage contract.

Pelham   Tedious but useful.

Durand *gives* **Pelham** *a document.*

Pelham   And the dowry?

Sir John (*to* **Durand** *giving him the key*)   Bring Mister Pelham's dowry from the safe box in the master bedroom.

Pelham   Will Frances not sit with us?

Lady Sarah   She is disturbed by sighting the Inigo Jones bed.

Pelham   I hear that one only has to look at it and one imagines the beast with two backs.

Sir John   Two, three or four backs.

Lady Sarah   As Puritans ourselves, we're having it turned into kindling.

Pelham   Is it an aphrodisiac?

Sir John   No, we use it to get the fire going.

Enter **Durand** *with the two money bags.* **Durand** *then offers* **Pelham** *a quill. He leaves the safe box key on the desk.* **Lady Sarah** *sees this and moves towards it.*

Sir John   The dowry, two thousand in coin, as promised, and contracts.

Pelham   Excellent.

He signs and passes the contract to **Sir John***. When they're busy signing,* **Lady Sarah** *surreptitiously takes the key and sticks it in her bosom.* **Pelham** *takes both money bags and sits holding them. Enter* **Connie** *from the street.*

Connie   The moneylender says he will call in shortly.

Pelham   You're borrowing money?

Lady Sarah   No! Usury is a sin!

Sir John   Why would I want to see the moneylender?

Lady Sarah   To close him down.

Sir John   I am ending his reign! We cannot have the citizens of Hull tempted by Mammon.

Pelham   I saw the mayor leaving. What do I tell John Pym about you associating with Royalists and Papists? You know he has a proper priest's hole?

Sir John   I didn't. Our only intimacy has been a handshake.

Pelham   The Duke of York and Prince Rupert are in Hull. Or so it is rumoured. It would advantage us and please Parliament if they were arrested.

Durand   But we are not at war, yet, by law they are but Englishmen and free.

Pelham   Prince Rupert is a German.

Sir John   So an Englishman and a Germanman, but both free.

Pelham   You speak as if you have some sympathy with the malignant party.

Sir John   No, no, no.

Durand   The malignant party? That phrase has no inherent meaning.

Pelham   The Royalists.

Durand   If you were a Royalist, *malignant party* would mean Parliament. Ergo, the words 'malignant' and 'party' are empty vessels waiting to be filled with meaning by others cognisant of your own position.

Sir John   You're not marrying him.

Durand   The use of such solipsistic patter is lazy, vain and self-gratifying.

Pelham *stands, insulted.*

Lady Sarah   You'll only see him at Christmas!

Sir John   He's a mere barnacle on a beautiful ship! Our two families bound in bondage! My fecund estates and your gold!

Pelham   I've heard you shit off the bridge.

Door knock. **Connie** *opens it.* **Albert Calvert** *is there.*

Calvert   Albert Calvert. I'm told you require a loan?

Sir John   A story I concocted to contrive this three-way conjunction. You know Mr Pelham?

Calvert   Aye, that damned Puritan's been trying to close me down for six years.

Sir John   And in that, as in religion and politics, he and I are united. No longer shall I permit you to flaunt your balls in public.

Calvert   I'm a freeborn Englishman.

Sir John   Oh suddenly you're English are you?!

Calvert   Hull. Born and bloody bred, aye. Where's the law in this?

Durand   *Jus est, ars boni.*

Calvert   First it's mi balls, and now it's mi arse.

Durand   The law – *jus* – is the art – *ars* – of what is good – *boni.*

Calvert   And what does the law say about the two hornifying soldiers tekking ovver mi house, eating mi food and contriving new experiences for mi daughters? Without no compensation!

Sir John   You will be remunerated in full for the billeting of troops. Tomorrow.

Door knocker knocks twice. **Sir John** *opens the door, looks out.*

Sir John   Argh!

He closes the door and draws his sword.

Sir John   Durand! Take refuge in your room!

Calvert   Do you arrest me?!

Sir John   No! Behind that door stand the king's son, the Duke of York, and Prince Rupert. I have tricked them into meeting me here so that I can arrest all three of them.

Pelham   Two. The Duke of York and the king's son is one and the same person.

Sir John   Good, well that should make it easier.

Durand *goes up to his room. Knocking louder, and with impatience.*
Pelham *stands, holding the money bags.*

Pelham   You plan to arrest these Cavaliers with violence?

Sir John   I know the merit of force, whilst respecting the
dangers.

Calvert   I'm loyal to the king. Don't look to me for service.

Sir John   But you cannot leave, so protect yourself. Get in
the trunk!

Calvert   I will not!

Pelham   Prince Rupert is known for his intemperate will. If
war breaks out in this room you will not have time to explain
your allegiances.

Calvert *gets in the trunk.*

Sir John   Drudge!

Drudge *opens the hatch and comes up the stairs.*

Sir John   Mr Pelham, hide your dowry in the coal cellar,
these godless cavaliers see all gold as the spoils of war.

Lady Sarah   *Avec moi.*

Pelham   *Enchanté.*

Sir John *kicks the hatch shut trapping* **Pelham**'s *fingers.*

Pelham   Aargh!

Sir John *gives* **Drudge** *a sword from the fireplace.* **Drudge** *takes
the sword gift as an invitation to wear the helmet too, the visor of
which blinds him, and he goes around blindly attacking stuff
including the vase. Further knocking.*

Connie   The door?

Sir John   Don't let them in yet.

He lifts the trunk lid.

Sir John (*fierce whisper*)   Could you loan me a thousand?

Calvert   But –

Sir John   – everything I said before was for the benefit of that Puritan arseworm! How much would the charge be?

Calvert   Thirty pounds in a hundred.

Sir John   Thirty!? In a hundred?! That's nearly twenty-five per cent! What's the rate for Jews?

Calvert   I only have one rate.

Sir John *slams the lid down, trapping* **Calvert**'s *fingers.*

Calvert   Aargh!

Sir John *knocks out* **Drudge** *with the vase and hangs him on the hook where the helmet/sword combo was.* **Sir John** *heads for the door. Enter* **Durand** *from his room.*

Durand   Father!

Sir John   Get back in your room!

Connie *stands on the hatch.* **Frances** *enters.*

Frances   Father, what –

Sir John   – get back in there, you randy minx! Connie! The hatch!

Sir John *opens the door, with a bow. Revealed are* **York** *and* **Rupert**.

Sir John (*fierce whisper*)   Shhhh! Your majesty, welcome.

York   May I present Prince Rupert of the Rhine.

Connie   Hiya!

Sir John *genuflects, on his knees.*

Sir John   Sir, welcome, I am your servant.

York   But, Hotham, you are retained by Parliament. Our warm welcome surely is not advised by John Pym?

Sir John   No, this over-buttered obsequiousness is mine own design.

Enter **Frances** *down the stairs. She gives them a letter each.* **York** *gives her a letter.* **Rupert** *gives her a letter. She goes off and tears at the letters, devouring them.*

Sir John   You know each other?

Rupert   We use the same messaging service.

Frances *mimes tearing her heart out and giving it to* **York**. **York** *mimes tearing his heart out and giving it to* **Frances**.

Sir John   But listen! Your majesties, there is treachery for you within this house, an assassin!

York   Assassin?

Sir John   Mr Peregrine Pelham MP is hiding in the coal cellar. He thinks I am loyal to Parliament so I want him to believe that I am arresting you, which I'm not, honestly, I'm actually making plans with you to hand over the arsenal. So I beg of you, humour me a lunatic pageant, think of it as a masque, it is in the interest of your safety. (*Shouted.*) I COMMAND YOU! LAY DOWN YOUR ARMS OR YOUR LIFE, LIVES I SHALL CURTAIL! FACE DOWN, YOU GERMAN CAVALIER DOG!

Rupert *gets on his knees.* **Sir John** *pulls him up.*

Sir John   No, no. You don't have to do that.

AND YOU, THE OTHER CAVALIER DOG!

York *drops to his knees, but* **Sir John** *jumps in with a whisper.*

Sir John   No, no, I will not harm you, your majesty.

YOU CHALLENGE ME! ERGO YOU FORFEIT YOUR LIFE!

Sir John *starts fencing* **Drudge**'s *sword, just for the noise of it. Meanwhile* **Frances** *has opened* **Rupert**'s *letter and is now miming that she loves him too.*

Sir John   AH! SOME WITTY GERMAN SWORDPLAY, PRINCE RUPERT!

He attacks **Drudge**'s *sword, but this time* **Drudge** *fences back, which amazes* **York** *and* **Rupert** *who both draw their swords and prepare to attack* **Drudge**.

York   Assassin!

Sir John   No, he's on our side.

Sir John *fences* **Drudge** *all the way to the trunk, takes his sword off him and knocks him out. Then he fences himself, ending up pinning himself against the wall with the two swords.*

Sir John (*shouts in unintelligible mock German whilst fighting then*)   SPARE ME, I HAVE FIVE WIVES AND SEVENTEEN CHILDREN.

(*Shouting at the closed hatch.*) I am hit! Arghh! I mean, arrgghh! I am hit!

More sword clattering.

HA HA! THE TABLES HAVE TURNED! LAY DOWN YOUR WEAPON!

He throws a sword down.

SUBMIT! I SHALL NOT SHOW MERCY TO GERMAN PAPIST SCUM. I'm so sorry, Prince Rupert. (*Ad lib re 'doing it for show', etc.*)

Calvert *opens the trunk lid quickly. He is puzzled: expecting to see a cavalier pinned to the ground he sees* **Sir John** *and the cavaliers grouped together. On seeing* **Calvert**, **Sir John** *takes* **York**'s *sword and holds it up to his own throat.*

York   Assassin!

Rupert   *Preparen Sie* to die, noble sir!

As **Rupert** *and* **York** *step forward to kill* **Calvert**:

Sir John   No! *Nein!*

Enter **Jack**, *who, seeing the two Cavaliers with swords drawn, draws his own sword.* **Calvert** *starts edging towards the door.*

York/Rupert   Assassin!

Jack   Prince Rupert! Assassins!

Rupert   *Nein!* We are not assassins!

York   And we are not at war yet, sir!

Jack   And you're the king's son!

York   Is regicide your aim?

Jack *charges the two Cavaliers, who defend themselves.* **Calvert** *escapes out the main door.* **Jack** *and* **Rupert** *sword fight.* **York** *knocks out* **Jack** *from behind with the vase, and just as* **Rupert** *goes in for the kill, enter the child* **Ghost**. *She takes the vase from* **York**. **York** *and* **Rupert** *are struck dumb.* **Rupert** *stabs her through the neck and yet she is extant. She puts the vase back on the table, turns and walks through the wall into the master bedroom.* **York** *follows to the wall she has just passed through.*

York   A soul in purgatory?

Sir John   A girl murdered by her father for breaking a vase.

York   So our assassin is your own son?

Rupert *draws his sword again as if to murder* **Jack**.

Sir John   No! Don't kill him, that is not my son Jack.

York   Prove it?

Sir John   How old would you say this man is?

York   He's young.

Rupert   Twenty-five?

Sir John   Indeed, but Jack fought in the Eighty Years' War and the Thirty Years' War, so my son is at least a hundred and ten.

Rupert   *Ich* cannot argue *mit das*.

York   Sorry.

Sir John   Good. Now go! And disguise yourselves, for I shall tell Mister Pelham that you are both arrested and imprisoned by Captain Moyer.

York *and* **Rupert** *leave.*

Sir John   Drudge! Go into Durand's room and kick and bang on the door. Make it sound like two men trying to break out.

Drudge *goes up the stairs to* **Durand***'s room, and starts banging on the door.* **Sir John** *rubs meat blood on his shirt.* **Drudge** *goes in, and starts banging on the door.*

Sir John   You can come up now!

He opens the hatch. Enter **Lady Sarah** *and* **Pelham** *up the stairs.*

Pelham (*fearful*)   Sir, you're bleeding heavens hard!

Sir John   Ah, it'll wash out!

Lady Sarah   Jack! Is he dead?

Sir John   Unconscious, knocked out by that feathered German Bedlamite.

Pelham (*fearful*)   Where are the Cavaliers now?

Sir John   Secure in that upstairs room, but as you can hear, they're trying to break out.

They listen, nothing.

AS YOU CAN HEAR, THEY'RE TRYING TO BREAK OUT!

Drudge *starts banging violently.*

Sir John   The door is locked, they are secure for now, and Captain Moyer is called, but as you can tell their blood is up!

Drudge *breaks a panel in the door and tumbles onto the balcony.*

Sir John   They took Drudge hostage with them! But he's escaped! Well done, Drudge!

He draws his sword.

Sir! There is no time to lose! If you value your life, leave now!

Pelham   My money is hidden in the coal.

Sir John   I'll secure it in the safe box.

Pelham   But –

Sir John   – it'll be safe under lock and key. The contract is signed, that is your money.

Lady Sarah   Come and see me tomorrow, to collect.

Pelham *exits. The door closes,* **Sir John** *leans against the door, and breathes.* **Lady Sarah** *heads for the hatch.*

Sir John   Stop!

Lady Sarah *stops.*

Sir John   Don't think I don't know what you're up to, you grasping tart! Drudge, recover the gold from the coal cellar. (*To* **Lady Sarah**.) You. The key!

Lady Sarah *hands over the key and goes into the bedroom.* **Sir John** *slips down the wall exhausted.*

Connie   My sweet muffin. Why did you rub meat on yer sen?

Sir John   I have no feculent idea! Look at me, I'm sweating like a kestrel.

Connie   You're doing what any man would do. Protecting your family from the danger of ending the war on the wrong side.

Sir John   Oh, Connie. At least you understand me.

The other knight's helmet falls and lands on his head.

Act Three

Scene One

The day after. Outside the Beverley Gate, so the outer town wall is upstage. People throng and trade. **Saltmarsh** *lurks.* **Sweet Lips** *solicits. The drawbridge is down and the gate open. The* **Ranters** *sings.*

Song: 'Enclosure'

They hang the man, and flog the woman,
That steals the goose from off the common;
But let the greater villain loose,
That steals the common from the goose.
The law demands that we atone
When we take things we do not own
But leaves the lords and ladies fine
Who takes things that are yours and mine and . . .

Enclosure tramples all that's in it's way,
Leaves the poor man a slave.
Enclosure, and we can't do shit but rant and rave
Fenced in til the grave.

The poor and wretched don't escape
If we conspire the law to break;
This must be so but we endure
Those who conspire to make the law.
They hang the man, and flog the woman
Who steals the goose from off the common
And geese will still a common lack
Until we go and steal it back and . . .

Enclosure. This England, this our common land.
Earth, mud, clay and sand.
Enclosure. Now we watch these bloated farms expand.
Shall we not make a stand?
Enclosure, so rail as the railings rise

Or watch the country's demise.
Enclosure. No one selling, someone buys
While old Albion dies.
While old Albion dies.

Enter **Connie**. *She is collecting stones in an iron bucket so they make a noise.*

Connie
    If a man denies a king
    He himself a traitor makes
    And every high-born noble man
    Sleeps ill, and every landless man wakes

    And God has shown us revolution
    In the garden way back when
    When Adam delved and Eve span
    Where then was the gentleman?

Enter **Lady Sarah** *who is approached by* **Saltmarsh**.

Saltmarsh   Turnip!

Sarah   Parsnip, my sweet!

Saltmarsh   Do you have good news?

Sarah   Yes, Sir John returned the money bags to the safe box in the bedroom of the governor's house.

Saltmarsh   So he has the key?

Sarah   Indeed.

Saltmarsh   Turnip, that is not good news.

Sarah   I made an impression in soap.

Saltmarsh   Of Sir John?

Sarah   Of the key! One of the smiths I used to visit is forging a duplicate as we speak.

Saltmarsh   We must rescue the coin before the king arrests Sir John.

Lady Sarah   What if the king does not constrain him?

Saltmarsh   How can a citizen challenge a king and not be detained?!

They move off. Enter **Rupert** *and* **York**, *both disguised as girls, with a barrow full of fish.*

York   I always wanted to be a princess.

Rupert   *Mich auch.* I used to dream of being locked in a tower, growing my hair, zen one day rescued, kissed, *unt* taken roughly from behind.

York   Hiding in plain sight as girls is our best policy. And if Frances likes fresh fish, then she will be drawn to our stall.

Rupert   *Wunderbar!* Then we can sell her some fish.

York   No! Then we can engage with her on matters of love!

Rupert   Do you love her, cuz?

York   I want her.

Rupert   For a night, *oder* forever?

York   I know not which, but I shall have her.

Rupert   Yet it is me she loves. I have more letters.

He laughs.

York   More maybe, but her letters to me are longer, and fulsome!

Durand *is seen.*

York   Now *he,* her brother, has got my blood up more than her.

Rupert   You love him? Socratische? Pederastical?

York   Rupert, feelings of love are like a rainbow.

Rupert   Are you saying that sexuality is a spectrum?

York   I love girls, exclusively. My love is red. The first colour of the rainbow. What are you, Rupert? Orange? Yellow? Green? Blue?

Rupert   Keep going.

York   Indigo? Violet?

Rupert   I find Joan of Arc attractive.

York   Short hair, looks like a boy? Rupert, you're violet!

Rupert   Was it so obvious?

Sir John *approaches the stall.*

Rupert   *Pass auf!* Here comes the governor.

York   Haddock! Cod! Sea bass! Coalie!

Rupert   Come on, *mutter*, sort it out!

Sir John   Fair maid, are you German?

Rupert   *Ja*, I followed *ze* herring.

Sir John   Which one?

Rupert   *Diese*.

Sir John   I shall buy it, if you continue to follow it. Will you?

Rupert   *Jawohl!*

Sir John *buys the herring and puts it in his pocket suggestively.* **Pelham** *approaches.*

Pelham   Hotham! Are the two effeminate Cavalier dandies arrested?

Rupert *draws a dagger but* **York** *holds him back.* **Sir John**, *and* **Pelham** *promenade, out of earshot to* **York** *and* **Rupert**.

Sir John   Imprisoned in the bilges of Captain Moyer's ship. You won't see them again, unless they escape.

Pelham   And when is the king expected?

Sir John   Eleven. But he's the king, so he can be late if he wants can't he, or not turn up at all. It's not a sensible way to run a country.

Pelham   And I can trust you to bar his entrance?

Sir John   My orders from Parliament are almost unequivocal.

Pelham   Good. It will be an honour to have such a brave man as a father-in-law.

Sir John   And I don't think of it as losing a daughter. I'm gaining a religious zealot.

Pelham   There she is now. With your permission, I will engage with her.

Sir John   Speak of love, it's her only subject.

Pelham *moves off.* **Barnard** *approaches.*

Barnard   Hotham! I need to know, are yer gonna let the king in?

Sir John   I have my orders, Lord Mayor.

Barnard   'ull folk are stomachful o' Parliament and nine out o' twelve of 'em are Royalist.

Moyer *approaches threateningly.*

Sir John   Captain Moyer tells me it's only three-quarters.

Barnard   Nine-twelfths is three-quarters!

Sir John   Don't be ridiculous!

Barnard   If yer divide nine by three, and twelve by three –

Sir John   – let's just agree to differ!

Barnard   If yer don't let the king in, and if yer continue to billet the soldiers without no compensation, well, the mob, they'll gerrodofyer and brae 'ell outa yer!

Sir John Lord Mayor, I am loyal to my king, and what comes next is for show.

Citizens! We might witness here in Hull, today, the birth of constitutional parliamentary democracy. And what is needed at a birth is an experienced midwife with an oiled finger. I am that oily finger. But no baby can guarantee an easy birth –

Sweet Lips – it might have its head stuck the wrong way round.

Sir John Yes –

Female Citizen – our Dennis had 'is cord wrapped round 'is neck.

Sir John Yes! And –

Male citizen – might be twins!

Sir John Oh forget it, forget it!

He storms off, the citizens following, **Moyer** *calling after him* 'Sir John . . .?'. **Frances** *enters, holding her book.*

Rupert Fraulein, would you like to buy this cod?

Frances Haddock. Dark blotch above the pectoral fin.

York What's in a name? That which we call a haddock. By any other word would smell as sweet.

Frances Miss, don't mock me because I'm reading *Romeo and Juliet*!

York I do not bite my thumb at you, dear lady.

Frances You still bite your thumb, stupid girl?!

York A quote from the play.

Frances Yes, I didn't understand that bit.

York Does the play move you?

Frances Like Juliet, I am tragically, hopelessly in love.

York   With whom?

Frances   A boy!

Rupert   Is he good looking?

Frances   Ohhh yes! He's, ooooh, and he's really eeerghh!

York   What do you feel for him?

Frances   Oooooh, nnnnnn, pheewwewe.

Rupert   She's mad.

York   What would you do for him?

Frances   Everything.

York   Did you dream of him last night?

Frances   No, I dreamt of his cousin, with the uniform. Who is equally handsome but is a bit bigger.

York   His cousin?! But his cousin is –

Frances   – a bit bigger! Yes!

Rupert   Tell us the dream.

Frances   I was shipwrecked on an island made of white linen and I had no clothes on and there was a big horse wearing a uniform, kneading dough, and I climbed on top of the horse and then it rained and we both got wet. (*Beat.*) What do you think it means?

York/Rupert   No idea

Frances   But you're both girls, do you have dreams like this?

Rupert/York   *Ja!*/No.

York   You love the tall one, but you love the other man too?!

Frances   I love them both. Urgh! But I am promised to that Puritan there! Do you know a good way to kill yourself that doesn't hurt?

They shake their heads. She runs off. **York** *collapses to his knees.*

York   I am hit! Now that she is unattainable, I want her with my life.

Rupert   She loves me more.

York   Rupert, I am second in line to the English throne. What are you?

Rupert   Eight hundred and seventh.

York   *And* you don't like girls. So cuz, step aside.

Rupert   What of my feelings?

York   You can dream of her brother.

Rupert   And what about our commission, the taking or destruction of the arsenal?

York   All I know is that I am less inclined to take up arms in a civil war than I am ripe to ride out and slay Durand and 'his loveless party'. But here's her future husband, my mortal enemy.

Pelham *approaches.*

Pelham (*averting his eyes*)   Have you no sense of decency? Cover your fish!

York   Whyfor sir?

Pelham   So that they don't excite lewd thoughts!

Rupert *covers the fish in a blanket, which leaves their heads showing.*

York   You are to be married soon, Mr Pelham?

Pelham   A man needs a wife.

York   To love, to adore, to worship?

Pelham   To breed. The Lord said go forth and multiply, I can't do that on my own.

Pelham *moves off.*

York   Another member of the loveless party. Let us declare war on them, Rupert!

Rupert   *Jawohl!*

York   Let us raze Durand's citadel of reason and then advance on Pelham's desert heart!

Messenger *at pace.*

Messenger (*Hull accent*)   Charlie's ower yonder now!

Moyer   Does the king have an army?

Messenger   Aye, I reckon near two hundred horse.

Sir John   How many foot?

Messenger   'bout fifty 'ead o' foot.

Sir John (*aside/improvisation*)   You, madam! How many soldiers is fifty head of foot if every soldier has one head and two feet?

Audience member   Fifty!

Sir John   Is that a guess or is it based on your own military experience?

Messenger   I'm gerrin' inside!

Messenger *runs within the walls. A trumpet sound near.*

Citizen   Here's Charlie!

Moyer   Everyone! Within the walls!

Sir John   Announce the curfew as designed!

Moyer   CURFEW! CURFEW! CURFEW!

The citizens rush to get within the walls as the drawbridge shows signs of rising.

Barnard   You said you would allow the king access!

Calvert   Let the king in I say, Hotham!

Sweet Lips   And taste the pleasures!

Moyer   Draw the bridge!

Ad libs from **Calvert**, **Sweet Lips**, *etc, 'Long live the King!', etc.*

The drawbridge starts to rise as the citizens scramble in behind the walls. Everyone gets inside the walls except for **Drudge**, *who is left on the wrong side of the raising bridge.*

Connie   Drudge!

Moyer   Curfew!

Connie   Drudge!

Moyer   Curfew!

Connie   Drudge!

Drudge *grabs the edge of the drawbridge as it rises, slowly being hauled up with the bridge to be pulled over the walls by the citizens as the bridge clanks into place. Enter the forward train of* **King Charles I**, *cavaliers, foot soldiers, and then* **Charles** *sat on a tiny white horse, a wooden prop. The citizens are now standing on the walls looking down.*

Soldier One   Oi! Keep the noise down I'm tryna have a lie-in!

Laughter.

Charles   I am Charles Stuart, King of England.

Soldier Two   Go wipe your arse!

Laughter.

Charles   I wish to speak to the governor.

Soldier One   Who, with any wit, would choose a white horse?!

Soldier Two   There's a little shit showing on top.

Charles   Hotham! Why is this bridge raised up?!

Sir John   According to Your Majesty's orders.

Charles   I gave no such instruction.

Sir John   Through your Parliament you did. Parliament is the instrument of the king, ergo you have ordered me not to let you in.

Charles   Duplicitous words, Hotham!

Sir John   Thank you!

Charles   Who the hell do you think you are?

Sir John   A supplicant, and it is my honour today to kneel before you, even in the lowly role of traitor.

Charles   Do you want to be the first dark cloud which will soon overspread this land and cast all into thunder?

Sir John   I am not a dark cloud, I am a lovely day. You have here in Hull, not only a magazine of military provisions, but also a magazine of hearts. The love that we feel for you is unbounded, and being unbounded it bounds everywhere in Hull's streets like an unbound hound of love.

Charles   The ordinance here is mine! Accumulated for the Second Bishops' War.

Sir John   Every last ounce of gunpowder is intact. I am merely protecting it for you.

Charles   Where's the mayor?

Barnard (*off*)   Gissa skeg!

Barnard's *head shows above the parapet.*

'ow do, mi Liege, how glad I would have been to welcome you –

A soldier smacks him on the head and **Barnard** *collapses behind the walls.*

Charles   This town –

All   – city!

Charles   This city is mine by name! Kingstown upon Hull. Show me your orders, Hotham! Come out here with the document!

Sir John   That cannot be done.

Charles   Why not?!

Sir John   If they won't let the gate down for you, they're not going to do it for me are they?

Charles   Throw him off the walls!

Sir John   No, that would be dangerous.

Uproar and fighting on the walls. **Barnard** *and another Royalist alderman grab* **Sir John** *and try to throw him off the walls.* **Drudge** *and* **Pelham** *fight back, and save* **Sir John**. *Fanfare.*

Charles   Proclaim the dog a traitor!

Herald   Sir John Hotham, 1st Baronet of Scorborough, is a traitor, guilty of high treason, by order of Charles Stuart, King of England.

Charles   I will have your head, Hotham!

The king's train leave. Drums.

Sir John   That went quite well.

Drum flourish. Blackout.

Interval.

Act Four

Scene One

Later that same day. The governor's house, main room. Enter
Drudge *with a huge log splitter maul. He heads for the vase and
places it on the floor like a golf ball. He swings the maul and whacks
it hard into the back wall. It doesn't break. The* **Ghost** *enters from
the master bedroom and snatches up the vase.*

Ghost No, sir! It's my vase.

Drudge *tries to get the vase back.*

Ghost I am Mary Ascough. This vase is the last of a pair. I
broke the other, which is why my father, drunk and enraged,
killed me. My task in purgatory is to protect the vase, but in
performing it, I cannot move on.

Drudge *holds the vase like a baby.*

Ghost You will protect the vase? Then I am free and can be
with God. It must not be broken, but if that happens then
you must kill whoever breaks it.

Draws a knife and mimes defending the vase against all comers.

Drudge Ayyyyeeeaaaaa!

Ghost Be diligent, sir. I can now be with God.

The **Ghost** *walks through a wall. Enter* **Frances** *and* **Lady Sarah**.

Drudge *is fiercer than ever.*

Frances Is it right that we, the gentry, who own nine-tenths
of the land, are acquiring the rest by the aggressive
enclosure of common pasture?

Lady Sarah Yes. Drudge! Put that knife down!

Frances   But it says here that the people have never endured such a painful yoke from foreign tyrants as from our own gentry – us. Why didn't anybody tell me that?

Lady Sarah   You'd give everyone the vote would you?

Frances   Why not?!

Lady Sarah   Imagine what kind of idiots would get elected.

Frances   When Adam delved, and Eve span, where then was the gentleman?

Lady Sarah *snatches a Diggers pamphlet from* **Frances***'s hand, looks at it and screws it up.*

Lady Sarah   The Diggers!

Frances *goes into her room in a huff.*

Connie   In times of turmoil masterless men crowd the streets like flies round a cow's –

Lady Sarah   – ah Connie, go back to mumbling! I'm going to take advantage of the shops now that we're in Hull.

Connie   I was surprised there's no white bread bakers.

Lady Sarah   I'm not interested in bread. Hats.

She exits.

Connie (*to* **Drudge**)   I'd like a baker's shop. Master, mistress of my own destiny. Not wiping the –

Enter **Sir John** *and* **Durand** *from the street.*

Sir John   – Connie! Where's the enemy?!

Connie   She found a hat shop.

Sir John   Women!

(*Aside.*) I bar the king of England, I'm declared a traitor, certain death if the monarchy wins the war, and what does my wife do?! She goes shopping!

(*Improvisation. Aside to a man with wife.*) What's this one like?
Eh? Any trouble?

Heated banging on the door. **Durand** *opens it to* **Barnard** *who*
storms in.

Barnard   What mekks yer think yer can deny the king of
England and live?! The image of Christ as God on earth!

Sir John   If God's four foot nothing with a cleft palate God
help us.

Barnard   The folk of 'ull saw what yer done and they'll not
wait no more now. They want their rightful money. For the
billeting of troops.

Sir John   Their money has been weighed, successfully, and
has left London in a ship.

Barnard   And how's a ship gonna gerrup the 'umber?

Sir John   Oak, wind and floating devices.

Barnard   The king's ship, *The Providence*, is in the estuary!

Sir John   Sodom!

Durand   The king's fleet is in the Humber?

Barnard   Packed wi' powder and troops from 'olland!

Sir John   But how did it get there?!

Barnard   Erk, wind and floating devices!

Sir John   If this is true why has Captain Moyer not
informed me of this?

Barnard   In haste, he's sailed out the 'arbour on *The 'ercules*
and is engaging *The Providence* right now!

Sir John   No, no, no, lies! There is no king's fleet. This is an
invention, to pressure me to turn over to the king's side.
Nothing more than a masque –

Cannon fire is heard.

an elaborate masque with naval cannon sound effects.

More cannon fire.

How do I know you haven't rented that schooner?

More cannon fire.

Barnard   You're all alone now, Hotham.

Sir John (*aside*)   The scales suddenly tip toward the royal party, like a see-saw with two evenly weighted children happily playing when suddenly an enormous ox falls out of a tree and lands on one end. What to do?! Am I a man, or am I two horses in double harness? Two horses pulling in opposite directions. The horse called 'Honour' pulls towards Parliament; the horse called 'Advantage' draws me to the King. Honour/Advantage. Honour/Advantage. Choose honour and I am disadvantaged. Choose Advantage and I am dishonoured. Honour/advantage/dishonour/ disadvantage.

Barnard   With events going agin yer I'll wager yer as ripe to roll over as a tuppeny whore.

Sir John   I don't use tuppeny whores. Prudently, I save all my pennies and treat myself on Christmas Eve to –

Durand   – he's calling you a cheap whore, father!

Barnard   All you care about is keeping your estates. Whoever wins the war.

Durand   Not once, not twice, but thrice you besmirch my father's reputation!

Barnard   Besmirch do I?

Sir John   My honour has ne'er been so much such besmutched!

Barnard   'ull folk are direct. My truths, which you call insults, are the least of your worries. How yer gonna manage without an 'ead?

Sir John   I shall adapt.

Barnard   Yer can't educate pork!

He leaves, passing a **Messenger** *in the doorway.*

Sir John   Connie! What to do?

Messenger   You have mail!

Frances *flies out of her room. She grabs letters but also gives letters.*

Frances   A letter from James, but nothing from Rupert?

Messenger   How many followers do you have?

Frances   Two. James and Rupert.

Messenger   Rupert? Sorry, nothing.

Messenger *exits.*

Frances (*in a negative swoon*)   Rupert has unfollowed me!

Sir John   Give me that!

He tears the letter open and reads.

James. The Duke of York?! 'My fair lily . . .'

She staggers around the room and then faints and rolls over the sofa, collapsing panting.

Durand   James loves my sister? What does he say?

Sir John   It's all acronyms, written in haste. C.U.L F.T.F. K.O.T.L.

Connie   See you later, face to face, kiss on the lips.

Durand   He loves her!

Sir John   Wait! If that sliver of quivering whimsy marries the Duke of York what would I be, to him?

Durand   Father-in-Law.

Sir John And I would be the king's brother-in-law and the king would be my king-in-law, which might be enough to make him think twice about beheading me.

Connie Stick that where the sun don't shine, John Pym.

Durand But by law and contract Frances is to marry Peregrine Pelham.

Sir John Argh! But we can't be allied to Parliament any longer! Not now, with the king's fleet in the Humber.

He sinks to his knees in despair.

Connie? How do I give the town over to the king and yet –

Connie – avoid the betrayal of Parliament?

Durand And the inevitable execution.

Sir John Yes!

Connie Your first problem is the mob.

Durand Yes.

Connie Pay them for the billeting or you will never see another day.

Durand Yes.

Sir John With Pelham's dowry from the safe box?

Durand No!

Sir John Why not?

Durand That is no longer our money. I like you a lot father, but I love the law.

Connie Borrow a thousand from the moneylender.

Sir John Albert Calvert, the Jew?

All He's not Jewish!

Connie (*to* **Durand**) Get him over here. Tell him it's for the billeting.

Durand   What shall I say has changed?

Sir John   Tell him I have a secret that I had not previously disclosed.

Durand *leaves.* **Sir John** *holds* **Connie**, *kisses the top of her head.*

Sir John   Oh Connie if only you weren't low born I could be happy and want for nothing. But since you're a coarse peasant with no breeding, there's an end to that.

Knocking at the door. **Connie** *opens the door to* **York**, *dressed as a fishwife.*

Connie   No hawkers or costers!

York *elbows his way in.*

Connie   Oi!

York   I am not a fishwife! I beg an audience. I am James, the Duke of York.

Sir John   You're a man, are you? Prove it.

York   I shall not expose myself.

Sir John   Reasonable.

He goes up and puts his hand under her skirts to check gender. This takes an inordinate amount of time, and searching, and consideration until –

Sir John   Ah! There it is. (*Genuflects.*) Welcome, your majesty!

York   Good sir, your daughter!

He runs to her, moved that she might be dead.

Sir John   She read your letter.

York   Is she not well?

Sir John   She's as mad as a sack full of wet chickens. And would make a perfect wife. This is her daily swoon.

York   My father is a mercurial beast.

Sir John   He declared me guilty of high treason!

York   Yes, but he'll return, and when he does, invite him in to inspect the arsenal, and I guarantee that he will relent, annul your death sentence, and treat you like family.

Sir John   Like a brother-in-law?

York   Yes, and who would kill their brother?

Sir John   Cain, Medea, Eteocles, Polyneices, Claudius, Romulus –

York   – my father was not raised by wolves.

Sir John   But my turning, away from Parliament, back to my only true calling, your father, must be a secret or Captain Moyer will clap me in irons.

York   The king will send an emissary.

He makes to leave.

A letter for your son, Durand.

Sir John   He's not here.

He takes the letter, sniffs it.

York   From a lady admirer.

Sir John   She's wasting her time, he has no interest in love.

York   Or girls?

Sir John   For his fourteenth birthday I gave him a shilling, so he could have a whore, but he spent the money on a book about pigeons.

*He gives **York** the letter back.*

York   This girl is different. He might be interested in her.

He leaves.

Sir John   Connie, if the king returns how can I bar him but also let him in?

Connie   How can a person be outside the walls and inside the walls at the same time?

Sir John   Yes! Is that possible, or is it against nature?

Connie   It is only possible if the person is a king.

Sir John   The king is a king!

Connie   When people say 'the king is coming', they don't mean a man on his own. No king travels alone. You can let the king in, but bar his attendants.

Sir John   Connie, you're an ill- bred, uncouth, plebeian, damned feculent miracle!

Enter **Durand** *and* **Calvert**.

Sir John   (*rocks back and forth chanting the Shema – in Hebrew that is clearly totally made-up gibberish*)

   Shema yisroel Adonai elohenu Adonai ehad
   Baruch Shem kavod Malchuto laolam vaed . . .

Calvert   Are you Jewish?

Sir John   Where there's smoke there's salmon.

Calvert   Circumcised?

Sir John   Abraham himself was not circumcised until he was ninety.

Calvert   He did well then, getting to ninety without an interest-free loan. What kind of Jew isn't cut?

Sir John   We Berber Jews have dispensation from circumcision because the Atlas Mountains, where we live, are quite draughty, and you need all the layers you can get.

Calvert   But then anyone could tell me they're a Berber Jew and get a discount.

Sir John   Ah! So you do favour the old religion?

Calvert   The only tribes I favour are those who repay. I'll lend you a thousand, interest free, because that is the only way I shall be paid my fourteen shillings for the billeting of troops. I'll draw up a contract.

Sir John   Bring the money today!

Calvert *leaves.*

Sir John   Yes!

Frances *wakes up with a start.*

Frances   Yes! If I'm Jewish I can't marry Pelham!

She runs off, joyfully.

Durand   I didn't know we were Jewish.

Sir John   We're not!

Connie   And neither is he.

Sir John   I got the money didn't I! Here, a letter for you.

Durand   For me?

Sir John   From a lady.

Durand   Does she need legal advice?

Sir John   No, she needs something more enjoyable and less expensive.

He hands over the letter. **Durand** *takes it into his room.*

Sir John   Connie! You may have saved my head!

He hugs and kisses her. Enter **Pelham** *at pace. He catches them in the act.*

Pelham   Sir John! What –?!

Sir John   – she'd swallowed a key, accidentally, I was sucking it out.

He sticks his fingers down **Connie***'s throat and comes up with a key, actually the key to the safe box.*

Sir John   Be more careful next time, you stupid mare!

Connie *takes the key.*

Sir John   What is it, Pelham?

Pelham   The king!

Sir John (*aside*)   My brother-in-law!

Pelham (*aside*)   What did he say?

The king has returned, he's before the Beverley Gate. Haste, man!

He exits.

Scene Two

The streets, inside the walls. **York** *and* **Rupert** *are there with the fish stall.* **York** *is watching* **Durand** *promenade.* **Rupert** *organises the fish stall.*

Rupert   *Wir* need parsley.

York   We're not here to sell fish, Rupert.

Rupert   *Selbsverstendlich! Der* fish stall *ist ein* Trojan Horse for getting inside the arsenal!

York   Yes, and then I'd like to prove that statue of conceit Durand human, and restore love to its rightful place above the law as the pinnacle of human achievement. He approaches! We will find out.

Rupert *heads off. Enter* **Durand**.

York   Fresh sea bass, sir!

Durand   Miss, your letter offered me truth, not fish.

York   I know a truth you don't know.

Durand   Ill-bred wench, you don't even know your own fish. That's a cod. Not a sea bass. Cod have beards, like men, see, it is an unchanging variance of their species.

York   You're a man, and you don't have a beard.

Durand   Because unlike a cod, victim to fate, I reason, I cogitate, I change my destiny by shaving each morning. A daily chore with which you girls are lucky not to be burdened.

York   We have other things to think about. Do you shave to please a lady?

Durand   To please no woman.

York   You don't like women?

Durand   I shave to soothe my chin.

York (*aside*)   Violet.

Actually, my mistress is quite boyish.

Durand   Tribadic?

York   She'll try anything once. She finds pleasure in the sight of your chin. Smooth, like a sea bass, unlike a cod. In fact the seabassnessness of your chin is the only conversation on this fish stall.

Durand   I have no time for love, nor it for me. Truth is my only passion.

York   A shame for truth is abstract.

Durand   Miss, truth is tangible in the law, and fairer than any woman, and shall become more perfect with age through the incorporation of precedent, until it is, eventually, flawless.

York   The law is the custody, the safeguard of all private interests, liberty, property and honour, but what it can't do is hold you, kiss you, and transport you into raptures of bliss.

Durand   By what name does your lady –

York   – Rupert . . . ia Rupertia.

Durand   And is she pleasing on the eye?

York   Does that concern you?

Durand   Not at all. I need the information to recognise her.

York   She has a moustache. She eschews fashion, believing it to be nothing more than socially approved construct.

Durand (*aside*)   A moustache, and tediously pedantic, like me!

She seems an exceptional intellect, for a fishmonger?

York   Ice was her idea.

Durand   How does she like to pass the time?

York   She has a bookish interest in books.

Durand   Building a library?

York   Specialising in semiotics and pigeons.

Durand (*aside*)   Mine own two passions!

York   I have often heard her say that the word 'modern' has no inherent meaning.

Durand   It doesn't. Modern is –

York   – don't tell me, tell her.

Rupert *approaches.*

York   Here he is now – she is now!

Durand   Quickly. Give me a fish.

York   Two farthings.

Durand *is handed a fish.* **Rupert** *approaches.*

Durand   Dear lady, miss, I have bought this fish.

Rupert   *Sehr Gut!* Best before sunset.

Durand   How *modern* is this fish?

Rupert   It is *frisch*, fresh, very modern.

Durand   But what does the word *modern* tell us about this fish?

Rupert   *Ich weiss nicht.*

Durand   You speak German, a language over four hundred years old, and yet we call it a *modern* European language. This fish, which we also call modern, is not four hundred years old. Therefore the word modern contains no meaning, and only tells us that there were fish before this fish. I will keep it. As a bookmark.

He puts the fish in his book. **York** *puts his arm through* **Rupert**'s *arm and hands* **Durand** *a rose.*

Durand   *Fur mich?*

Rupert   *Dich.*

Durand   Thank you, Rupertia. *Danke.*

He walks off backwards.

Rupert   I think he likes me.

York   Yes, and now we must make a proper Malvolio of him.

He takes up a quill and writing paper and writes.

Clothing – yellow, a codpiece –

– a false nose!

Yes, he's already declared for noses!

Enter **Sir John**. *He is joined by* **Durand** *and approached by* **Barnard**.

Barnard   Good news! Hotham! Gerr'ere! The Earl of Newcastle has ridden south with most of the Royalist gentry and is already at Wetwang.

Sir John   Wetwang?

Barnard   Wetwang.

Sir John   Wetwang?

Barnard   Wetwang! And with the king's fleet in the 'umber, we will have our day soon enough. Keep yer word!

He skulks off. **Pelham** *approaches.*

Pelham   The king is before the Beverley Gate with about fifty horse.

Sir John   Any foot?

Pelham   None brother.

Sir John   Fifty horse and no feet?!

Pelham   Your orders from Parliament require you to bar him.

Sir John   A second time. He's behaving like Hull was his favourite pub.

Fanfare. Enter a **Soldier** *running.*

Soldier   They got the king on a ladder sir!

Charles *appears atop a ladder overlooking the walls.* **Soldiers** *take aim.*

Sir John   Hold your fire! Let me reason with him!

Charles   Hotham! An opportunity to make amends for your earlier affront.

Sir John   Your Majesty, I have never said you can't come in. Only your troop, your horse, your foot cannot enter.

Pelham   Remember your orders, Hotham!

Sir John   Alright!

Charles   So a king is invited to enter this nest of rebels *alone*?! I will need at least thirty attendants for security.

Sir John   Six.

Charles   Twenty-five!

Sir John   Fourteen! That's my final offer. Fourteen is already thrice six!

Charles   I shall not reprise King Lear! Harassed from daughter to daughter, begging a meal!

Sir John   What's he talking about?

Soldier One   King Lear. Shakespeare's old king.

Sir John   I don't know it. What happens?

Soldier Two   The king goes mad and dies.

Sir John   Is that it?

Soldier One   Yes.

Sir John   Three and a half hours?

Soldier Two   And the rest.

Sir John   Your Majesty, we do not wish you to go mad and die. You are our king, and welcome in Hull, alone. I have prepared a bed chamber for you in my house.

Charles   You pile indignity on affront! This disobedience of yours will cause much loss of blood, which could be avoided if you perform your duty as a subject. War is inevitable now, and on your conscience!

He is lowered out of sight. The Parliament troops heckle and chant.

Soldiers   War! War! War!

Sir John *retreating, with 'No, no, no!' as the song begins.*

The **Ranter** *sings.*

Song: 'A Song of War'

The Familists are recruiting, the Levellers fall in
The Roundheads are preparing, the war will soon begin.
The Royalists, may knock us down, they won't expect it
    when
The people of Hull rise up and then they rise up once again.

Let's sing a song of war.
Fathers, brothers, sons.
Let's sing a song of war.
Get your muskets, pikes and drums.
Let's sing a song of war.
A song for everyone.

The rebellion will rise up, size up the enemy.
They'll hear the dreadful cries 'up with Parliament and
    Hull'.
So, brothers, come and sign up, line up the enemy
Straighten your spine up, and pray for a miracle.

Let's sing a song of war.
Fathers, brothers, sons.
The rebellion will rise up, size up the enemy
Let's sing a song of war.
Get your muskets, pikes and drums.
They'll hear the dreadful cries 'up with Parliament and Hull'
Let's sing a song of war.
A war for everyone.
Brothers come and sign up, line up the enemy
A war for everyone.
Brothers come and sign up, line up the enemy
A war for everyone.

Act Five

Scene One

The house. Enter **Lady Sarah** *and* **Saltmarsh** *from the street.*
Lady Sarah *has two hat boxes.*

Lady Sarah   There is no one in. My husband is currently charming the king.

Saltmarsh   But we must be swift! If he is arrested, all your goods will be confiscated and the money commandeered. Where's Pelham's dowry?

Lady Sarah   Secure in a safe box in the bedroom. This newly minted key is not tested.

Saltmarsh   Not the bedroom with the Inigo Jones bed?

Lady Sarah   Yes. But you must not look at . . . oh sod it, I'd like to show you the bed, come with me.

They go into the bedroom.

Saltmarsh (*off*)   Oh my God!

Lady Sarah (*off*)   Not now, Parsnip!

Lady Sarah *comes out running, with* **Saltmarsh** *after, who grabs her and kisses her. Enter* **Drudge** *from the street carrying the vase like a baby.*

Lady Sarah   Drudge? What's happening?

Drudge *mimes that it's all over and that* **Sir John** *is coming back.*

Lady Sarah   He's coming back! Quick! Get in the coal cellar.

She opens the hatch and **Saltmarsh** *goes down into the cellar. Enter* **Sir John**, **Durand**, **Frances** *and* **Connie**.

Sir John   Drudge, put that damn vase down.

Drudge *draws a knife.*

Sir John   Give me the knife! Or you're going on the hook!

Connie   He doesn't have a hook here.

Sir John   The knife or I'll put up a hook!

Connie *goes down into the cellar, but shouts up.*

Connie (*off*)   Who the bloody 'ell are you?!

Sir John   Who is it, Connie?

Saltmarsh (*off*)   I am Sir John's cousin.

Sir John   A cousin? Ask him if he's the mad one from Heslerton.

Connie (*off*)   Are you the mad one from Heslerton?

Saltmarsh (*off*)   Yes.

Sir John   Let him up.

Saltmarsh *appears,* **Connie** *after.*

Sir John   If you needed coal, Mister Saltmarsh, just ask? But I would have thought seventeen wives was enough to keep a man warm.

Saltmarsh   That is not how the Family of Love works.

Sir John   I want you to stop using your cant to excite the people.

Saltmarsh   It was a different kind of cant that closed the gates on the king.

Sir John   I was commissioned by Parliament.

Saltmarsh   Parliament is just another emperor, but by another name.

Sir John   And what name is that?

Saltmarsh   Parliament.

Sir John   You're a gentleman, you have the vote.

Saltmarsh   Which I will never use until every Englishman is so entitled. Parliament is the gentry legitimising their illegitimate powers.

Lady Sarah   He has renounced his birthright.

Sir John   What an idiot.

Saltmarsh   I have chosen to be a wretch.

Sir John   You would have every man, regardless of his station, given the vote?

Saltmarsh   And every woman.

Sir John   You would give my wife the vote?

Saltmarsh   Why not your wife, sir?

Sir John   Because a compendious knowledge of shoes and sitting down to piss does not qualify one to elect a national assembly!

Saltmarsh (*re* **Connie**)   And this woman.

Sir John   She's a servant!

Saltmarsh   Master and servant has no grounding in the New Testament.

Sir John (*re* **Connie**)   Conceived in a ditch?! Out of wedlock. Quickly, without poetry or payment. A hedgehog has a finer pedigree!

Saltmarsh   She seems to me a credit to God. With a fine wit.

Sir John   No learning! No land! No money! What would she vote for?

Connie   Learning, land and money.

Sir John   No! *My* learning, my land and my money!

Saltmarsh   Why, if you have 'all your land', should she not have 'all your land'?

Sir John   You would have us all levelled?!

Saltmarsh   At one time this woman owned England.

Sir John   Sceptical nonsense!

Saltmarsh   She owned the land in common with others, before it was stolen from her by enclosure.

Connie   Middleton-on-the-Wolds actually.

Sir John   Enclosure was not theft!

Durand   It was an issue of Parliament.

Connie   In which, without the vote, my father could not participate.

Sir John   Oh, not you Connie. Not you, you're all –

Saltmarsh   – why should one man have four thousand pounds a year and another exist on but a single pound?

Sir John   Because I am Sir John Hotham! A Hotham! A damned feculent gentleman, from an unbroken line dating back to the eleventh century. Get out! This is enough revolution for one lifetime. Out!

(*To* **Lady Sarah**.) Go with him if you must!

Saltmarsh *and* **Lady Sarah** *leave. The door closes. A knock.* **Connie** *opens it. A messenger is there with letters.* **Frances** *devours the letters and gives some back then runs back up to her room. Then she realises that one of the letters is for* **Durand***, and gives it on.* **Durand** *gives the messenger a letter. This is all done amazingly swiftly.*

Sir John   Like the twitter of birds.

Durand *takes it and retires to his room, but only after giving the messenger a letter.*

Sir John (*to* **Connie**)   Forgive me.

Connie   The hedgehog bit?

Sir John   Yes.

Connie   Money did change hands.

Sir John   Ah. You said your mother was enterprising. My lunatic cousin has confirmed my worst fears.

Connie   The mob?

Sir John   What might the people want if they begin to imagine? A lowly smith, a carter, a glover, might fancy himself my equal.

Connie   Yeah . . .

Sir John   Forget Parliament or king, if the mob act they could level the rich of both parties.

Knocking on the door. **Connie** *opens it,* **Moyer** *and* **Frottage** *enter.*

Moyer   Sir, events, sir, events! My ship *The Hercules* engaged with the Royalist schooner in the Humber –

Sir John   – schooner? You mean the king's fleet?

Moyer   One ship, sir, which fled, running aground near Paull.

Sir John   Who's Paul?

Moyer   Paull is the name of a small village up a creek east of here.

Sir John   Damn stupid name for a village up a creek.

Moyer   The Cavaliers fled on foot, and my crew took their mariners prisoner.

Sir John (*aside*)   The painful wind of history has blown and an elephant has landed on the Parliament end of the see-saw. The see-saw has see-sawed back again, which is why they're called see-saws, back to favour Parliament. And I stand in the middle, not knowing which end of the see-saw to ride, like a man with two horses but only one arse. But she's a loin exciter.

(*To* **Moyer**.) And is this the Royalist captain?

Moyer   This, sir, is a lady.

Sir John   I can see that, Captain Moyer.

Moyer   Aristocracy, and French.

Frottage   *Parlez vous Francais?*

Sir John   *Oui! Wilkommen!*

Moyer   She is Queen Henrietta's lady of the bedchamber.

Frottage   *Enchanté.*

Sir John   *J'arrive!*

Moyer   She gives her name as Mademoiselle Félicité de Frottage d'Aquitaine. She is a prisoner –

Sir John   – *une* guest *d'honneur.*

He kisses her hand.

Moyer   The other prisoners are secure in irons in the fo'c'sle but she, being a lady and so fair, I didn't know . . . could you iron her here?

Connie (*aside*)   To iron. Verb. To clap in irons.

Sir John   *Pro bono.* She shall have the Inigo Jones bed, in the king's room.

Moyer   But I thought your wife was in there, sir?

Sir John   She was.

Soldier   Sir . . .!

Moyer   I must return to the walls. The papists are camped only a mile off.

Sir John   Our king is hardly a papist, Captain Moyer.

Moyer   His queen is. Or do you soften, sir?

Sir John   Soft?! *Moi*?! *Non! J'ai bois!*

Moyer   Good! After today's display of defiance the
company and I are much emboldened. Let this war begin!
And in Hull!

Sir John   *Au revoir, mon brave!*

Moyer *exits.* **Sir John** *closes the door and considers his new
adventure.*

Sir John (*to himself, re:* **Frottage**)   Once more into the
breach.

Frottage   Monsieur?

Sir John   *Encore une fois! Entrer nous dedans la* breach. *C'est
une* famoose Anglaisy speechy Monsieur William
Shakespeare.

Frottage   *Qui?*

Sir John   I have the keys to all the rooms. The master suite
is your prison cell, with the bed designed by Inigo Jones.

Frottage   Inigo Jones the libertine?

Sir John   I presumed he was a bed designer. One look at
the bed, and you will be conquered.

Frottage   The mere sight of the bed fires the passions?

Sir John   They can't use straw for the mattress. They use
duck down from non-flammable ducks. You're speaking
English?

Frottage (*whisper*)   I am not Mademoiselle Frottage. That
was a part I played for Captain Moyer. (*Re:* **Connie** *and*
Drudge.) The servants.

Sir John   Connie, Drudge, leave us alone!

Connie (*aside*)   How many times have I seen this moment?
His passion lasts a year, two years, and then one day he'll
seek me out, and describe at length the witch he fell in love
with, and beg some comfort, which I give him, for he is all I
have.

She exits into the coal cellar.

Frottage   I am Lady Digby, of the king's court, a messenger.

Sir John   But if somebody sees me talking to a member of the royal party –

Frottage   – I entreat you, reconsider your position vis à vis the king.

Sir John   You're speaking French again?!

Frottage   Hand over the arsenal and you will regain his favour.

Sir John   No! Ten minutes ago he had a ship in the Humber and looked like taking the town, then he lost that ship. And now Parliament again prevails and anyway the king declared me a traitor!

Frottage   Give him the munitions and he will pardon you.

Sir John   As well as not beheading me, would he give me a baronetcy?

Frottage   You're already a baron.

Sir John   I've always wanted to be a double baron.

Frottage   He will let you keep your head, is that not enough?

Sir John   Lady Digby, how can I?! Parliament is in the ascendant. It would be suicide for me. But I will not betray you to Captain Moyer, you must stay the night.

Frottage   No, get me a horse, I shall ride to the king.

Sir John   But you haven't seen the bed yet. And anyway, it's Holy Horse Day today.

Frottage   A holiday for horses?

Sir John   A Hull tradition. Once a year they can wear what they like, eat pancakes and shit in the road. Let me show you the room that the bed's in, the one you can't look at.

Sir John *opens the door. She goes in and he is about to follow when* **Durand** *opens his door, and comes out.* **Sir John** *slams his door.* **Durand** *is now dressed in a yellow costume decorated with roses, a codpiece, and a huge nose.*

Sir John   What the feculent hell is that?!

Durand   Pater. Tis I.

Sir John   You look like a daffodil with the horn. Two horns!

Durand   I am an object of desire.

Sir John   A woman?

Durand   Possibly.

Sir John   But why dress like that?

Durand   To please her.

Sir John   From which end.

Durand   She is enchanted by my chin but finds my nose disappointing.

Sir John   But who built it, it must've taken weeks?

Durand   I made it out of pig skin and stuck it on with fish glue. I never knew before the ecstasy of purposeful suffering.

There is banging on the door and **Barnard** *enters.*

Sir John   You can't just come –

Barnard   – refuge! The mob besiege mi 'ouse! Why don't yer pay them!

Sir John   I shall send you the money today. Before dinner.

Barnard   I don't trust you, Hotham.

Barnard *sees* **Durand**.

Barnard   Bugger me! I'll 'ave to tek mi socks off!

Sir John   My son. He's in love.

Barnard   Oh that explains it then.

Durand   Do you doubt my father's word?!

Barnard   I doubt bloody everything about him! I doubt he is standing here before me! I have never in my entire puff met such . . . doubling duplicity, such a pestiferous purpose changer, such Janus-faced pharisaical frontage!

Sir John   And I'm glad that in insulting me you have finally found full use for your limited education! I demand you leave!

He pushes **Barnard** *to the door,* **Barnard** *resisting. There's beating on the door.*

Barnard   Refuge!

Sir John   The cellar.

Barnard *goes down into the cellar.* **Connie** *comes straight out.*

Connie   This is my coal cellar and I in't sharing it wi' no one! Who's that banging on the door!

Sir John   Don't open –

Connie *opens the door and lets in* **Calvert**.

Sir John   Shalom Aleichem!

Calvert   I have the contract for your loan. With an additional clause. Since you are indebted to me now in blood.

He produces a written legal contract.

Durand   Blood?

Calvert   A clown, Hotham?

Sir John   My son, he's in love.

Calvert   Oh, bad luck. Blood because my daughter has been tupped, and her maidenhead taken.

Sir John   I am neither taker nor tupper. I've been too busy, and in here.

Calvert   I know the ram! He is a Parliament soldier, quartered for nowt in my house, having no diversions but porter, wine and the horn, and now I contract for an equivalent injury from you!

Sir John   Your Hull's Shylock, eh? You want a pound of flesh?

Calvert   An ounce.

He gives **Sir John** *the contract,* **Sir John** *gives it to* **Durand**.

Durand   The party of the first part –

Calvert   – that's me.

Durand   – agrees to loan a thousand pounds to the party of the second part –

Sir John   – is that me?

Calvert   Yes, you.

Durand   As surety the party of the second part –

Sir John   – me.

Durand   – provides his foreskin.

Sir John   My foreskin?

Calvert   Your foreskin.

Sir John   My foreskin?

Calvert   Your foreskin.

Sir John (*re* **Durand**)   Would his foreskin suffice?

Calvert   No. I want yours.

Sir John   But it's the only one I have, and I use it a lot!

Calvert   I can only lend this money interest free to a Jew.

Durand   But you're not Jewish.

Calvert   I am a free man and can make my own terms. My daughter has been violated. An eye for an eye. A tooth for a tooth.

Sir John   You can have a tooth. Two teeth? Three teeth, one eye and a finger! And that's my last offer.

Calvert   Whenever you need it, the money's here.

He is gone. Enter **Moyer***.*

Moyer   We are alone, Sir John.

Sir John   No, no! My son is here.

Moyer   Alone in Yorkshire. Fairfax will not fight.

The hounds bark, go crazy, and just as quickly stop.

Durand   Fairfax?

The hounds bark, go crazy, and just as quickly stop.

Sir John   Which feculent son of a bachelor thought it was a good idea to bring a pack of hounds to Hull?!

Beat.

Can't a man make one mistake?!

Durand   With regard to Black Tom . . . what is the detail?

Moyer   He shall not raise a pike against his king.

Durand   He has signed a deed of neutrality?

Moyer   And Queen Henrietta has landed at Bridlington with a Dutch army. Do you have orders for me, Sir John?

Sir John   Yes. Cancel all leave.

Moyer *goes to leave.*

Moyer   Is Mademoiselle Frottage –

Sir John   Don't worry about her, I'll sort her out later.

(*Aside.*) An enormous blue whale falls out of the tree and lands on the see-saw slinging Parliament's elephant into the Humber. Victory for the king is inevitable. Thank God we have Lady Digby!

A messenger with letters passes him in the doorway. **Frances** *comes out of her room, rushes to the open door with letters, and they swap.* **Frances** *reads the latest letter.* **Lady Sarah** *enters from the street.*

Sir John What's my cousin offered you? Wife number eighteen?

Lady Sarah Equivalence. Rights. Respect.

Sir John Would you be free of me?! A divorce?

Lady Sarah No. I would profit more from your death, and the Hull mob might have that intent. My wit tells me to wait. (*To* **Durand**.) In love?

Durand Yes, Mater.

Lady Sarah Is it a girl?

Durand I'm not sure.

Frottage (*off*) Monsieur Hotham?! *Que se passe-t-il?*

Lady Sarah Why is there a French woman in the bedroom?

Sir John It's Holy Horse day. The horses get the day off, and you have to lock a French woman in the bedroom. Or it's six years' bad luck.

Frottage *emerges from the bedroom.*

Lady Sarah Where did he find you?

Frottage (*to* **Lady Sarah**) *Je suis* Mademoiselle Félicité de Frottage.

Lady Sarah Lady congratulations of rubbing?

Frottage – D'Aquitaine.

Lady Sarah Of water sports.

Frottage   *Je suis la dame de la chambre de lit de la* Reine Henrietta.

Lady Sarah   And my arse is the temple of Venus.

Sir John   She is an emissary from the king himself.

Lady Sarah   So you're the king's tart?! You're not French!

Sir John   She's masking a French lady, to fool Captain Moyer.

Lady Sarah   Connie! What is happening here?!

Connie   The Dutch are coming, Black Tom is not coming, and Newcastle's arrived. Now it would be wise to surrender Hull to the king.

Lady Sarah   Why?

Sir John   Don't you want to end the war on the winning side?!

Connie (*to* **Frottage**)   Will the king renounce the *traitor condemnation* if Sir John surrenders?

Frottage   That is already agreed.

Sir John   I can't surrender just like that, Captain Moyer would clap me in irons.

Connie (*to* **Frottage**)   Arrange for the king to advance, in large numbers, to surround the city and to make a show of firing on the arsenal –

Sir John   – but if the stores are hit we will all be blown to hell!

Connie   Which is why I said 'make a show of'.

Frottage   So the king fires once aiming to miss, and not at the arsenal.

Connie (*to* **Sir John**)   Then you, aware that one stray incendiary could fire the powder and kill every soul in Hull, you surrender the city to protect the innocent citizens –

Sir John   – who, seeing the wisdom of my decision might then decide not to tear me limb from limb –

Connie   – because you'd saved them.

Sir John   Oh Connie, if only you weren't a woman you might have made something of yourself.

Mob banging on the doors.

Durand   The mob again, father. We don't have the money to pay them off! And I'm not getting circumcised.

Connie   Mister Pelham's dowry, the two thousand is in the strongbox in the bedroom.

She produces the key.

Lady Sarah   What's she doing with the key?

Sir John   Don't you trust her?

Lady Sarah   No!

Connie *gives the key to* **Sir John**.

Durand   The money may be in our house, but it is not ours. Pelham took possession and signed a contract. It's his money, unless legally challenged.

Sir John   Legally challenged?

Connie   Or exposed as an adulterer, with another woman in the Inigo Jones bed.

Connie *looks to* **Lady Sarah**.

Lady Sarah   You impudent strumpet!

Sir John   This might just work! Pelham is more enamoured of you than Frances.

Lady Sarah   I will not –

Sir John   – Shut up, you eviscerated gold truffling sow.

Lady Sarah   Is this the law?

Durand   In common law a betrothal contract is annulled if either party is witnessed *in flagrante delicto* with another.

Connie   You invite Pelham into the bedroom, with that bed –

Lady Sarah   – I'm not playing the lead in this masque for no reward.

Sir John (*to* **Lady Sarah**)   Divorce, and eight hundred a year.

Lady Sarah   Where would I live?

Sir John   And a house.

Lady Sarah *looks unmoved.*

Sir John   Two houses. Three houses?! Alright! Bridlington?!

Lady Sarah   Agreed! Does it have to be *in flagrante delicto*? Or can it be just *in flagrante*?

Durand   The witnesses must consider Mr Pelham's intent to be obvious, let me explain –

Lady Sarah   – I know what you mean.

Sir John   Lady Digby, you have saved England! Ride to the king, tell him of our scheme and Hull is his! Drudge, saddle a horse!

Frottage   But I thought it was Holy Horse Day?

Sir John   For Christian horses it is, but we keep a Hindu mare well disposed for emergencies.

Connie   Avoid the mob, use the coal chute!

Drudge *exits down the hatch with* **Frottage**. **Sir John** *shouts down the hatch.*

Sir John   Lord Mayor. This lady is an agent of the king. I'm handing him the town.

Barnard (*off*)   Good lad!

Connie (*to* **Durand**)   How many witnesses d'yer need for proving adultery?

Durand   Five gentlemen or twenty-seven yeomen.

Sir John   Five gentlemen?! Where are we going to find five gentlemen in Hull?!

Lady Sarah   Lord Mayor Barnard, that's one –

Frances   – the princes! Yes, the princes! Father, please!

Sir John   Two princes! So, two plus one, that's our five!

Lady Sarah   – three!

Durand   Mr Calvert, the *money lender*.

Sir John   The Jew?!

All   He's not Jewish!

Durand   He is a man of property, which makes him a gentleman.

Sir John   Fetch him here!

Durand *exits*.

Lady Sarah   That's four.

Sir John   My cousin, your lover, Saltmarsh.

Lady Sarah   We are quorate!

Sir John   Connie! We need to tempt Pelham here. Tell him that now would be a good time for him to collect his money, as my wife has the key to the safe box.

He produces the key. Looks for **Lady Sarah**.

Sir John   Where has the damned feculent sapphist gone?

Lady Sarah   I'm here.

Sir John   Darling. Take this key and we need something of you to tempt him, something redolent of you. Maybe an old shoe.

Lady Sarah   He likes my hands. This glove will fire him.

She gives **Connie** *a glove.* **Connie** *leaves by the cellar.*

Sir John (*to* **Connie**)   Bring my cousin here. He will profit from this. (*To* **Lady Sarah**.) Go prepare the bedroom, and I pray Mr Pelham has leaping crabs.

Lady Sarah *leaves.*

Sir John   Mister Barnard! Come up here please, sir!

Barnard *comes up.*

Sir John   Sir, I am cuckolded by Mr Pelham. I need you to witness the Puritan's ardour.

Barnard   What am I looking for?

Sir John   It's not called ardour for nothing is it?

Frances   Shall I bring the princes? I am meeting James at four.

Sir John   Which is now.

Frances   But I intend being late, it will heighten his desire, this is the theory according to poetry.

Sir John   No, no, no. Now!

Frances *leaves.*

Sir John   Come! To the bedroom!

Song: 'Lo! The Bed!'

Lo! The bed!
Behold!
The bed!
The Inigo Jones bed!

Avert your eyes
Avert your eyes
Lest you be tempted by . . . The bed!
The bed! The bed! The bed!
Lo! The bed!

Scene Two

The bedroom. A fabulous bed with a chandelier over it. There are curtains, some oak panelling and a commode. A series of safe boxes built into the panel wall.

Sir John (*to the audience*)   Don't look at the bed! I said, don't look at the bed! Right now, bugger off all of you . . . (*etc.*)

Cherub   Wanker!

Barnard   Right, where do I hide?

Sir John   Under the bed!

Barnard *crawls under the bed. Enter* **Saltmarsh** *and* **Lady Sarah**.

Sir John   Cousin. We need to hide you somewhere. Under the bed with the Lord Mayor.

Saltmarsh *goes under the bed. Enter* **Calvert** *and* **Durand**.

Calvert   What is it, Hotham? I am dragged through the streets of Hull, the mob following and –

Sir John   – you are here, as a gentleman, to witness Mr Pelham's ardour.

Calvert   It will be a pleasure, I loathe the man.

Sir John   Behind the curtains!

Calvert *goes behind the curtains. Enter* **Drudge** *with vase*.

Sir John   Drudge! Get out! Get out! You can't watch!

Drudge *refuses to leave. Enter* **Frances** *with* **York** *and* **Rupert**, *both still in women's attire.*

Sir John   Ah, my daughter! With her friends!

Durand *struts across. Offering a rose. He kneels before* **Rupert**.

Durand   As Adonis was mortal and Aphrodite a goddess, I supplicate myself before your deity, and requite your rose. I renounce the law and am committed to employ all my learning in the art of love, *ars amandi*, *ars amatoria*, or if my advances do not please you, *ars moriendi*. I implore you, leave your home even if it be heaven and come and live in Hull.

Barnard   It is a cultured city.

Calvert   There's a fast route to Holland and cheap tobacco.

Sir John   You will not be inconvenienced by hills.

Lady Sarah   It's only twelve hours to Bridlington.

Connie   Pelham's in the lobby!

Sir John   Princes, find a place.

Frances *grabs* **York** *and drags him behind a curtain.* **Durand** *advances on* **Rupert** *and they kiss. Everyone watches. Enter* **Connie**.

Lady Sarah *dramatically throws off her shawl.*

Sir John   Bring him in!

Connie   Where will you hide?

Sir John   Where else is there?

Connie   The commode! Get in!

They take the pan out of the commode and **Sir John** *hides in the back.*

Connie   Madam?

Lady Sarah   I'm ready.

Connie *exits.* **Sir John** *pops up through the hole in the commode.*

Sir John   Show him the key, you top-heavy spleen farm!

Enter **Connie**, *with* **Pelham**, *averting his eyes from the bed.*

Connie   Mr Peregrine Pelham, ma'am, come to collect his money.

Lady Sarah   Mr Pelham! Come through.

Pelham   Good day, Lady Hotham.

Lady Sarah   Thank you, Connie. Tell me, where is Sir John?

Connie   He's inspecting the Myton Gate block house.

Lady Sarah   Did he say how long he would be?

Connie   About two hours, ma'am, but if he returns unexpectedly I'll –

Lady Sarah   – that's enough, thank you.

Connie *exits.*

Lady Sarah   You can look at the bed, Mr Pelham.

Pelham   No! I'll just take my money. I shall not be tempted! For if I look I will fall victim to mine own febrile concupiscence.

Sir John *pops up and encourages* **Lady Sarah***, and in doing so, creeps the commode forward.*

Lady Sarah   Did you return my glove?

Pelham   I have kept it here, in my breast pocket, next to my heart.

Lady Sarah   Have you held it?

Pelham   I touched it, yes.

Lady Sarah   What did it feel like?

Pelham   Inviting.

Lady Sarah   It's goat skin.

Pelham   It feels softer than that. I should know I touch a lot of goats.

Lady Sarah   They soak the hide in cold urine.

Pelham   Cold urine?

Sir John *pops up and suggests that she stop talking about urine.*

Lady Sarah   Yes, cold urine softens the skin, then they rub it until all the coarse hairs fall out, after which they stretch the hide over tenterhooks.

Pelham   You seem to know a lot about it.

Lady Sarah   I wanted to know what they were doing with my urine. Did you try the glove on?

Pelham   I did.

Lady Sarah   But you're a big man, with big hands.

Pelham   I am!

Lady Sarah   It must have been tight?

Pelham   Yes! It felt like I was entering a small goat.

Lady Sarah   That had been soaked in cold urine.

Sir John *pops up again protesting.*

Lady Sarah   If you feel the call of nature there is a commode over here.

Pelham   I dearly would like to but I fear my current mettle will not allow it.

Sir John *pops his head out watching.* **Calvert**'s *head appears from behind the curtains. Some of the witnesses peep.*

Calvert (*whispered*)   Ardour?

Sir John (*whispered*)   It needs to be harder than that.

Lady Sarah   Throw the glove on the bed, Mr Pelham.

Pelham   I cannot look at the bed or I shall be destroyed!

Lady Sarah   Do as I say.

Pelham *turns, holding the glove, and now he looks at the bed. The sight of the bed takes his breath away and gives him an erection.*

Lady Sarah   It's an empty stage, awaiting the players.

Pelham   An elixir for the imagination.

Lady Sarah   And who do you see on the bed?

Pelham   Lady Hotham.

Lady Sarah   Frances, the young lady Hotham of your engagement, or –

Pelham   – no! Please, not that fatuous, empty youth.

Frances *comes out of hiding but is dragged back in by* **York***.*

Frances   Oi –

Lady Sarah   – oi, oi, oi.

She undoes her stays dramatically. **Pelham** *rips his shirt off, buttons flying. The sound of love-making coming from behind the curtains.* **Lady Sarah** *coughs to cover it.* **Sir John** *pops up questioningly.*

Pelham   I hear love-making! And that commode has moved!

Lady Sarah   It is the effect of the bed. A fevered imagination infusing all the senses.

Pelham   This house has a ghost.

Lady Sarah   Yes, the ghost.

She intercepts him and throws her arms around him, they kiss and fall heavily on to the bed. The bed visibly bends down under the weight and we hear a cry from **Barnard** *as the springs dig into him.*

Barnard   'kinnell!

Pelham   I heard the cry of a man.

Lady Sarah   That was me, my voice deepens when I yearn.

(*In a deep voice.*) Argh! Oohhh! 'kinnell! Don't stop!

At that moment **Jack** *bursts in from downstage left. He is wearing the full uniform of a Roundhead, sword and scabbard and musket.* **Pelham** *hides under the sheets.*

Jack   Mother!

Lady Sarah   Jack!

Jack   Are you safe? The mob are at the windows!

He throws his sword and scabbard off, as well as his cloak.

They wouldn't let me pass, I had to climb in through one of the skylights.

Lady Sarah   They are intent on taking their money.

Jack   I have ridden hard from Beverley, two hours, not even stopping for nature. Mother! I need your commode!

Lady Sarah   Yes! Over there!

Jack *stands at the commode, urinates and vocalises his relief.*

Jack   Ooooh!

Sir John (*muffled*)   Oh, come on!

Urine runs out from the bottom of the commode. **Jack** *has spotted* **Drudge** *and leaps off and draws his sword.*

Jack   Drudge! You peep on my mother in her chamber?!

Sir John *pushes his head through the hole, still unseen by* **Jack.** **Drudge** *falls onto the bed. The bed collapses flat down so that we fear for the lives of the gentlemen underneath.* **Lady Sarah** *leaps up in the mayhem and goes to the safe boxes with the key. Plaintive groaning and wailing from* **Barnard.** **Sir John** *runs forward to* **Jack,** *still trapped in the commode and wet head sticking through the hole.*

Sir John   Jack! Sheathe your sword!

Jack   Father, why are you wearing a commode?!

Sir John   To unearth this fox!

Jack   What fox?!

Sir John *has no arms available since they're trapped in the commode, so* **Jack** *throws back the sheets on* **Pelham.**

Jack   Father! You are cuckolded!

Pelham *tries to escape but* **Jack** *has his sword and swiftly bars his way to the door.* **Lady Sarah** *has the money bags from the safe box.*

Sir John *runs around still trapped in the commode and tries to raise witnesses.*

Sir John   Mr Calvert! Witness this!

Calvert *shows himself.*

Sir John   Mr Calvert, open the curtains, I have no hands!

Calvert *opens the curtains to reveal* **York** *and* **Frances** *fucking.*
Sir John *goes to the other curtains.*

Sir John   And this.

Calvert *opens that and witnesses* **Durand** *and* **Rupert** *fucking.*

Sir John   MR PELHAM! You are betrothed to my daughter and the bride price is paid! And yet you consort with my wife in her chamber! I declare the engagement nul and void, and require you to return the dowry forthwith.

Pelham   Your word alone is not enough.

Sir John   I have five witnesses to this perfidy! Mr Calvert, his majesty the Duke of York and Prince Rupert.

Pelham   Your numbers fail you once again, Hotham.

Sir John   Barnard and Saltmarsh are under the bed.

He looks down at a trickle of blood coming from under the bed.

Pelham   They may not live.

Sir John   Move the bed!

Calvert, **Durand**, **York** *and* **Rupert** *lift the bed and* **Barnard** *and* **Saltmarsh** *crawl out.* **Barnard** *is groaning and covered in blood, but* **Saltmarsh** *is alright.*

Sir John   The Lord Mayor of Hull, and my fifth witness, another landed gentleman, is John Saltmarsh.

Pelham   Then I am undone. I confess, I was in thrall to my lust, and I shall return home and flagellate myself as is God's want.

He takes a leather belt and starts flagellating himself as he leaves.

Lady Sarah   Turnip!

Saltmarsh   Parsnip!

Lady Sarah *throws the money bags to* **Saltmarsh**, *who escapes.*

Sir John   Vixen! The money! My cousin! I have been tricked!

Lady Sarah   You should have divorced me when you had the chance.

She runs past him. He chases her and hits the door frame at pace. He can't get out the door as the width of the commode won't get through the door.

Sir John   Who will rid me of this turbulent commode?! Jack! Stop her!

Jack   Who!

Sir John   My wife! She's taken the money we need to appease the mob!

Jack *chases after* **Lady Sarah** *and* **Saltmarsh**. **Barnard** *and* **Calvert** *pull the commode off* **Sir John**. **Durand** *and* **Rupert** *step back into the curtains kissing. Enter* **Connie**.

Sir John   Where's your lady?!

Connie   She left the house.

Sir John   How can she?! The mob are breaking in!

Connie   Through the coal chute.

Enter **Jack** *at a pace.*

Jack   They've broken through a skylight. We must barricade ourselves in!

Sir John   Secure the door!

Jack, **Barnard** *and* **Drudge** *secure the door. We hear the mob at the bedroom door, and see the door flex from the pressure.*

Barnard   What we gonna do? Hotham! You have to pay off the mob!

Calvert   I have your loan here, in coin.

He shows it.

Sir John   Your Shylock loan?! The price is too high!

Calvert   I've offered the governor a loan, secured with –

Sir John   – a terrible sacrifice!

Jack   Father! Inaction will cost us all our lives!

Sir John (*to* **Calvert**)   They'll kill you too, Calvert!

Calvert   They know me, and I owe them nothing.

Connie   Sir John . . .

Sir John   Connie?

Connie   Don't matter.

York   Sir! Do the deed! Think of me! My father will reward your sacrifice.

Sir John   He would, wouldn't he.

Barnard   Come on, Hotham! What yer waiting for, man?!

Sir John   Connie, my razor.

He quickly carries out the circumcision and delivers the foreskin to **Calvert**. **Calvert** *hands over the coin. Enter, at pace,* **Moyer** *with two soldiers. They secure the door behind them. The mob is still there. All three soldiers draw their swords.*

Moyer   Hold! Rest easy! Sir John Hotham! I am arresting you for treachery to Parliament!

Jack   What is the nature of this treachery?

Moyer   A conspiracy to surrender the town to the papists!

Sir John   Captain Moyer, my dear chap, whatever are you talking about?

Moyer   You conspired with Lady Digby, Queen Henrietta's lady of the bedchamber, to surrender Hull to the king's party.

York (*drawing his sword*)   Sirrah, I am the Duke of York, heir to the throne, and no papist, I know of no one at court called Lady Digby.

Moyer (*drawing sword*)   Yes, Lady Digby and Mademoiselle Frottage were inventions of mine and Sweet Lips, designed to reveal Hotham's true intent, namely the betrayal of Parliament.

Sir John   I am tricked! Undone.

Rupert *steps out of the curtains, and draws his sword.*

Rupert   Ruprecht Pfalzgraf bei Rhein, Herzog von Bayern! The king's commander of horse!

York   Cuz! We are maligned, called papists!

Rupert   Then the English Civil War starts now. Who will make the first advance?

A stand-off. No one wishes to make the first move.

Moyer   Let it begin!

He picks up the vase and deliberately smashes it on the floor. **Drudge** *draws his knife and charges him with a blood-curdling scream. Sword fight involving everyone.* **Sir John** *takes his chance and escapes via the entrance that* **Jack** *had used to come in. The fighting freezes.* **Connie** *stands, holding two hat boxes, both looking rather heavy.*

Connie   My lord fled Hull on foot through the Beverley Gate, pursued by Captain Moyer and grapeshot.

Sir John *runs across the stage followed by* **Moyer** *with* **Drudge** *on his back beating him.*

Connie   I picked up the hat boxes, heavy for hat boxes, as their cargo was coin. Aye, I got the money, and Lady Sarah and lover boy got the stones.

(*Aside.*) Do you remember seeing me collecting stones? Towards the end of the first half. You can't remember. Do you know where you are, love?

The two thousand pounds. Enough to buy into the bakers' guild. I wanted to call my baker's shop 'Connie's' but the guild wouldn't allow a woman's name so I had to use my surname, alone, hence Greggs.

Enter **Sir John** *again. He meets a* **Commoner** *on a horse – a wooden prop or coconut shells.*

Connie   Sir John ran north where meeting a yeoman riding to Hull he declared himself to be the man's superior, and commandeered his horse.

Sir John   I'm a baron, and a knight, and you're less than nothing, so hand over your horse. What's he called?

Commoner   Radish.

Sir John (*jumping on the horse*)   Giddiyup, Radish!

Connie   At Beverley he came upon a Parliament troop of cavalry. He took over command from their captain and ordered them to escort him to the family estate at Scorborough.

Enter **Sir John** *slowly, with a troop of Parliament horse,* **Sir John** *acting the part of commander.*

Connie   However, Captain Moyer had made good speed from Hull, and –

Moyer (*taking the bridle of* **Sir John**'s *horse*)   – Sir John Hotham, you are my prisoner! I arrest you in the name of the Commonwealth.

Sir John   Since it must be so, I am content, and submit.

He kicks **Moyer** *in the groin and runs off again, this time pursued by everyone.*

Mob   Wanker!

Connie   Finally, he is cruelly beaten, secured and taken back to Hull, before being shipped to the Tower of London, and the scaffold where we began.

A tableau reprise of the Prologue.

This man in his time played many parts,
Soldier, politician, baronet, lover,
Husband, father, loyalist, liar,
Turncoat, renegade, traitor.

Beheaded by the victorious Parliament party
For his offer to the royals, the arsenal to bring,
Yet if the cavaliers had won the war
He would have been executed by the king.

His place in Hull and history is secure
And his own small act of revolution
In denying the divine right of the monarch
Began the English road to parliamentary constitution.

The **Ranter** *and* **Company** *sing.*

Song: 'Jerusalem'

There's a promise that is worth the years of toil,
And it needs somebody to be the pioneers.
It's a notion that was planted in our soil,
That we've watered with our blood and sweat and tears.
And we'd plough a thousand fields to help it flourish
And we'll harrow and we'll till until it grows.
For to nurture and to cultivate takes courage
It's far easier to deny than to propose

We were angered
We were looted
We were easy to condemn
But we'll be anchored
We'll be rooted
When we have built our Jerusalem.

And we'd face a thousand armies to protect it in the field
Our honour and our voices are our shield.

Our hope will be a beacon, a guiding light for all to see.
Now we've something to believe in, England's proud
    democracy

For we were angered
We were looted
We were easy to condemn
But we'll be anchored
We'll be rooted
When we have built our Jerusalem.

We were angered
We were looted
We were easy to condemn
But we'll be anchored
We'll be rooted
When we have built our Jerusalem.
When we have built our Jerusalem.

The End.

9 781350 183650